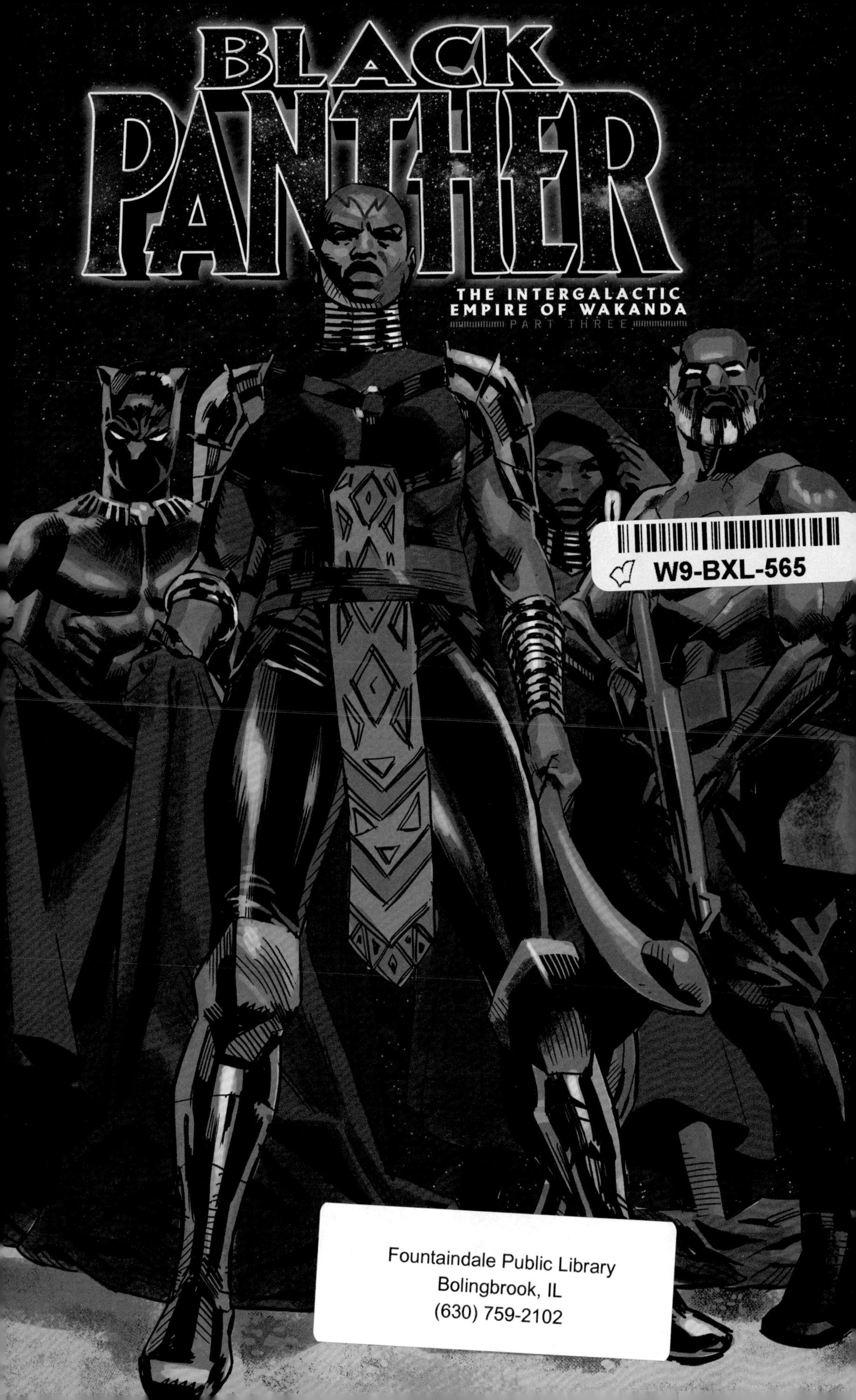
BLACK
PANTHER
THE INTERGALACTIC
EMPIRE OF WAKANDA
PART THREE

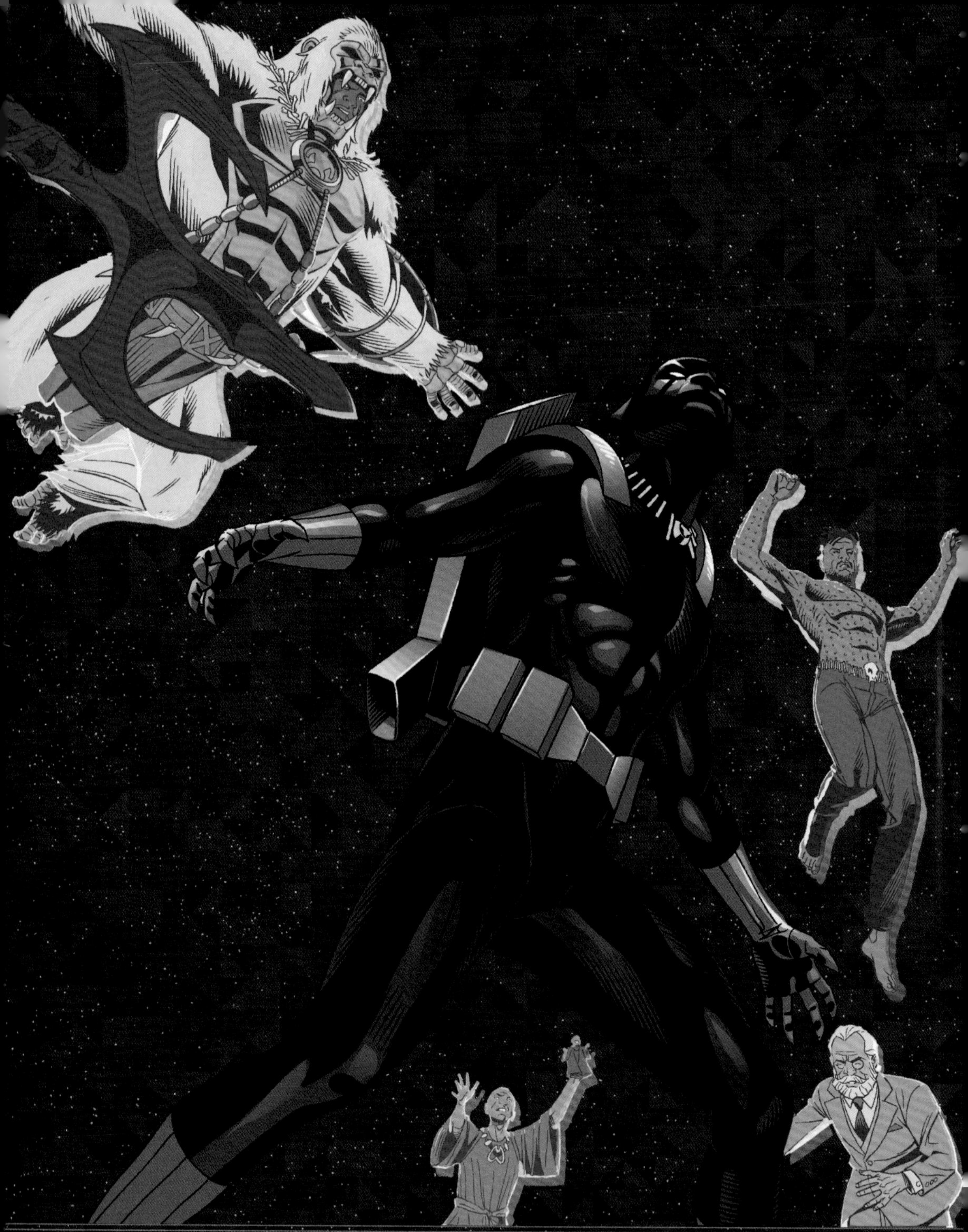

COLLECTION EDITOR **JENNIFER GRÜNWALD**
ASSISTANT EDITOR **CAITLIN O'CONNELL**
ASSOCIATE MANAGING EDITOR **KATERI WOODY**
EDITOR, SPECIAL PROJECTS **MARK D. BEAZLEY**
VP PRODUCTION & SPECIAL PROJECTS **JEFF YOUNGQUIST**
BOOK DESIGNERS **SALENA MAHINA** & **ADAM DEL RE**

SVP PRINT, SALES & MARKETING **DAVID GABRIEL**
DIRECTOR, LICENSED PUBLISHING **SVEN LARSEN**
EDITOR IN CHIEF **C.B. CEBULSKI**
CHIEF CREATIVE OFFICER **JOE QUESADA**
PRESIDENT **DAN BUCKLEY**
EXECUTIVE PRODUCER **ALAN FINE**

BLACK PANTHER BOOK 8: THE INTERGALACTIC EMPIRE OF WAKANDA PART THREE. Contains material originally published in magazine form as BLACK PANTHER (2018) #13-18. First printing 2019. ISBN 978-1-302-91446-2. Published by MARVEL WORLDWIDE, INC., a subsidiary of MARVEL ENTERTAINMENT, LLC. OFFICE OF PUBLICATION: 135 West 50th Street, New York, NY 10020.

Printed in Canada. DAN BUCKLEY, President, Marvel Entertainment; JOHN NEE, Publisher; JOE QUESADA, Chief Creative Officer; TOM BREVOORT, SVP of Publishing; DAVID BOGART, Associate Publisher & SVP of Talent Affairs; DAVID GABRIEL, VP of Print & Digital Publishing; JEFF YOUNGQUIST, VP of Production & Special Projects; DAN CARR, Executive Director of Publishing Technology; ALEX MORALES, Director of Publishing Operations; DAN EDINGTON, Managing Editor; SUSAN CRESPI, Production Manager; STAN LEE, Chairman Emeritus. For information regarding advertising in Marvel Comics or on Marvel.com, please contact Vit DeBellis, Custom Solutions & Integrated Advertising Manager, at vdebellis@marvel.com. For Marvel subscription inquiries, please call 888-511-5480. **Manufactured between 10/18/2019 and 11/19/2019 by SOLISCO PRINTERS, SCOTT, QC, CANADA.**

10 9 8 7 6 5 4 3 2 1

BLACK PANTHER

THE INTERGALACTIC EMPIRE OF WAKANDA

PART THREE

Ta-Nehisi Coates
WRITER

ISSUES #13-17

Daniel Acuña
ARTIST

Daniel Acuña with **CAFU** (#16)
COVER ART

ISSUE #18

Chris Sprouse
PENCILER

Karl Story
INKER

Marcio Menyz
COLOR ARTIST

Chris Sprouse, Karl Story & **Tamra Bonvillain**
COVER ART

VC's Joe Sabino
LETTERER

Sarah Brunstad
ASSOCIATE EDITOR

Wil Moss
EDITOR

BLACK PANTHER CREATED BY
Stan Lee & **Jack Kirby**

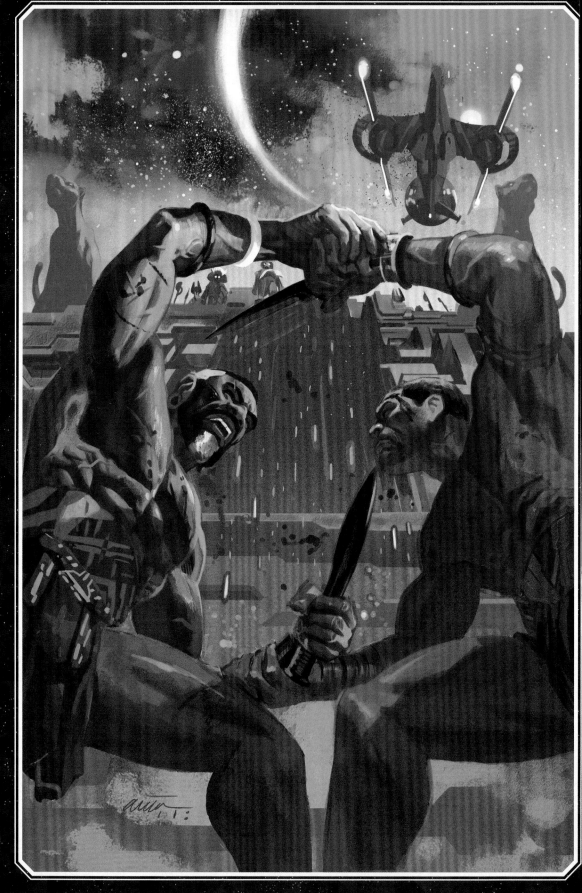

13

THE INTERGALACTIC EMPIRE OF WAKANDA

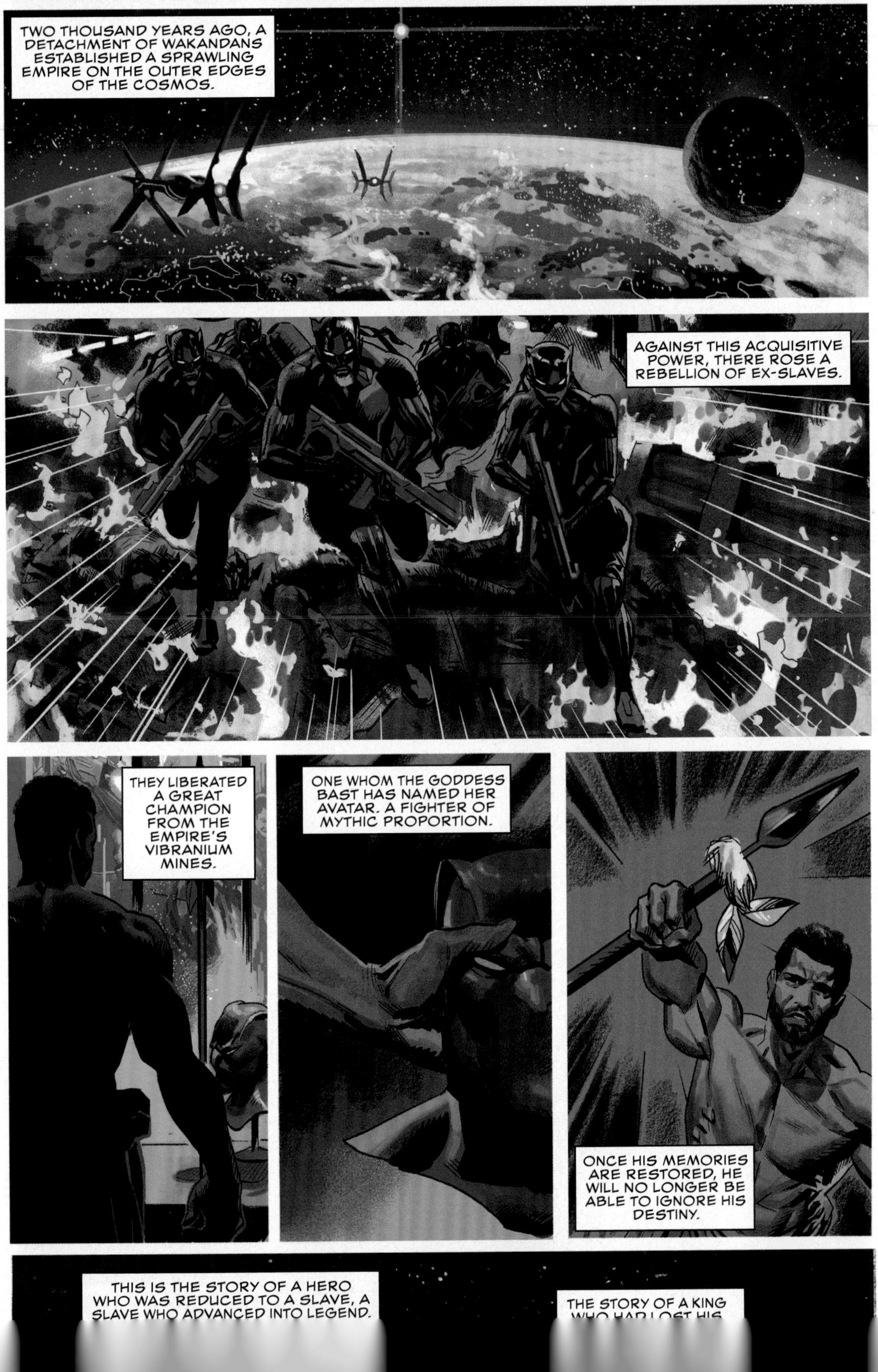
TWO THOUSAND YEARS AGO, A DETACHMENT OF WAKANDANS ESTABLISHED A SPRAWLING EMPIRE ON THE OUTER EDGES OF THE COSMOS.
AGAINST THIS ACQUISITIVE POWER, THERE ROSE A REBELLION OF EX-SLAVES.
THEY LIBERATED A GREAT CHAMPION FROM THE EMPIRE'S VIBRANIUM MINES.
ONE WHOM THE GODDESS BAST HAS NAMED HER AVATAR. A FIGHTER OF MYTHIC PROPORTION.
ONCE HIS MEMORIES ARE RESTORED, HE WILL NO LONGER BE ABLE TO IGNORE HIS DESTINY.
THIS IS THE STORY OF A HERO WHO WAS REDUCED TO A SLAVE, A SLAVE WHO ADVANCED INTO LEGEND.
THE STORY OF A KING

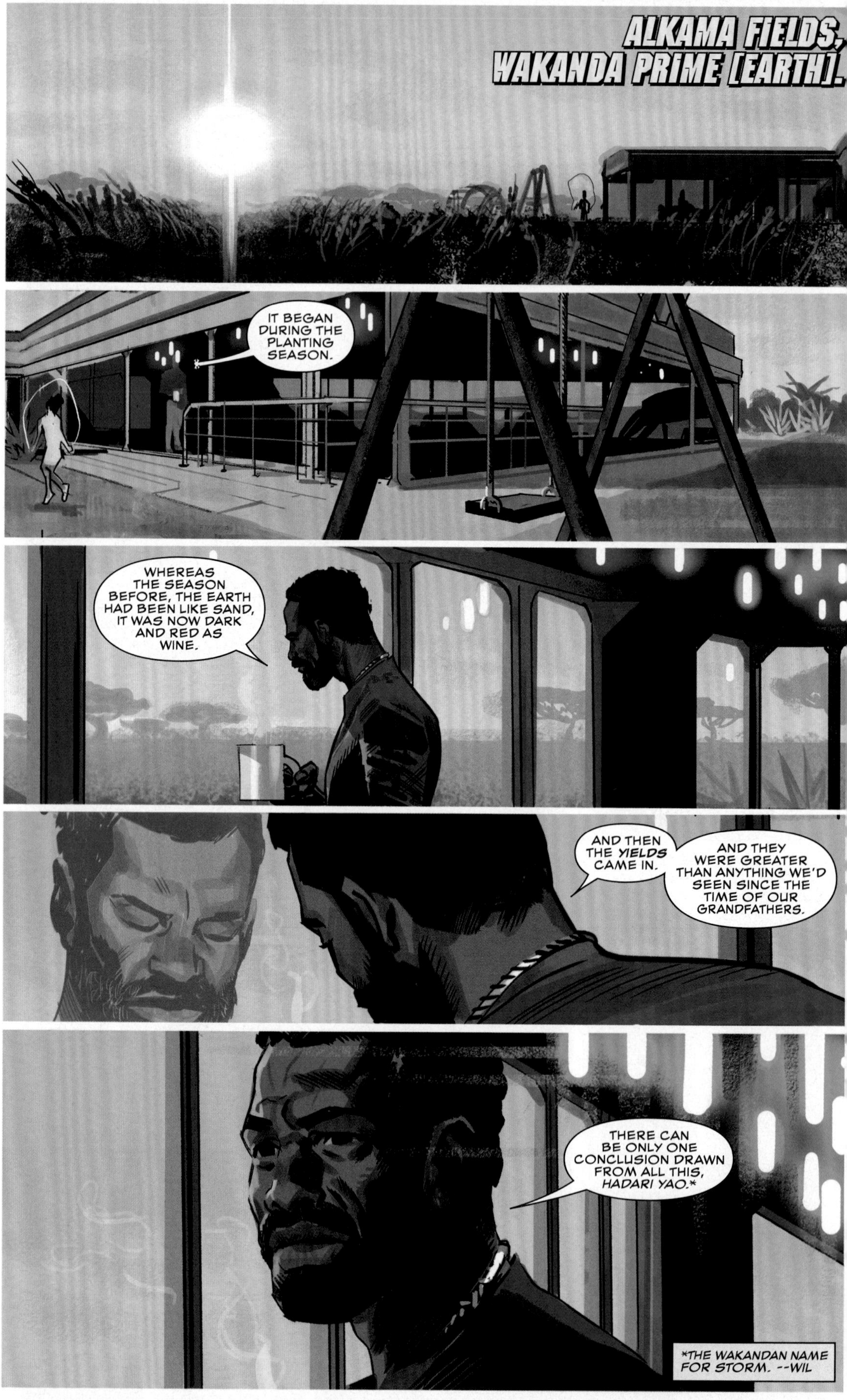
ALKAMA FIELDS, WAKANDA PRIME [EARTH].
IT BEGAN DURING THE PLANTING SEASON.
WHEREAS THE SEASON BEFORE, THE EARTH HAD BEEN LIKE SAND, IT WAS NOW DARK AND RED AS WINE.
AND THEN THE YIELDS CAME IN.
AND THEY WERE GREATER THAN ANYTHING WE'D SEEN SINCE THE TIME OF OUR GRANDFATHERS.
THERE CAN BE ONLY ONE CONCLUSION DRAWN FROM ALL THIS, HADARI YAO.*
*THE WAKANDAN NAME FOR STORM. --WIL

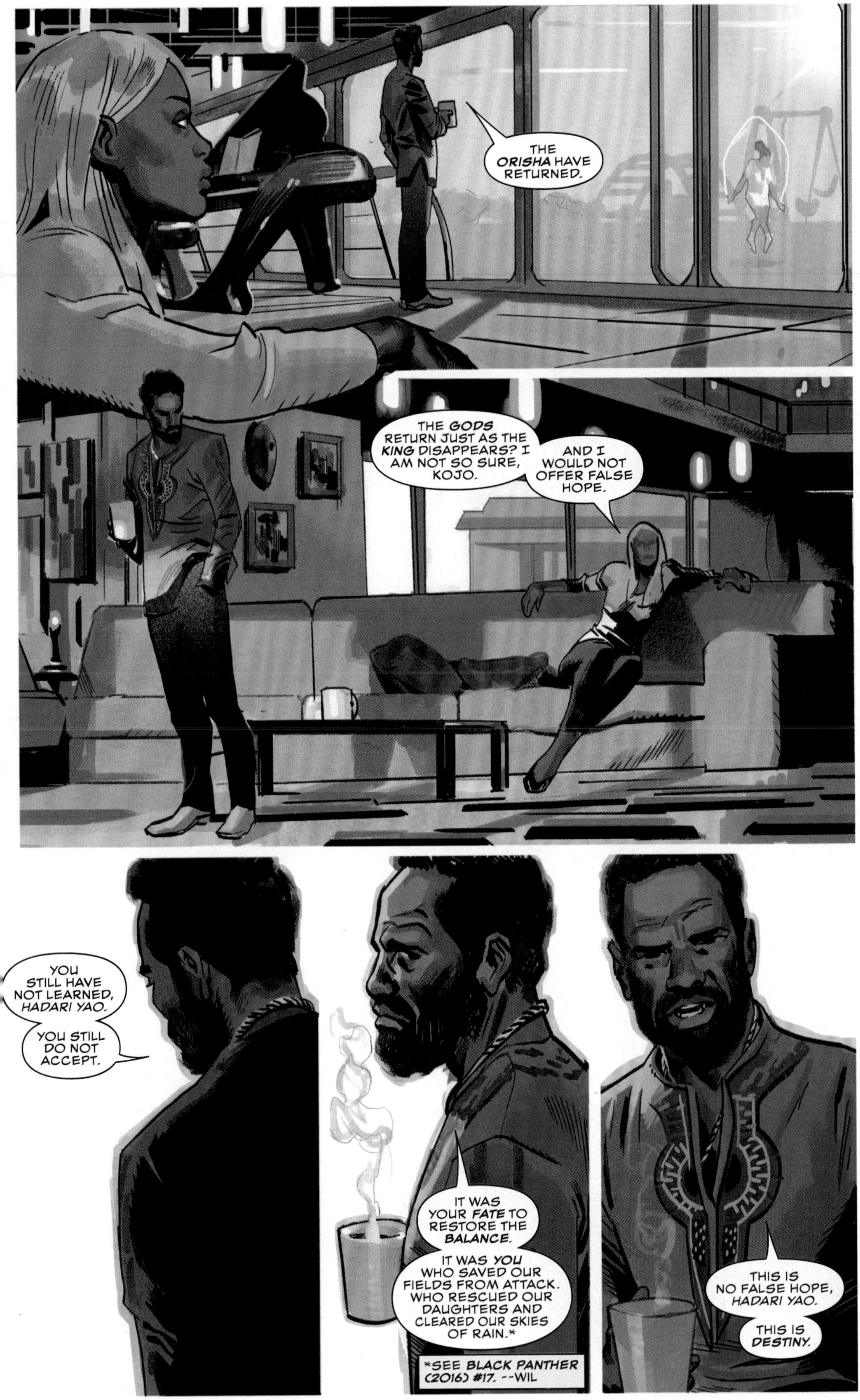

THE ORISHA HAVE RETURNED.
THE GODS RETURN JUST AS THE KING DISAPPEARS? I AM NOT SO SURE, KOJO.
AND I WOULD NOT OFFER FALSE HOPE.
YOU STILL HAVE NOT LEARNED, HADARI YAO.
YOU STILL DO NOT ACCEPT.
IT WAS YOUR FATE TO RESTORE THE BALANCE.
IT WAS YOU WHO SAVED OUR FIELDS FROM ATTACK. WHO RESCUED OUR DAUGHTERS AND CLEARED OUR SKIES OF RAIN.*
*SEE BLACK PANTHER (2016) #17. --WIL
THIS IS NO FALSE HOPE, HADARI YAO.
THIS IS DESTINY.

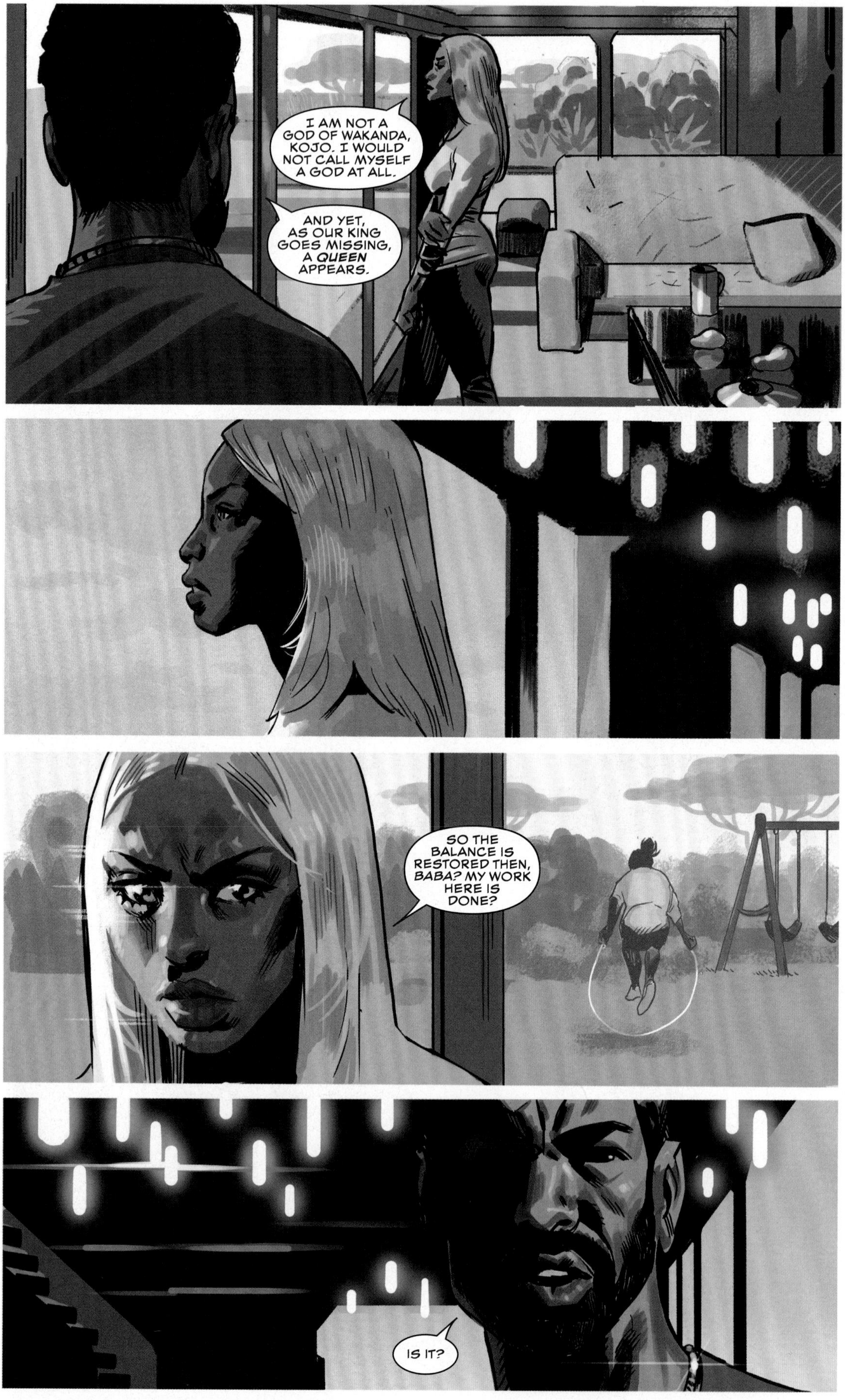
I AM NOT A GOD OF WAKANDA, KOJO. I WOULD NOT CALL MYSELF A GOD AT ALL.
AND YET, AS OUR KING GOES MISSING, A *QUEEN* APPEARS.
SO THE BALANCE IS RESTORED THEN, *BABA*? MY WORK HERE IS DONE?
IS IT?

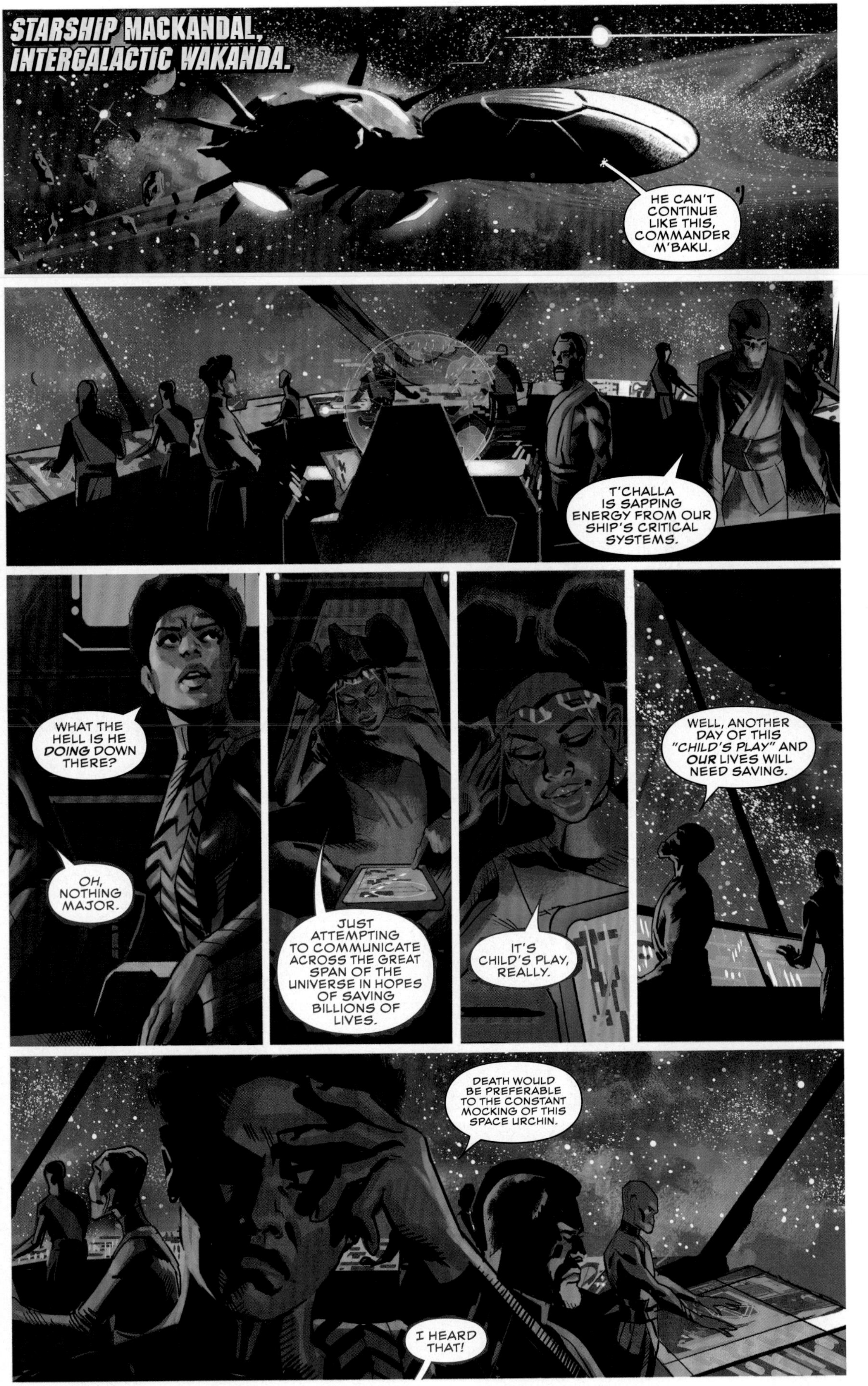
STARSHIP MACKANDAL, INTERGALACTIC WAKANDA.
HE CAN'T CONTINUE LIKE THIS, COMMANDER M'BAKU.
T'CHALLA IS SAPPING ENERGY FROM OUR SHIP'S CRITICAL SYSTEMS.
WHAT THE HELL IS HE DOING DOWN THERE?
OH, NOTHING MAJOR.
JUST ATTEMPTING TO COMMUNICATE ACROSS THE GREAT SPAN OF THE UNIVERSE IN HOPES OF SAVING BILLIONS OF LIVES.
IT'S CHILD'S PLAY, REALLY.
WELL, ANOTHER DAY OF THIS "CHILD'S PLAY" AND OUR LIVES WILL NEED SAVING.
DEATH WOULD BE PREFERABLE TO THE CONSTANT MOCKING OF THIS SPACE URCHIN.
I HEARD THAT!

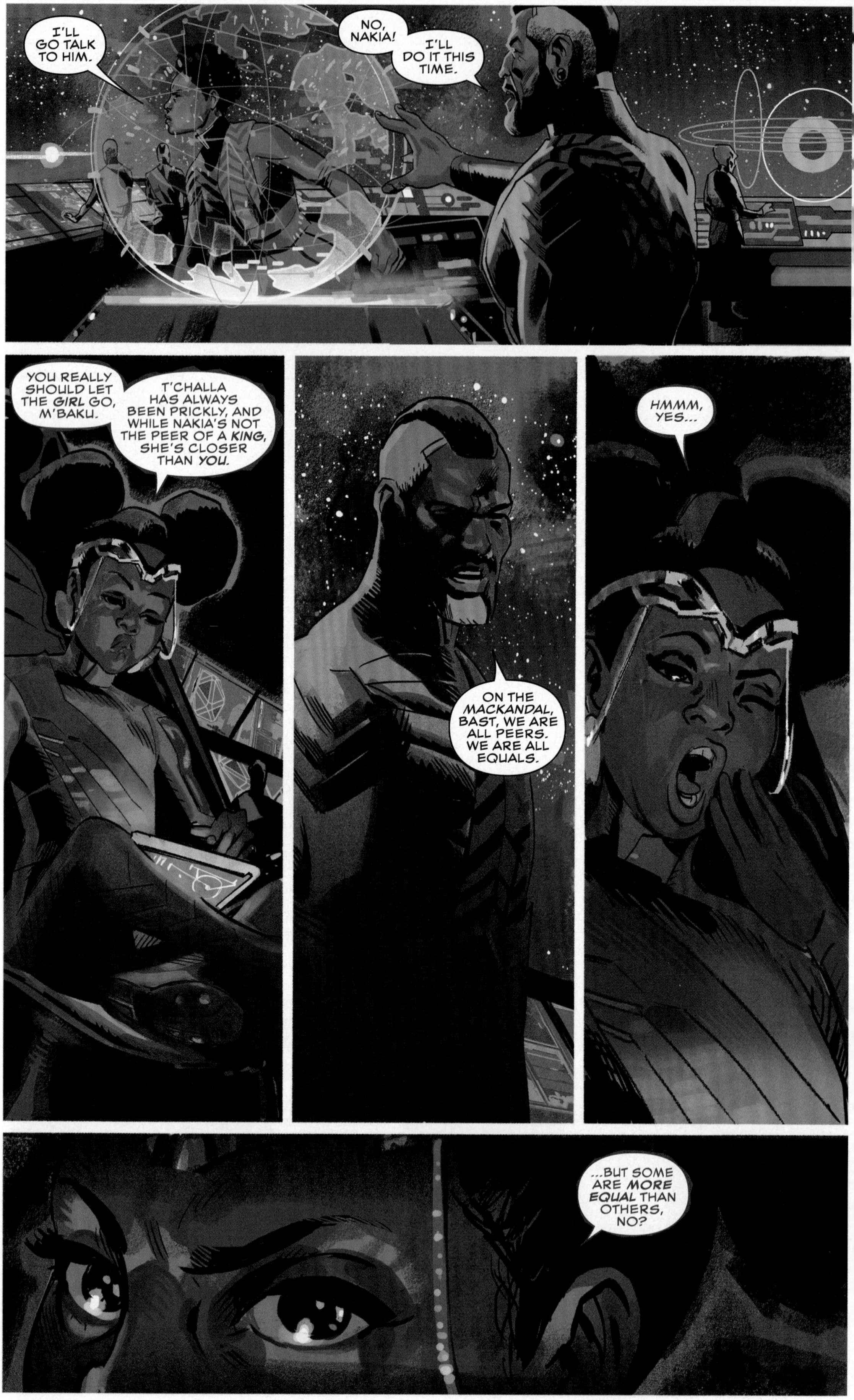
I'LL GO TALK TO HIM.
NO, NAKIA!
I'LL DO IT THIS TIME.
YOU REALLY SHOULD LET THE GIRL GO, M'BAKU.
T'CHALLA HAS ALWAYS BEEN PRICKLY, AND WHILE NAKIA'S NOT THE PEER OF A KING, SHE'S CLOSER THAN YOU.
ON THE MACKANDAL, BAST, WE ARE ALL PEERS. WE ARE ALL EQUALS.
HMMM, YES...
...BUT SOME ARE MORE EQUAL THAN OTHERS, NO?

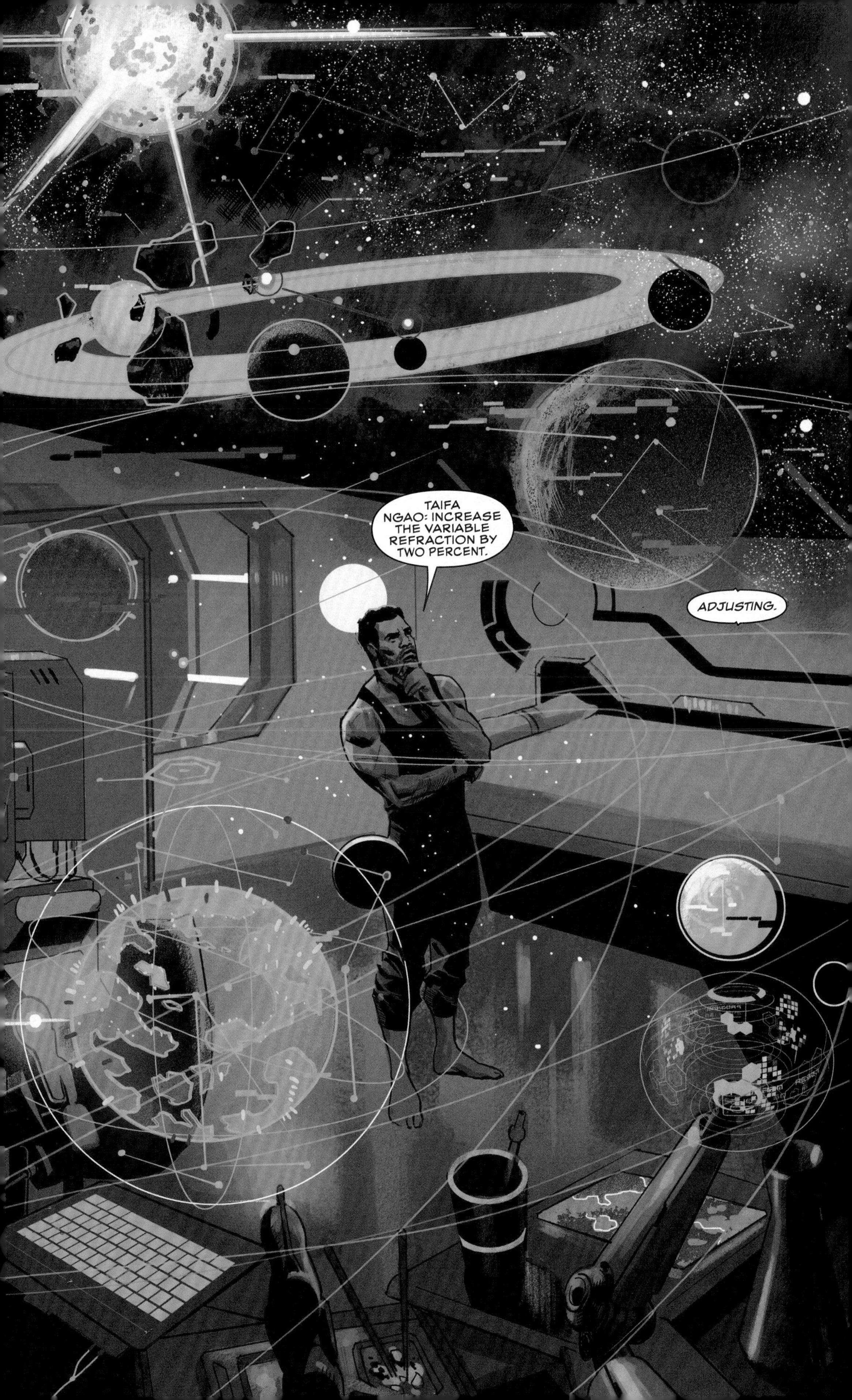
TAIFA NGAO: INCREASE THE VARIABLE REFRACTION BY TWO PERCENT.
ADJUSTING.

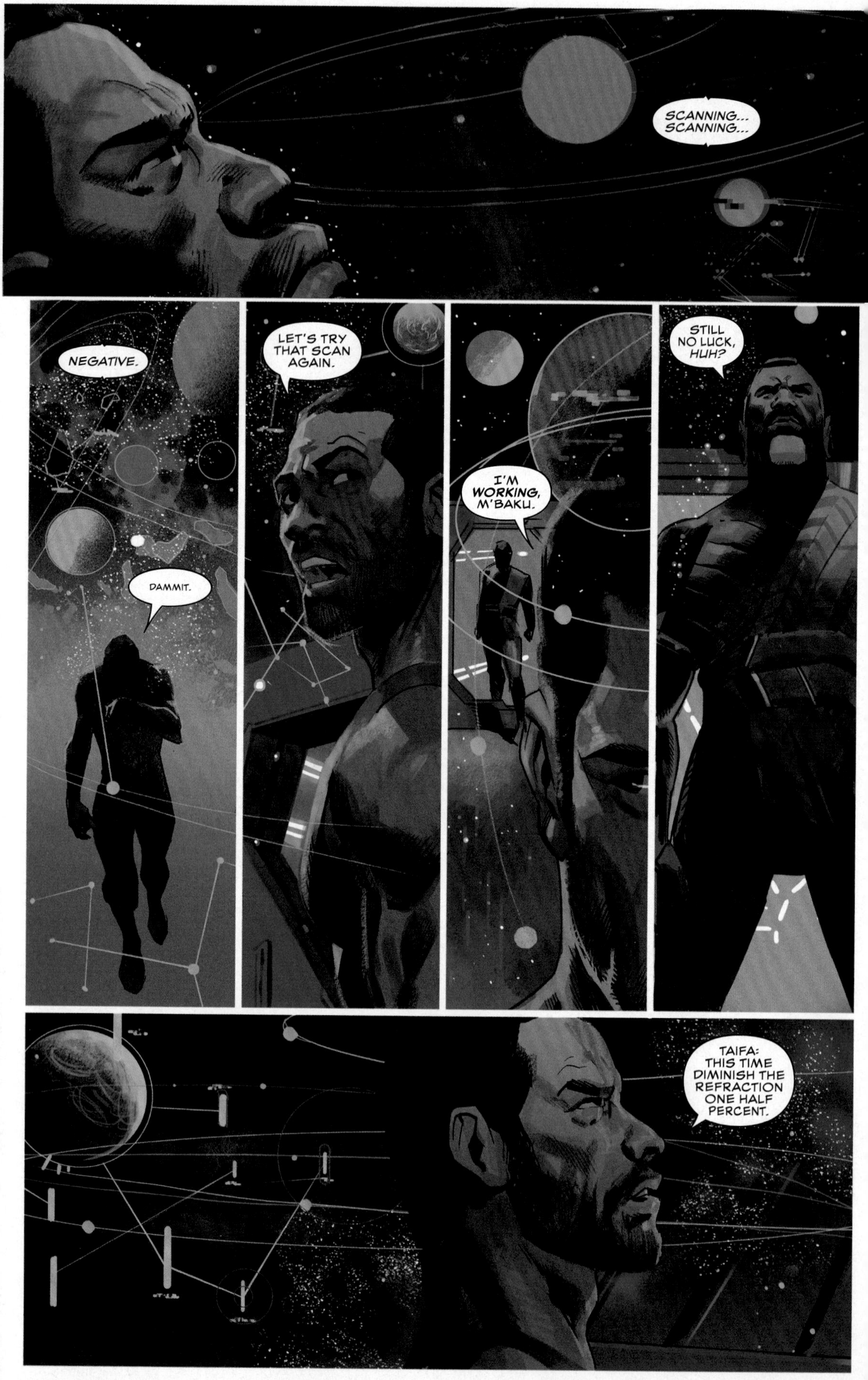
SCANNING...
SCANNING...
NEGATIVE.
DAMMIT.
LET'S TRY THAT SCAN AGAIN.
I'M WORKING, M'BAKU.
STILL NO LUCK, HUH?
TAIFA: THIS TIME DIMINISH THE REFRACTION ONE HALF PERCENT.

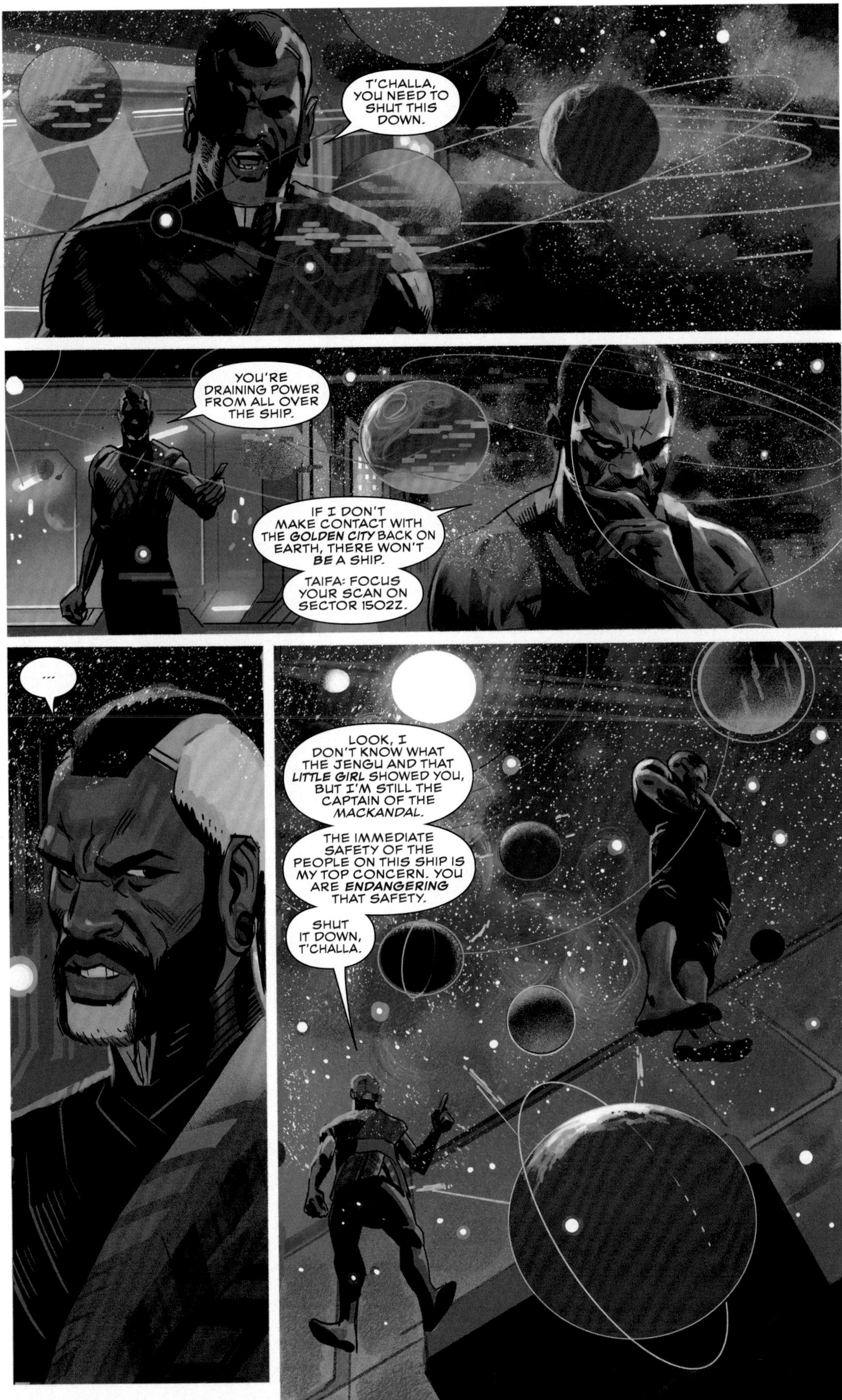

T'CHALLA, YOU NEED TO SHUT THIS DOWN.
YOU'RE DRAINING POWER FROM ALL OVER THE SHIP.
IF I DON'T MAKE CONTACT WITH THE *GOLDEN CITY* BACK ON EARTH, THERE WON'T *BE* A SHIP.
TAIFA: FOCUS YOUR SCAN ON SECTOR 1502Z.
...
LOOK, I DON'T KNOW WHAT THE JENGU AND THAT *LITTLE GIRL* SHOWED YOU, BUT I'M STILL THE CAPTAIN OF THE *MACKANDAL.*
THE IMMEDIATE SAFETY OF THE PEOPLE ON THIS SHIP IS MY TOP CONCERN. YOU ARE *ENDANGERING* THAT SAFETY.
SHUT IT DOWN, T'CHALLA.

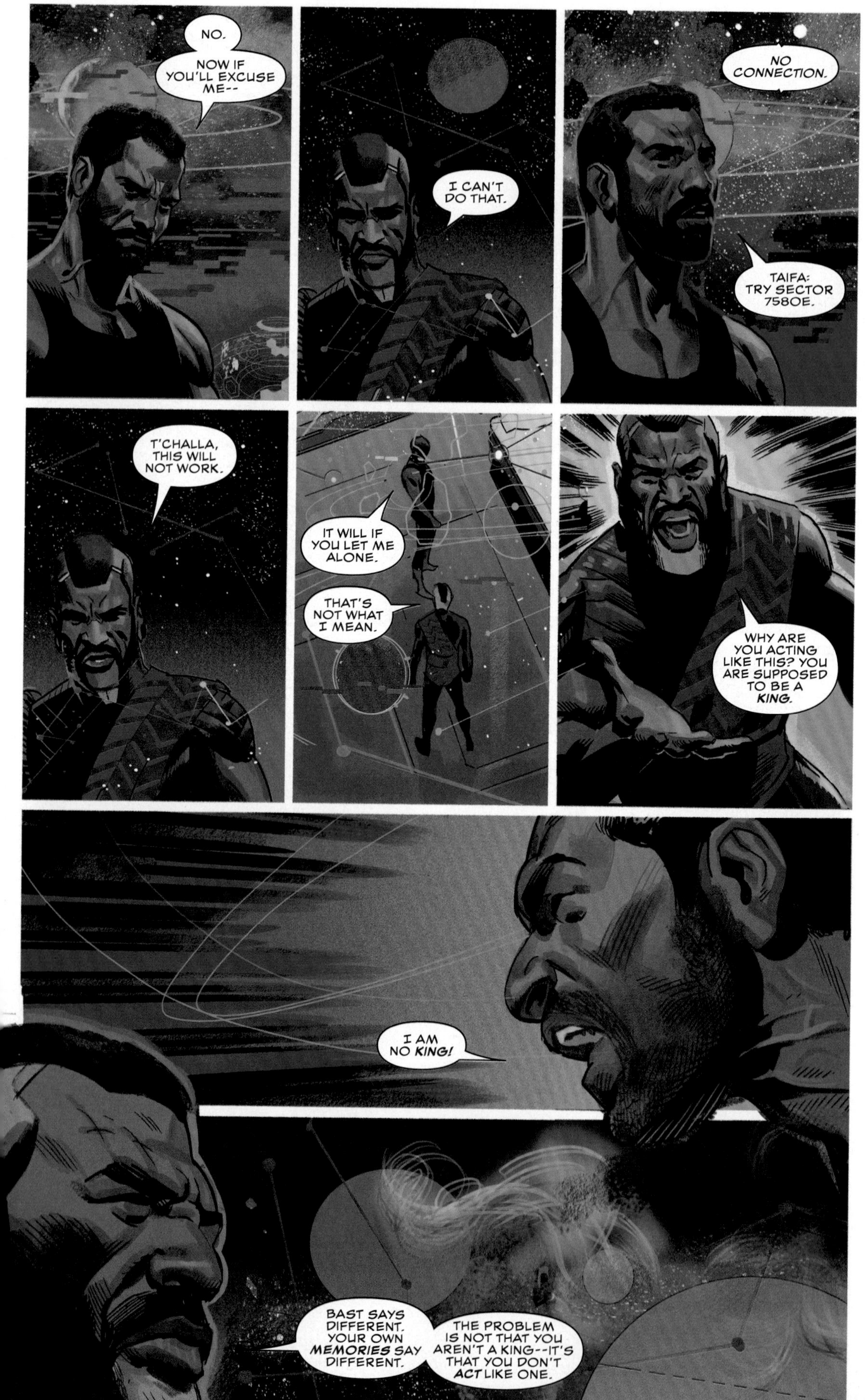
NO.
NOW IF YOU'LL EXCUSE ME--
I CAN'T DO THAT.
NO CONNECTION.
TAIFA: TRY SECTOR 7580E.
T'CHALLA, THIS WILL NOT WORK.
IT WILL IF YOU LET ME ALONE.
THAT'S NOT WHAT I MEAN.
WHY ARE YOU ACTING LIKE THIS? YOU ARE SUPPOSED TO BE A KING.
I AM NO KING!
BAST SAYS DIFFERENT. YOUR OWN MEMORIES SAY DIFFERENT.
THE PROBLEM IS NOT THAT YOU AREN'T A KING--IT'S THAT YOU DON'T ACT LIKE ONE.

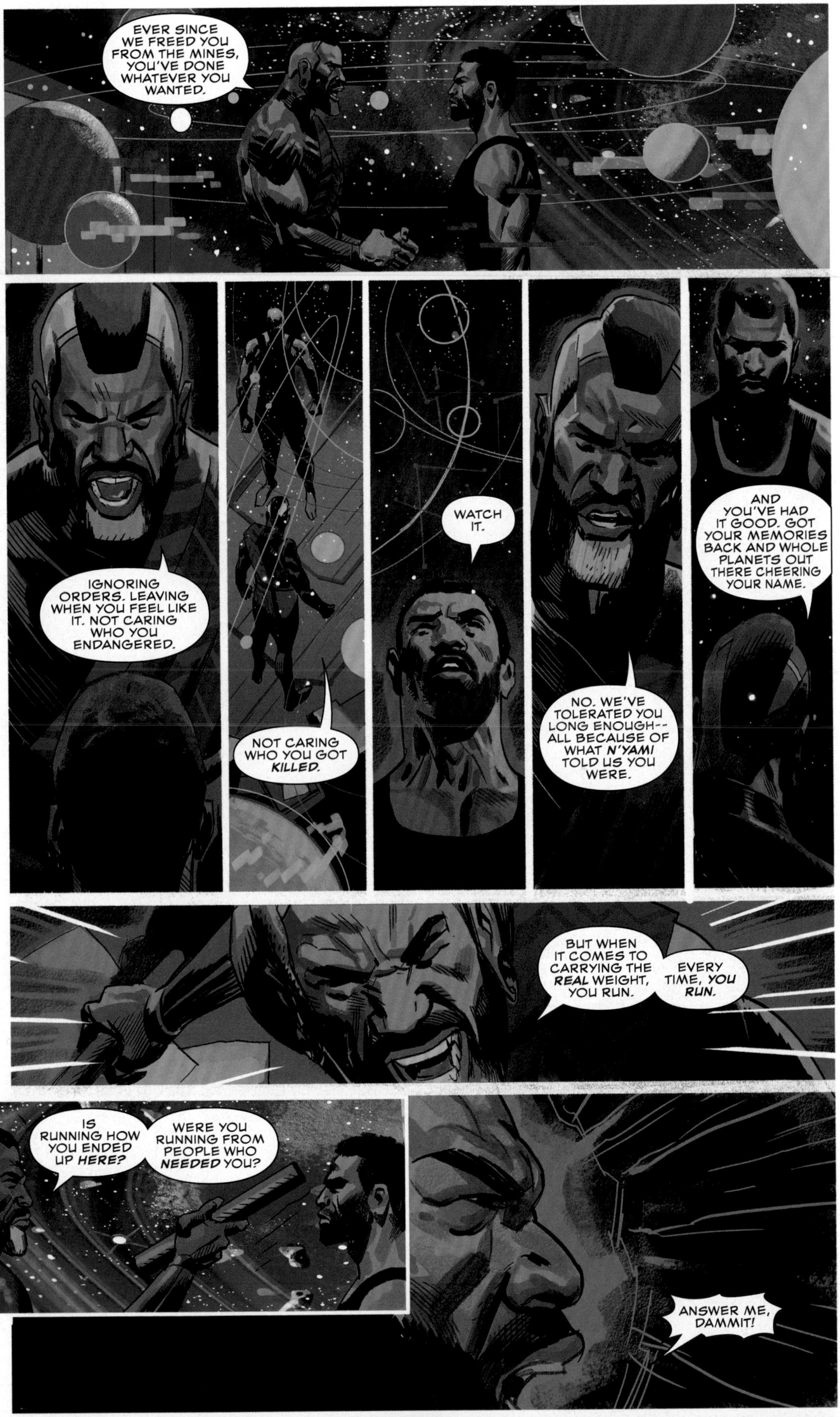
EVER SINCE WE FREED YOU FROM THE MINES, YOU'VE DONE WHATEVER YOU WANTED.
IGNORING ORDERS. LEAVING WHEN YOU FEEL LIKE IT. NOT CARING WHO YOU ENDANGERED.
NOT CARING WHO YOU GOT KILLED.
WATCH IT.
NO. WE'VE TOLERATED YOU LONG ENOUGH-- ALL BECAUSE OF WHAT N'YAMI TOLD US YOU WERE.
AND YOU'VE HAD IT GOOD. GOT YOUR MEMORIES BACK AND WHOLE PLANETS OUT THERE CHEERING YOUR NAME.
BUT WHEN IT COMES TO CARRYING THE REAL WEIGHT, YOU RUN.
EVERY TIME, YOU RUN.
IS RUNNING HOW YOU ENDED UP HERE?
WERE YOU RUNNING FROM PEOPLE WHO NEEDED YOU?
ANSWER ME, DAMMIT!

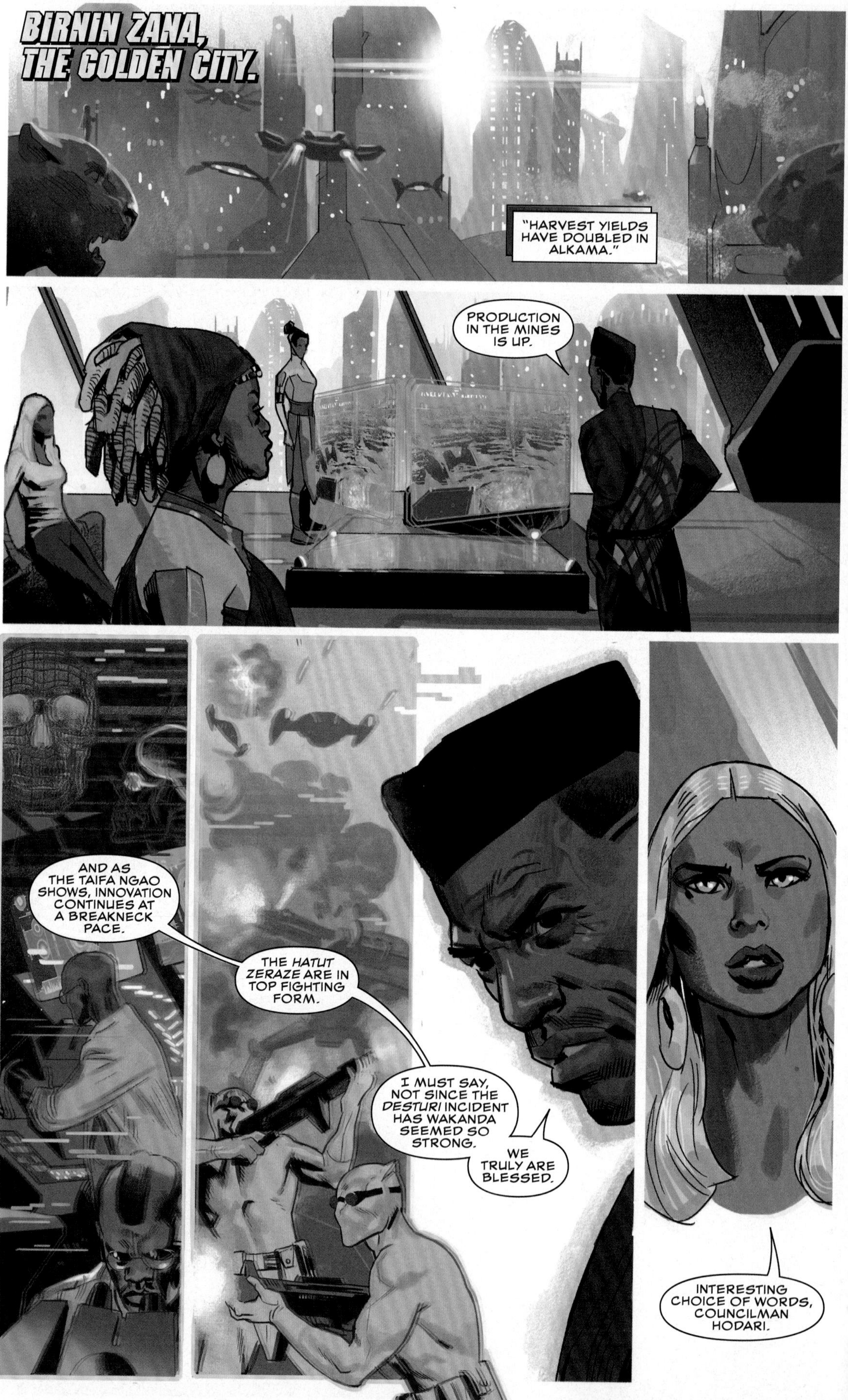
BIRNIN ZANA, THE GOLDEN CITY.
"HARVEST YIELDS HAVE DOUBLED IN ALKAMA."
PRODUCTION IN THE MINES IS UP.
AND AS THE TAIFA NGAO SHOWS, INNOVATION CONTINUES AT A BREAKNECK PACE.
THE *HATUT ZERAZE* ARE IN TOP FIGHTING FORM.
I MUST SAY, NOT SINCE THE *DESTURI* INCIDENT HAS WAKANDA SEEMED SO STRONG.
WE TRULY ARE BLESSED.
INTERESTING CHOICE OF WORDS, COUNCILMAN HODARI.

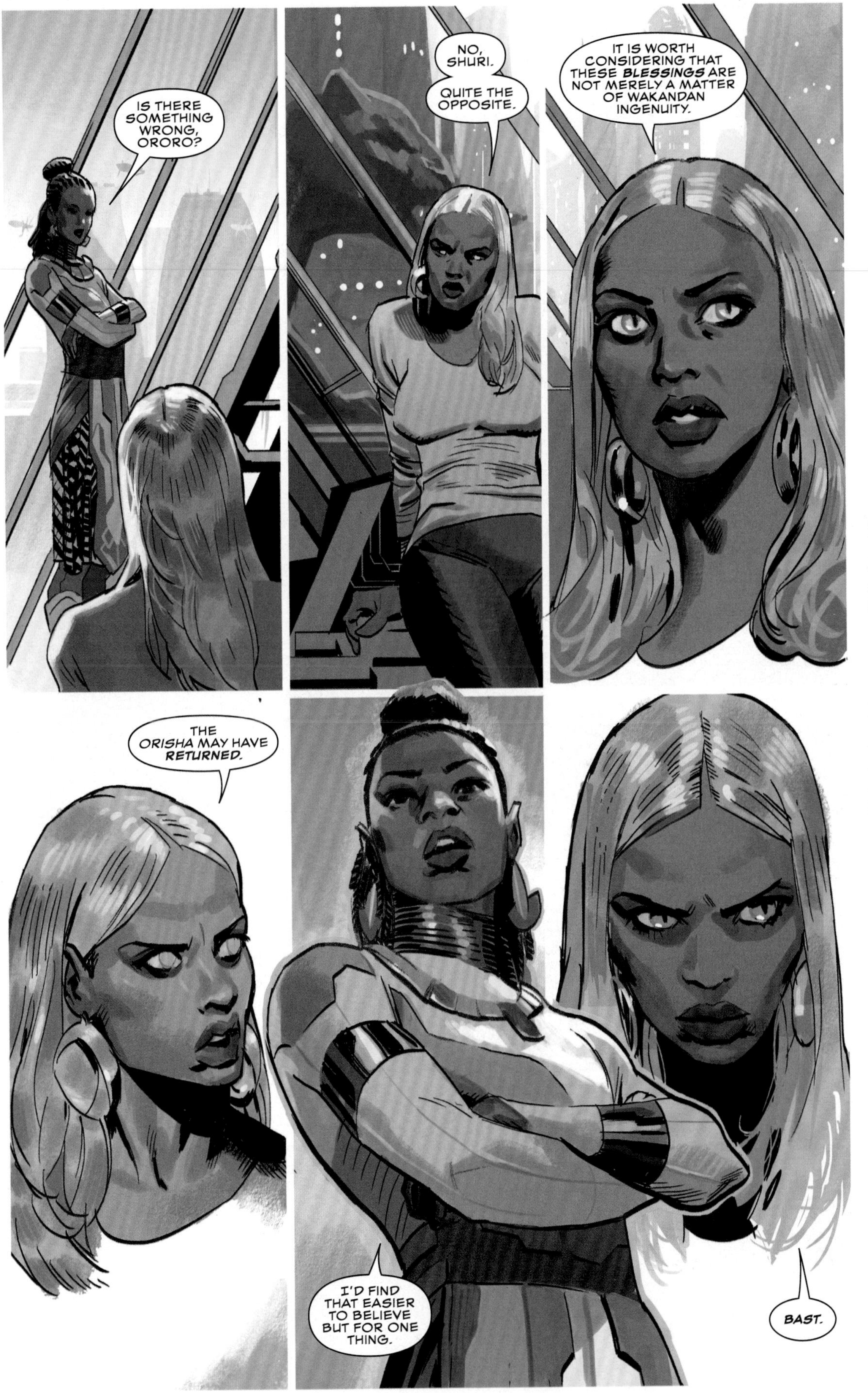
IS THERE SOMETHING WRONG, ORORO?
NO, SHURI.
QUITE THE OPPOSITE.
IT IS WORTH CONSIDERING THAT THESE BLESSINGS ARE NOT MERELY A MATTER OF WAKANDAN INGENUITY.
THE ORISHA MAY HAVE RETURNED.
I'D FIND THAT EASIER TO BELIEVE BUT FOR ONE THING.
BAST.

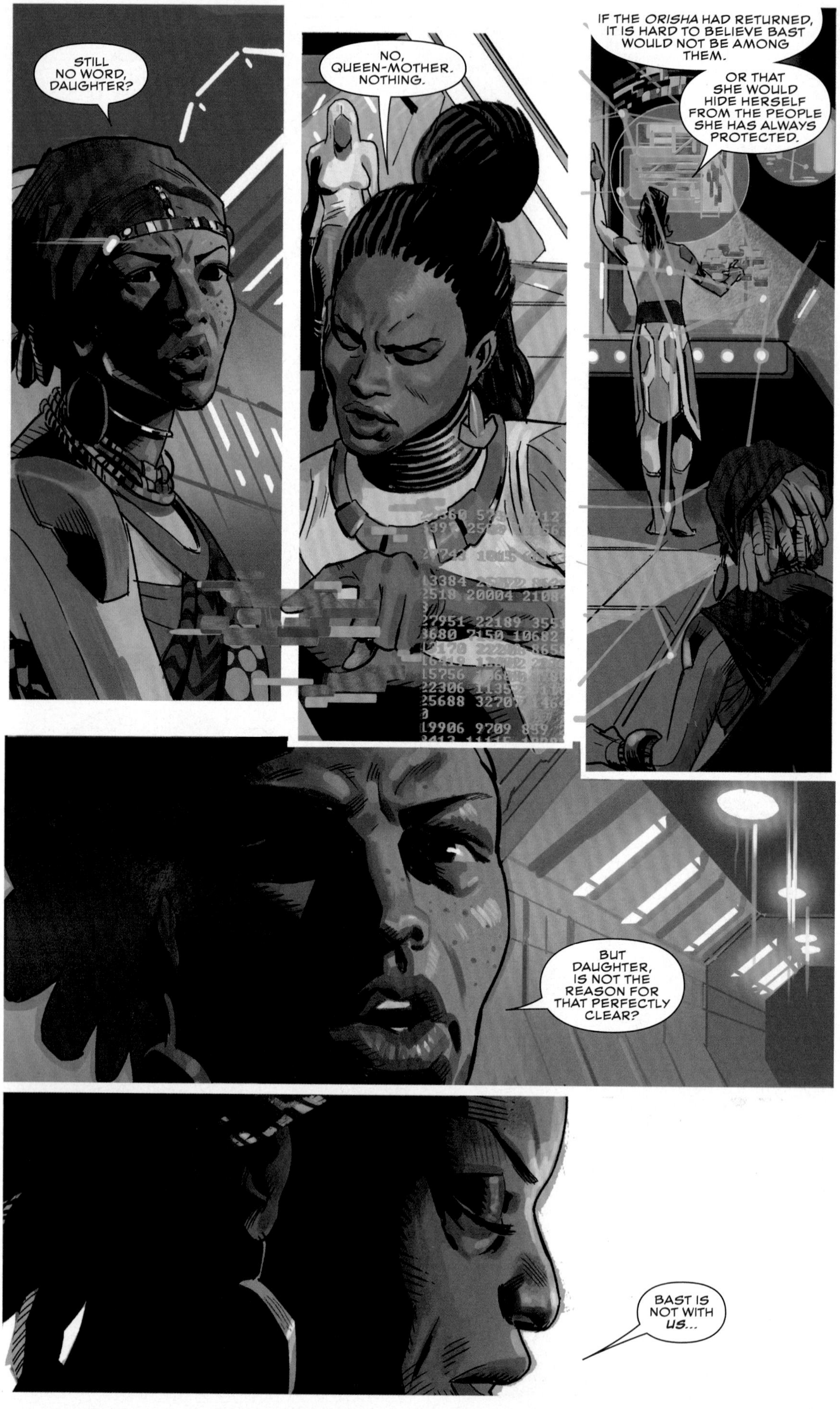
STILL NO WORD, DAUGHTER?
NO, QUEEN-MOTHER. NOTHING.
IF THE *ORISHA* HAD RETURNED, IT IS HARD TO BELIEVE BAST WOULD NOT BE AMONG THEM.
OR THAT SHE WOULD HIDE HERSELF FROM THE PEOPLE SHE HAS ALWAYS PROTECTED.
BUT DAUGHTER, IS NOT THE REASON FOR THAT PERFECTLY CLEAR?
BAST IS NOT WITH *US*...

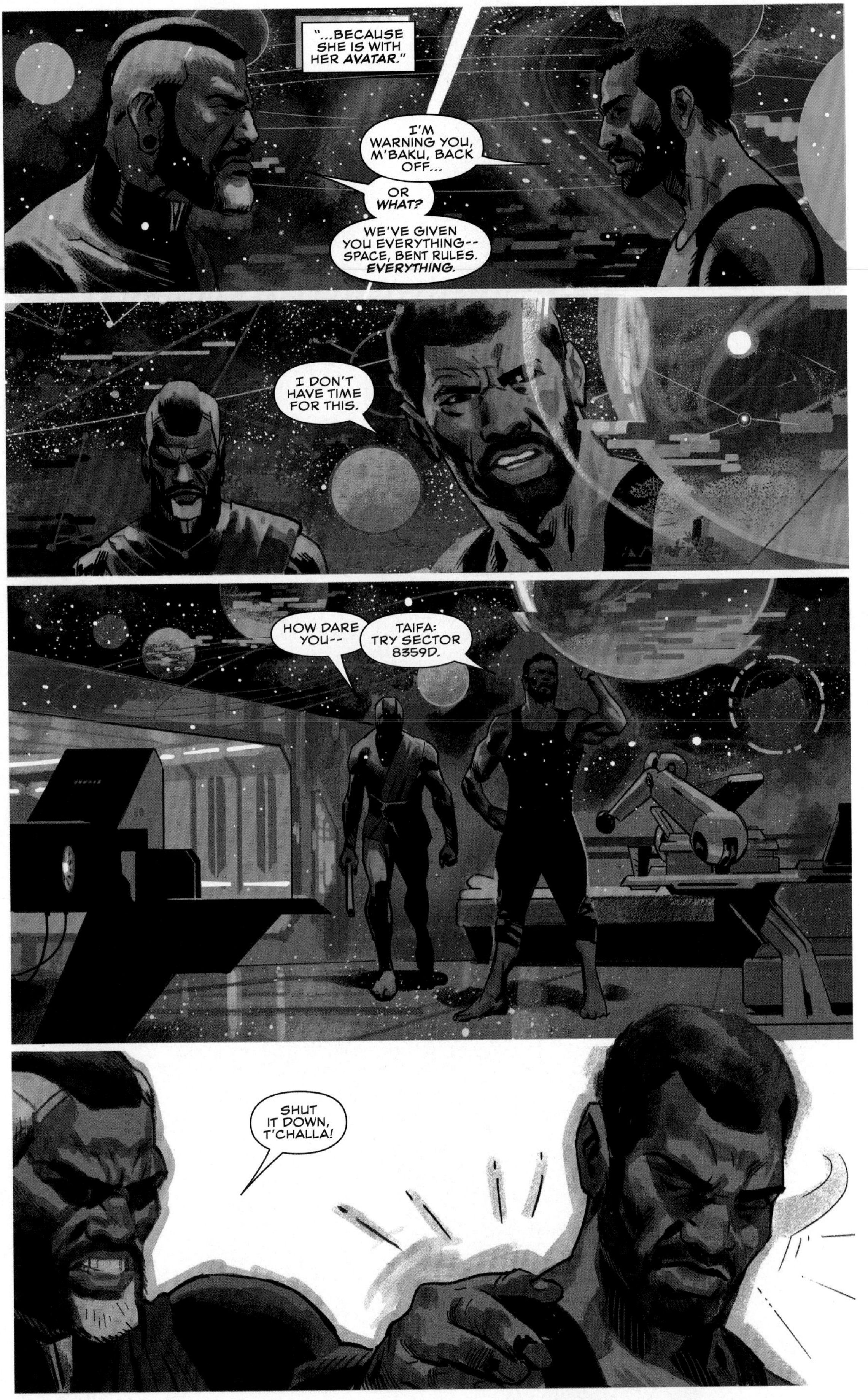
"...BECAUSE SHE IS WITH HER *AVATAR.*"
I'M WARNING YOU, M'BAKU, BACK OFF...
OR *WHAT?*
WE'VE GIVEN YOU EVERYTHING-- SPACE, BENT RULES. *EVERYTHING.*
I DON'T HAVE TIME FOR THIS.
HOW DARE YOU--
TAIFA: TRY SECTOR 8359D.
SHUT IT DOWN, T'CHALLA!

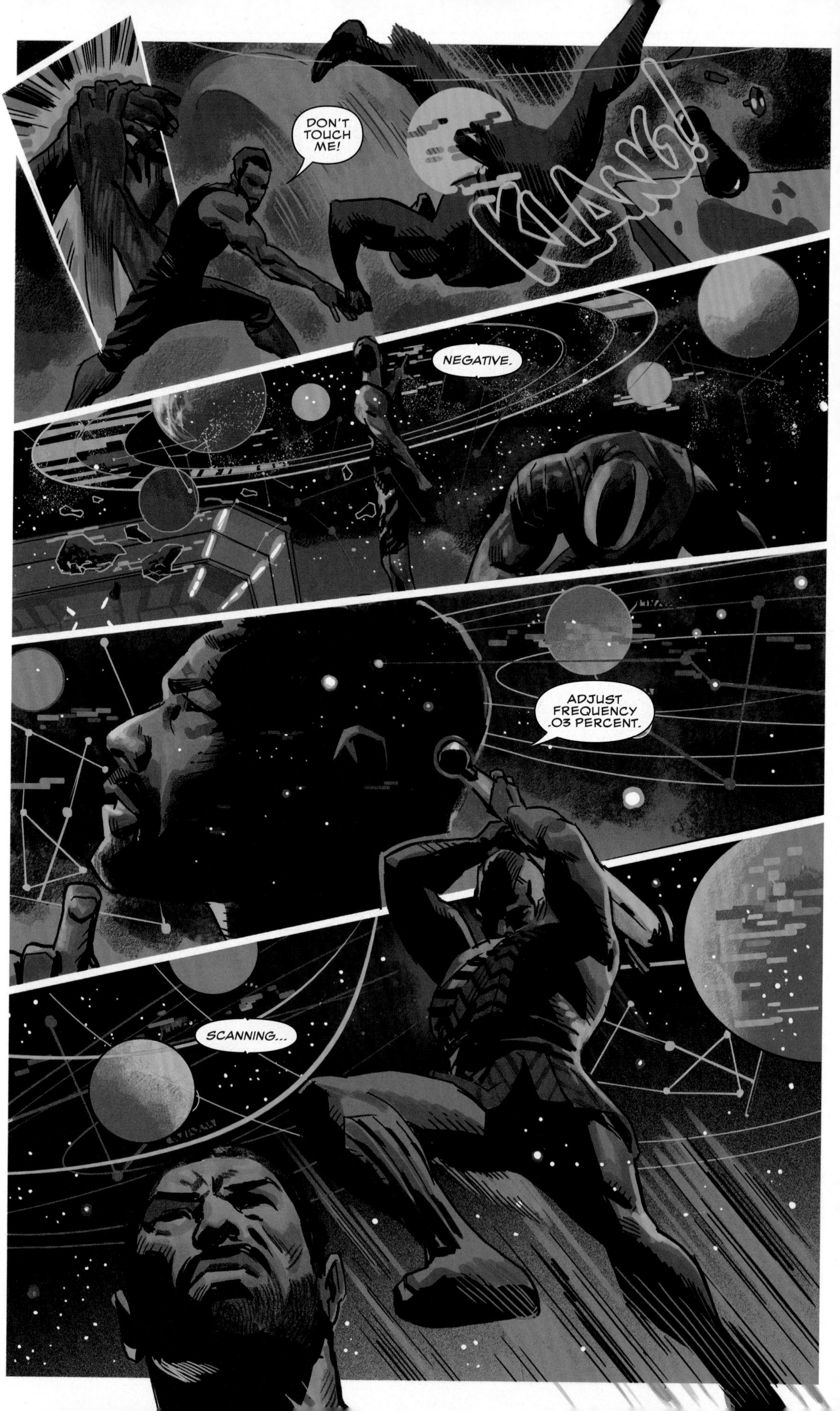
DON'T TOUCH ME!
KLANG!
NEGATIVE.
ADJUST FREQUENCY .03 PERCENT.
SCANNING...

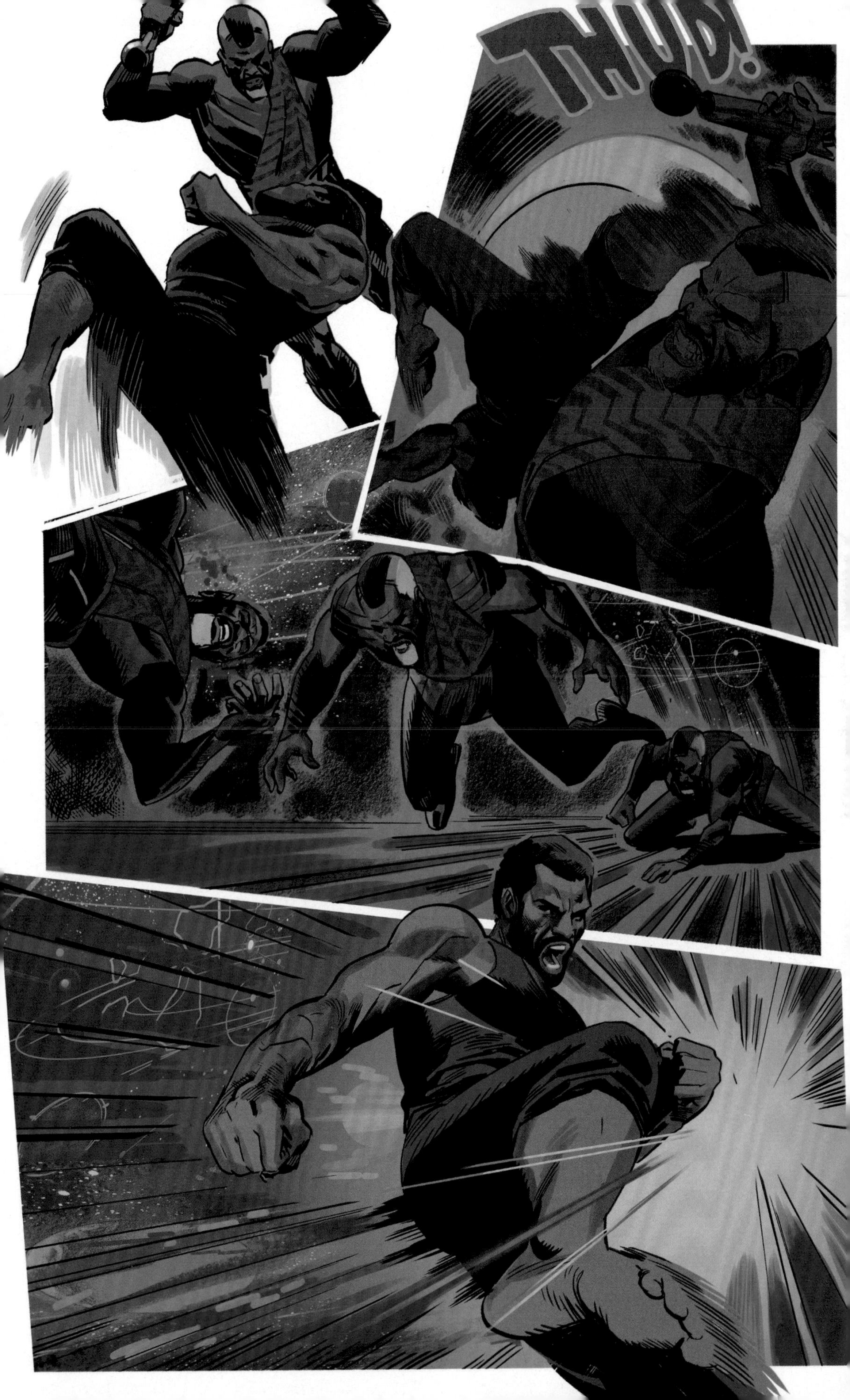
THUD!

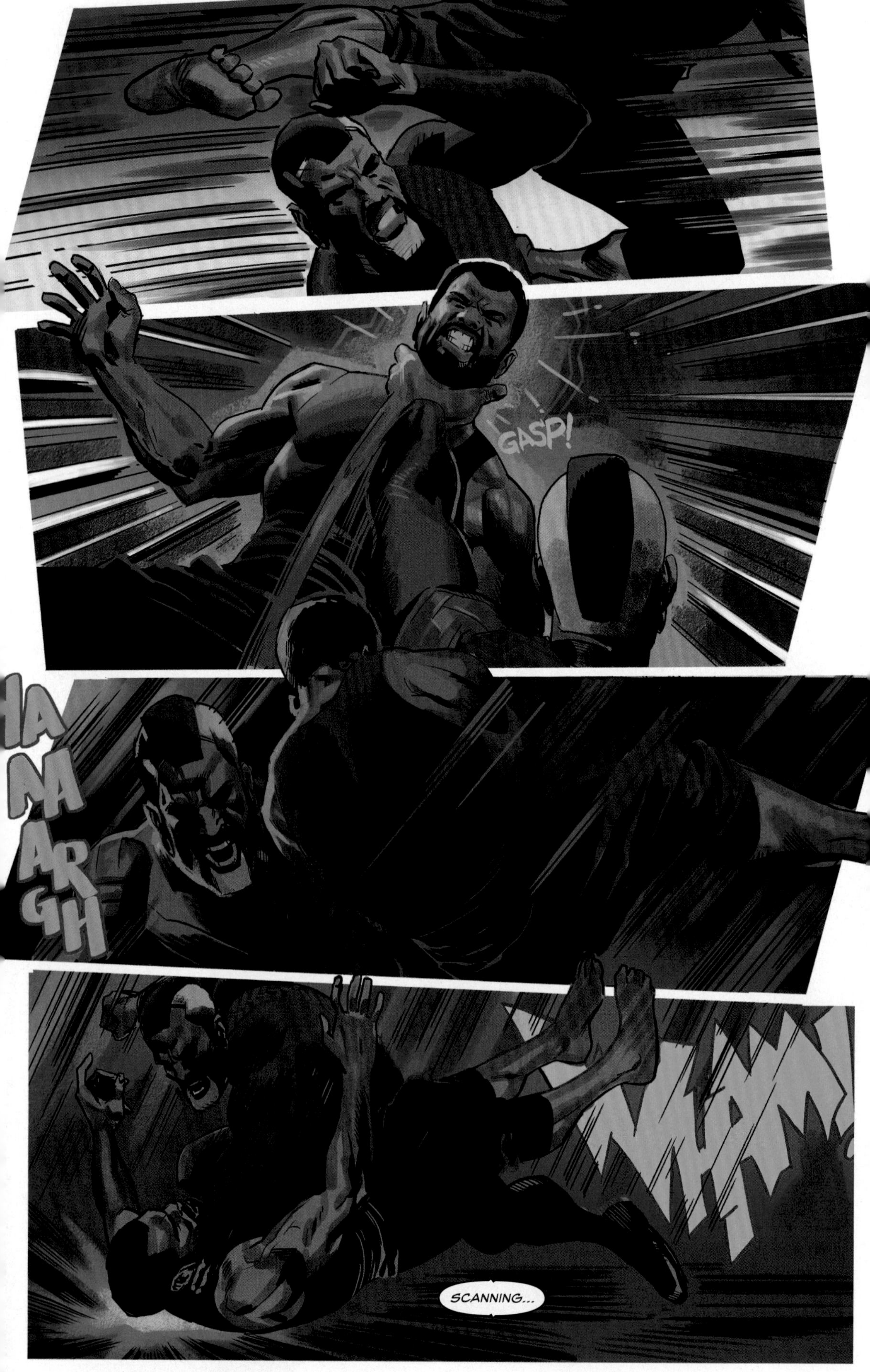
GASP!
HAAAARGH
SCANNING...

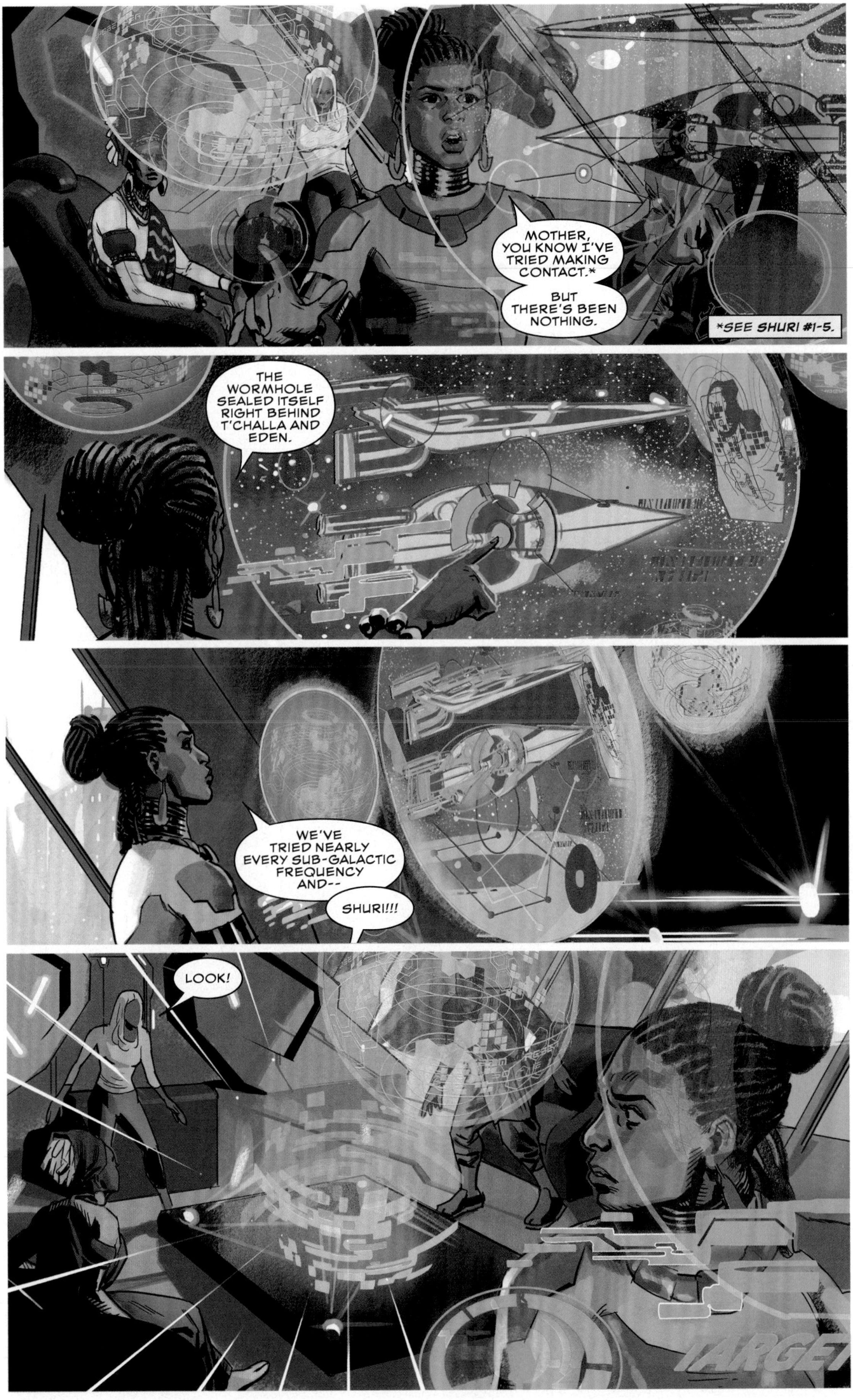
MOTHER, YOU KNOW I'VE TRIED MAKING CONTACT.*
BUT THERE'S BEEN NOTHING.
*SEE SHURI #1-5.
THE WORMHOLE SEALED ITSELF RIGHT BEHIND T'CHALLA AND EDEN.
WE'VE TRIED NEARLY EVERY SUB-GALACTIC FREQUENCY AND--
SHURI!!!
LOOK!
TARGET

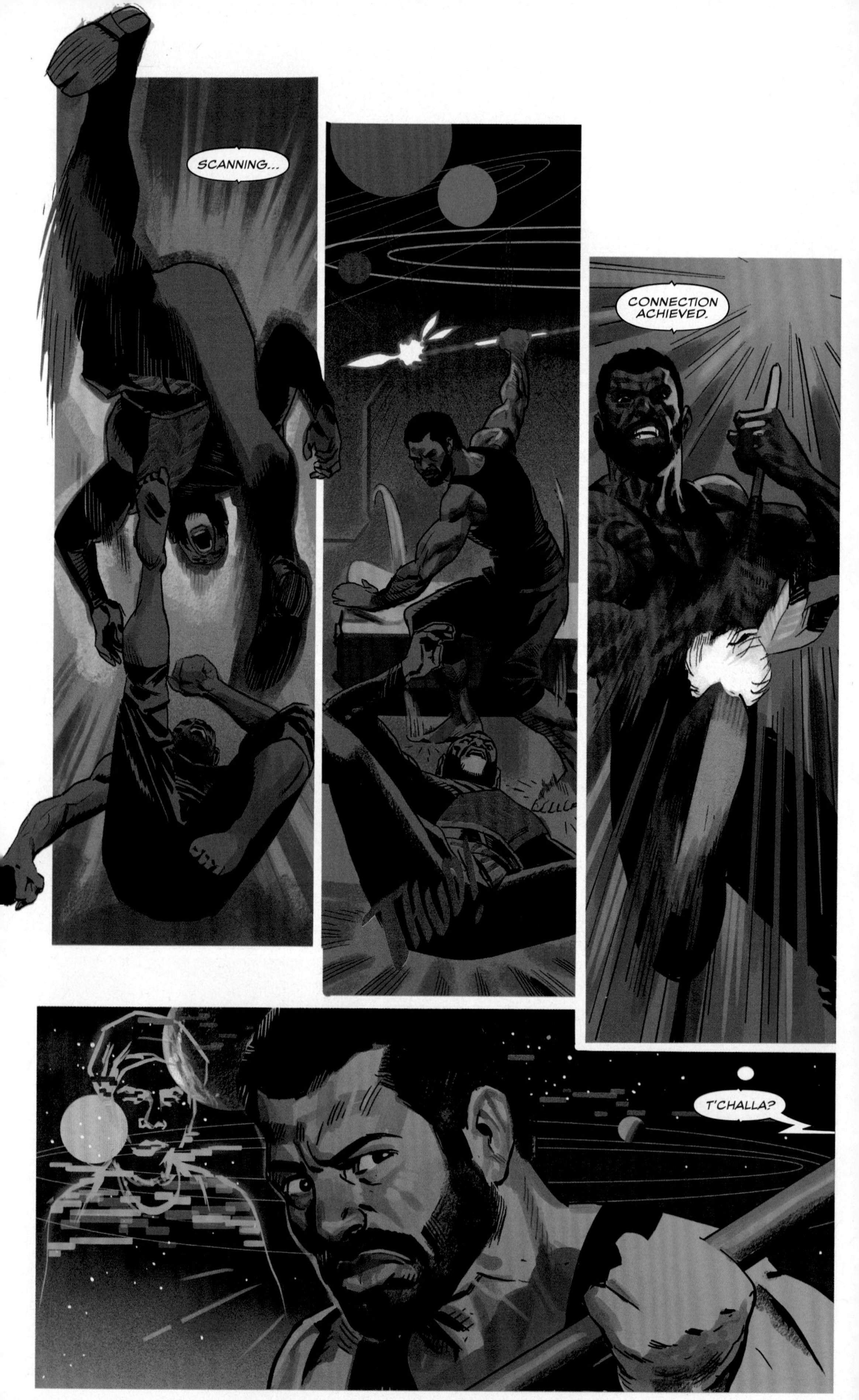
SCANNING...
THUD
CONNECTION ACHIEVED.
T'CHALLA?

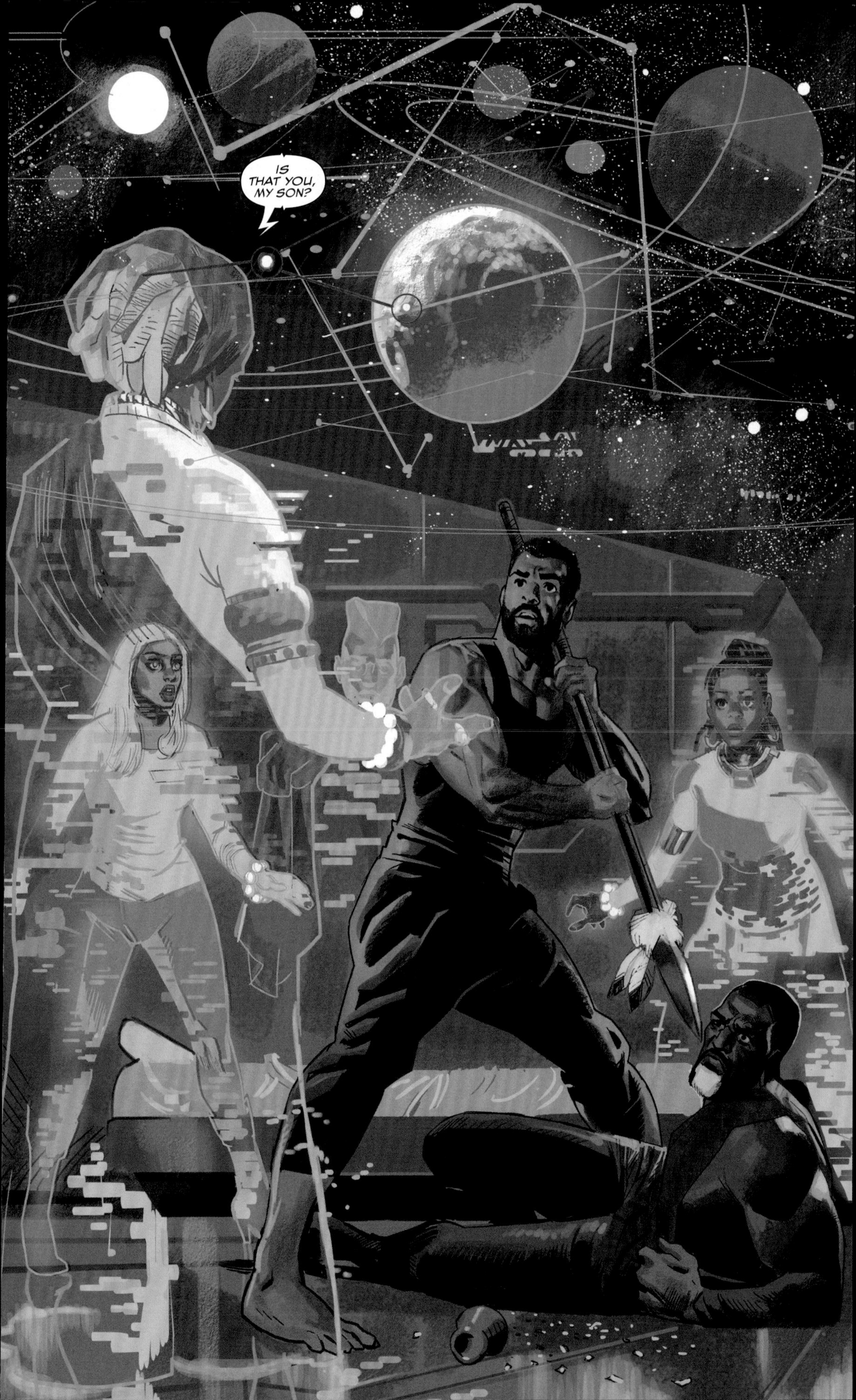
IS THAT YOU, MY SON?

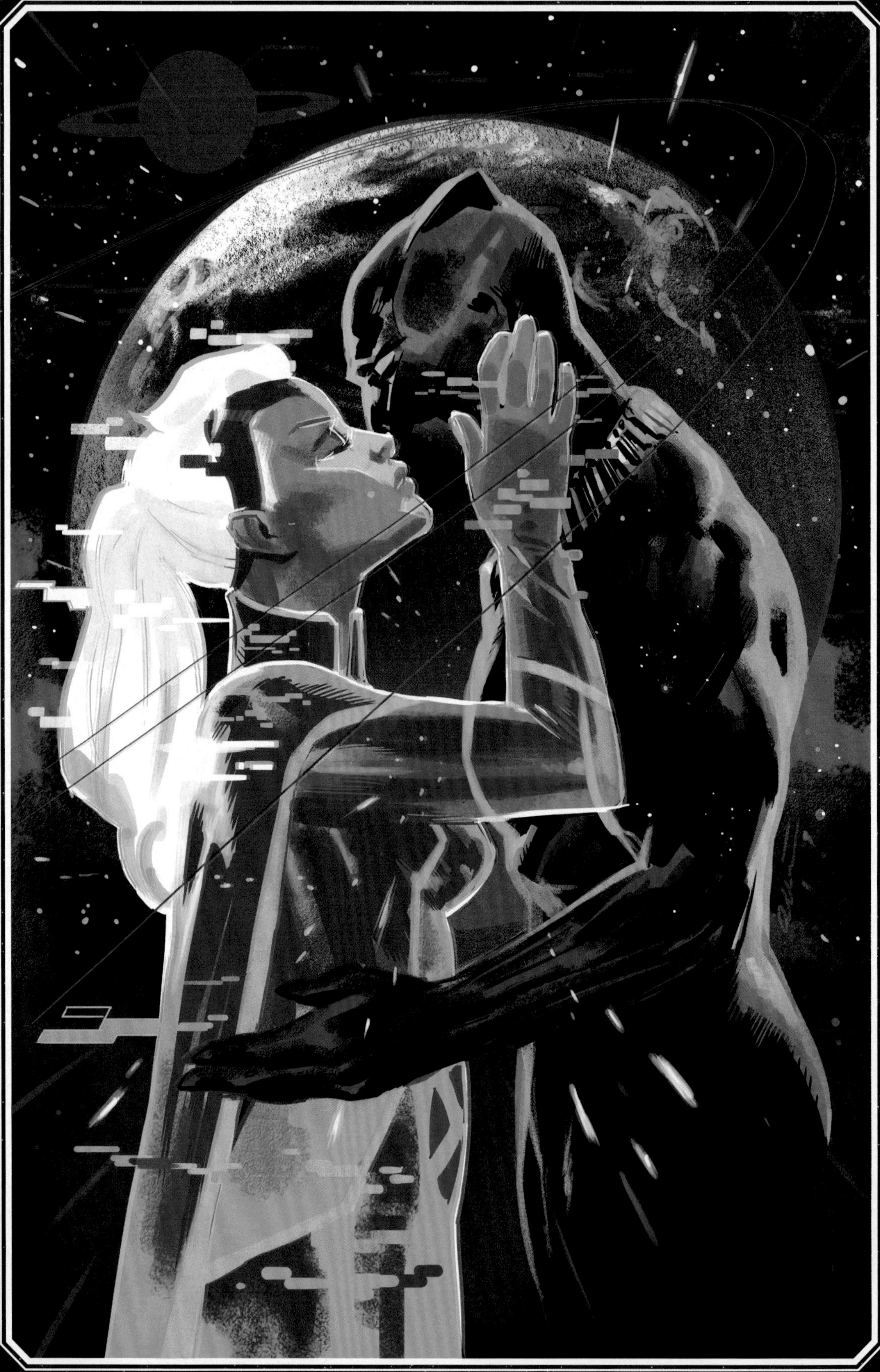

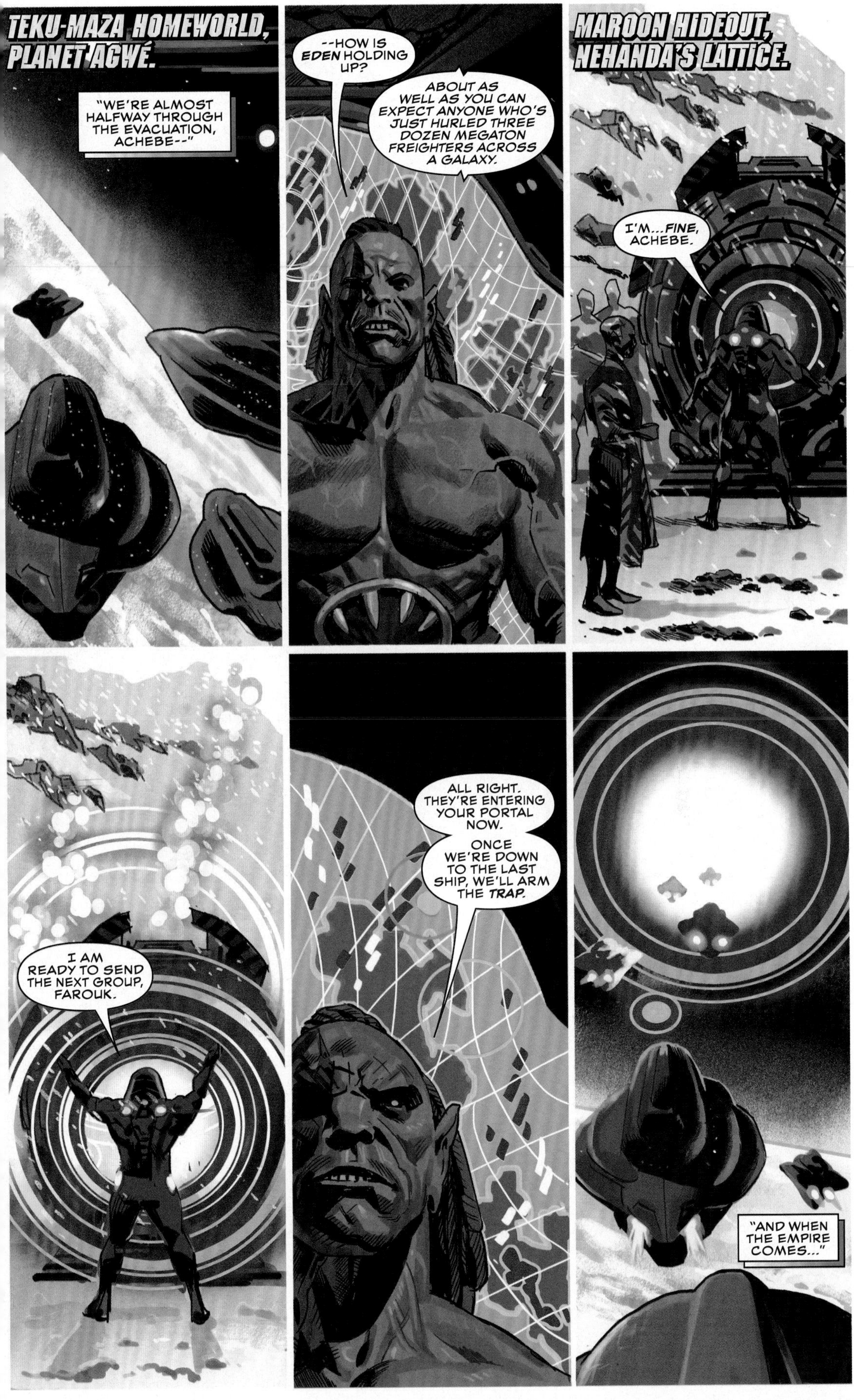
TEKU-MAZA HOMEWORLD, PLANET AGWÉ.
"WE'RE ALMOST HALFWAY THROUGH THE EVACUATION, ACHEBE--"
--HOW IS EDEN HOLDING UP?
ABOUT AS WELL AS YOU CAN EXPECT ANYONE WHO'S JUST HURLED THREE DOZEN MEGATON FREIGHTERS ACROSS A GALAXY.
MAROON HIDEOUT, NEHANDA'S LATTICE.
I'M...FINE, ACHEBE.
I AM READY TO SEND THE NEXT GROUP, FAROUK.
ALL RIGHT. THEY'RE ENTERING YOUR PORTAL NOW.
ONCE WE'RE DOWN TO THE LAST SHIP, WE'LL ARM THE TRAP.
"AND WHEN THE EMPIRE COMES..."

"...THE *CORE-KILLER* WILL BE WAITING."

THE LAST OF THAT GROUP HAVE GONE THROUGH NOW.

EXCELLENT. PREPARING THE NEXT FLIGHT TO--

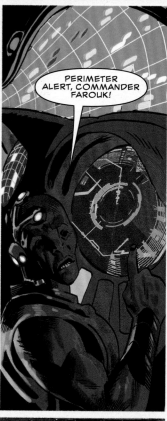

PERIMETER ALERT, COMMANDER FAROUK!

"FIVE FLIGHTS OF MASSAI FIGHTERS EMERGING FROM HYPERSPACE!"

NO...

SIR...

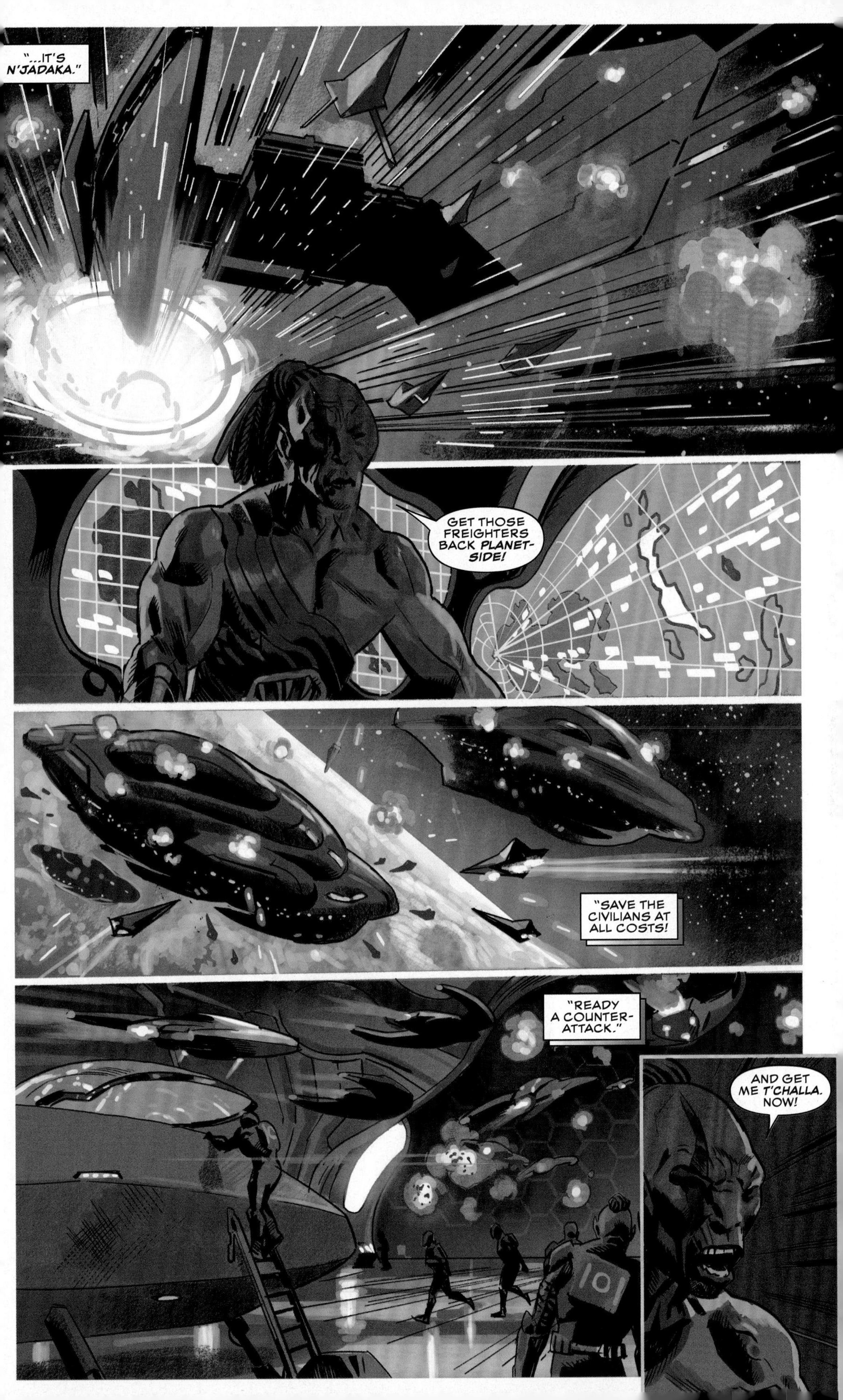
"...IT'S N'JADAKA."
GET THOSE FREIGHTERS BACK PLANET-SIDE!
"SAVE THE CIVILIANS AT ALL COSTS!
"READY A COUNTER-ATTACK."
AND GET ME T'CHALLA. NOW!

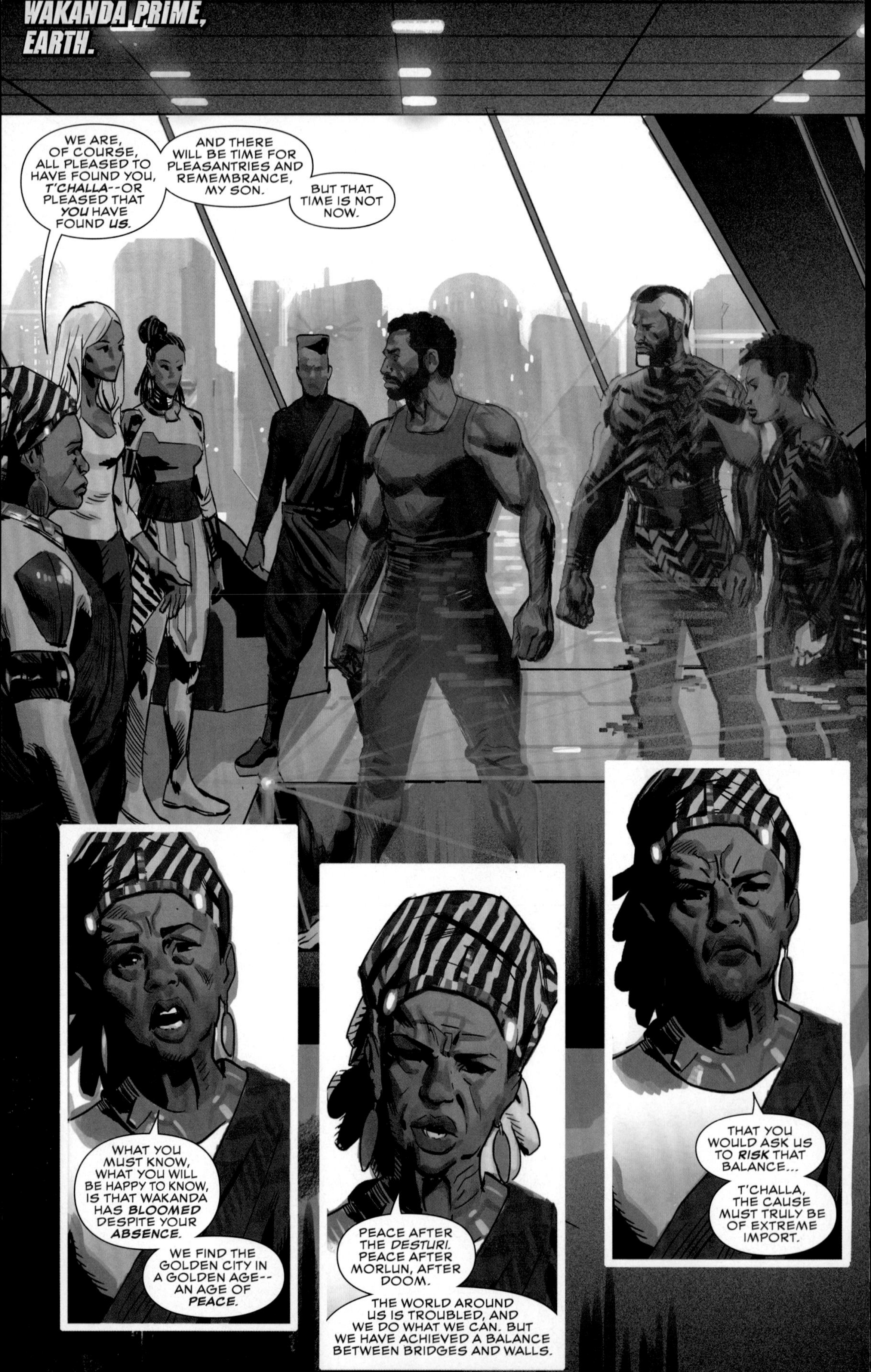
WAKANDA PRIME, EARTH.
WE ARE, OF COURSE, ALL PLEASED TO HAVE FOUND YOU, T'CHALLA--OR PLEASED THAT YOU HAVE FOUND US.
AND THERE WILL BE TIME FOR PLEASANTRIES AND REMEMBRANCE, MY SON.
BUT THAT TIME IS NOT NOW.
WHAT YOU MUST KNOW, WHAT YOU WILL BE HAPPY TO KNOW, IS THAT WAKANDA HAS BLOOMED DESPITE YOUR ABSENCE.
WE FIND THE GOLDEN CITY IN A GOLDEN AGE--AN AGE OF PEACE.
PEACE AFTER THE DESTURI. PEACE AFTER MORLUN, AFTER DOOM.
THE WORLD AROUND US IS TROUBLED, AND WE DO WHAT WE CAN. BUT WE HAVE ACHIEVED A BALANCE BETWEEN BRIDGES AND WALLS.
THAT YOU WOULD ASK US TO RISK THAT BALANCE...
T'CHALLA, THE CAUSE MUST TRULY BE OF EXTREME IMPORT.

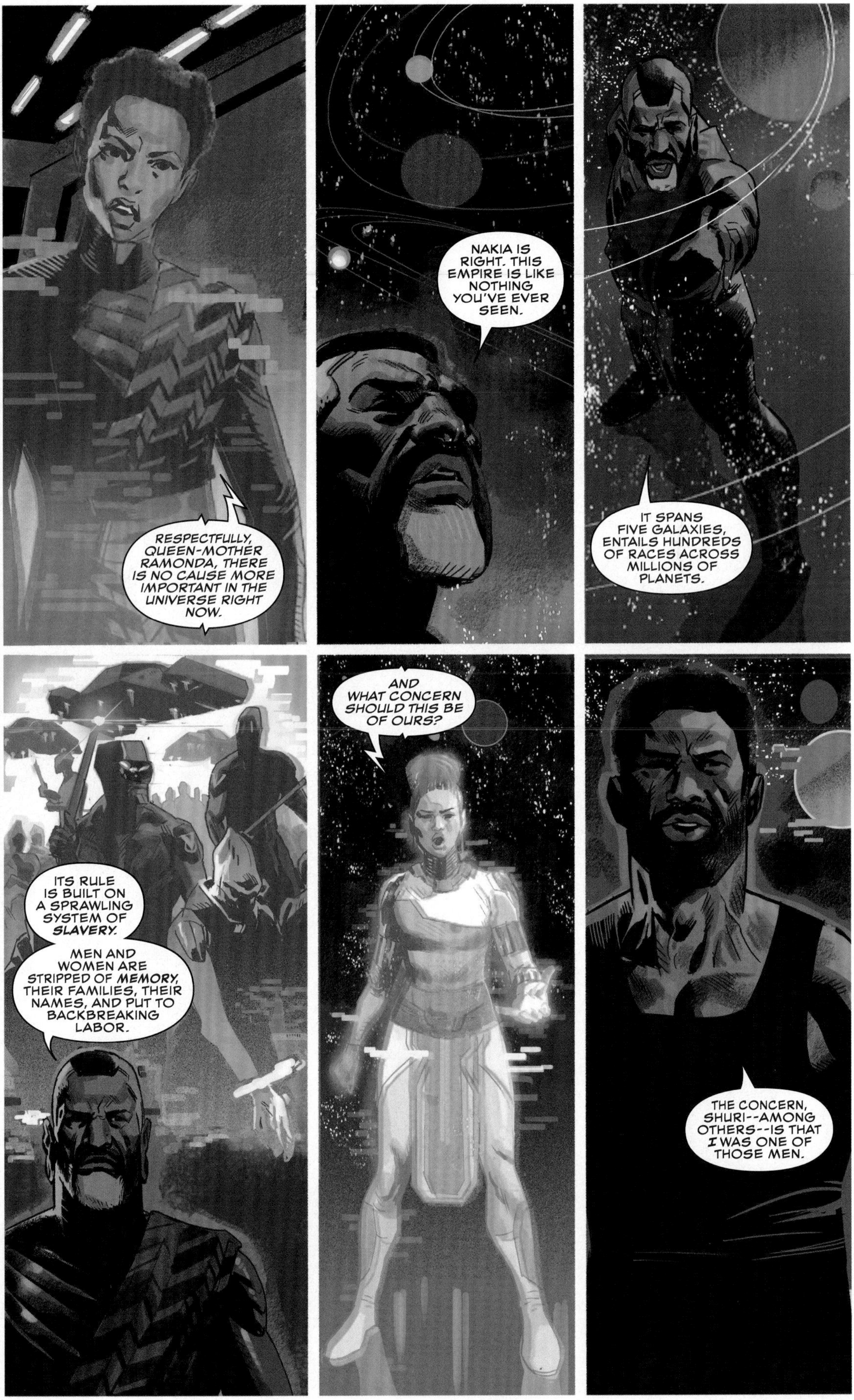
RESPECTFULLY, QUEEN-MOTHER RAMONDA, THERE IS NO CAUSE MORE IMPORTANT IN THE UNIVERSE RIGHT NOW.
NAKIA IS RIGHT. THIS EMPIRE IS LIKE NOTHING YOU'VE EVER SEEN.
IT SPANS FIVE GALAXIES, ENTAILS HUNDREDS OF RACES ACROSS MILLIONS OF PLANETS.
ITS RULE IS BUILT ON A SPRAWLING SYSTEM OF SLAVERY.
MEN AND WOMEN ARE STRIPPED OF MEMORY, THEIR FAMILIES, THEIR NAMES, AND PUT TO BACKBREAKING LABOR.
AND WHAT CONCERN SHOULD THIS BE OF OURS?
THE CONCERN, SHURI--AMONG OTHERS--IS THAT I WAS ONE OF THOSE MEN.

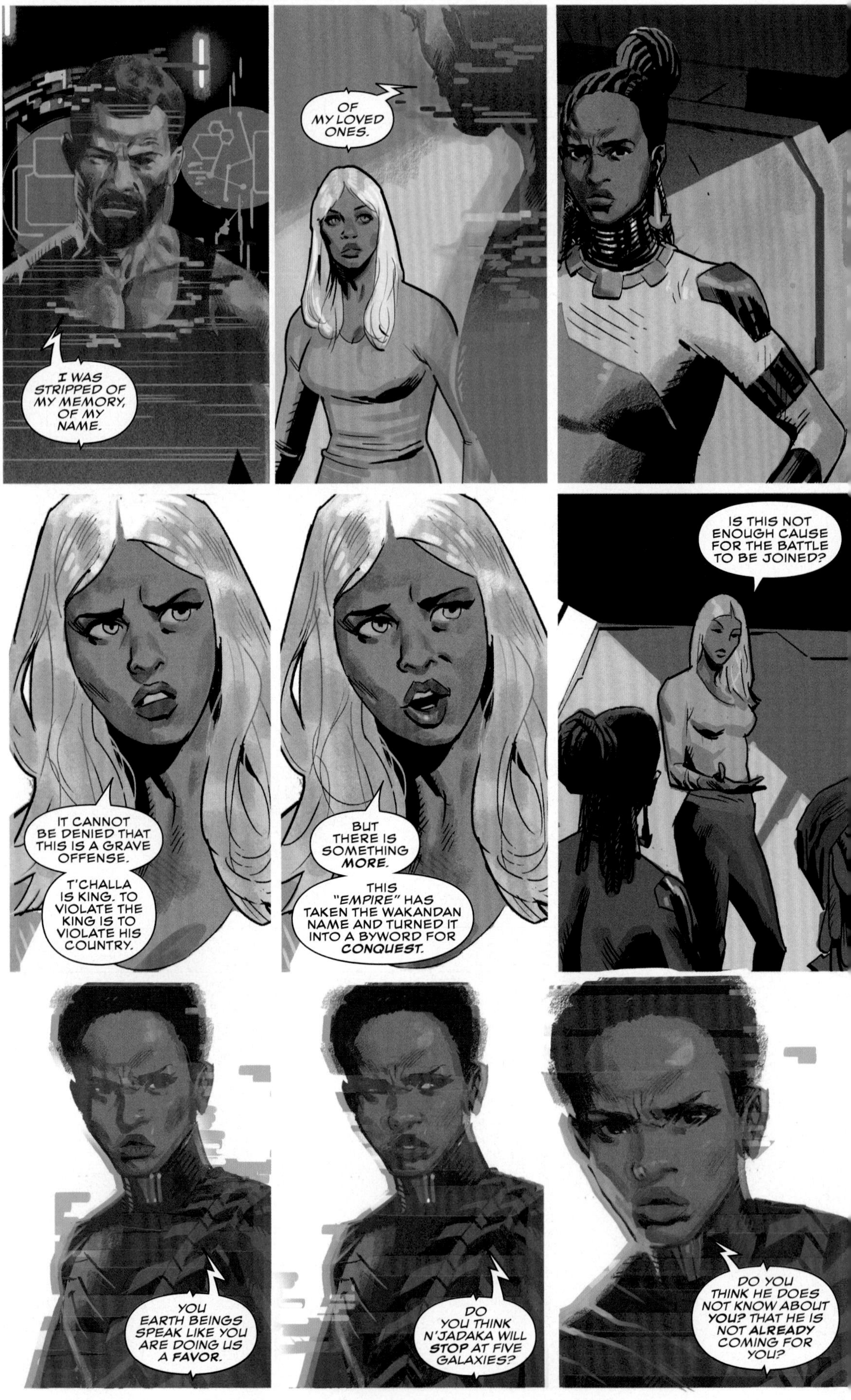
I WAS STRIPPED OF MY MEMORY, OF MY NAME.
OF MY LOVED ONES.
IT CANNOT BE DENIED THAT THIS IS A GRAVE OFFENSE.
T'CHALLA IS KING. TO VIOLATE THE KING IS TO VIOLATE HIS COUNTRY.
BUT THERE IS SOMETHING MORE.
THIS "EMPIRE" HAS TAKEN THE WAKANDAN NAME AND TURNED IT INTO A BYWORD FOR CONQUEST.
IS THIS NOT ENOUGH CAUSE FOR THE BATTLE TO BE JOINED?
YOU EARTH BEINGS SPEAK LIKE YOU ARE DOING US A FAVOR.
DO YOU THINK N'JADAKA WILL STOP AT FIVE GALAXIES?
DO YOU THINK HE DOES NOT KNOW ABOUT YOU? THAT HE IS NOT ALREADY COMING FOR YOU?

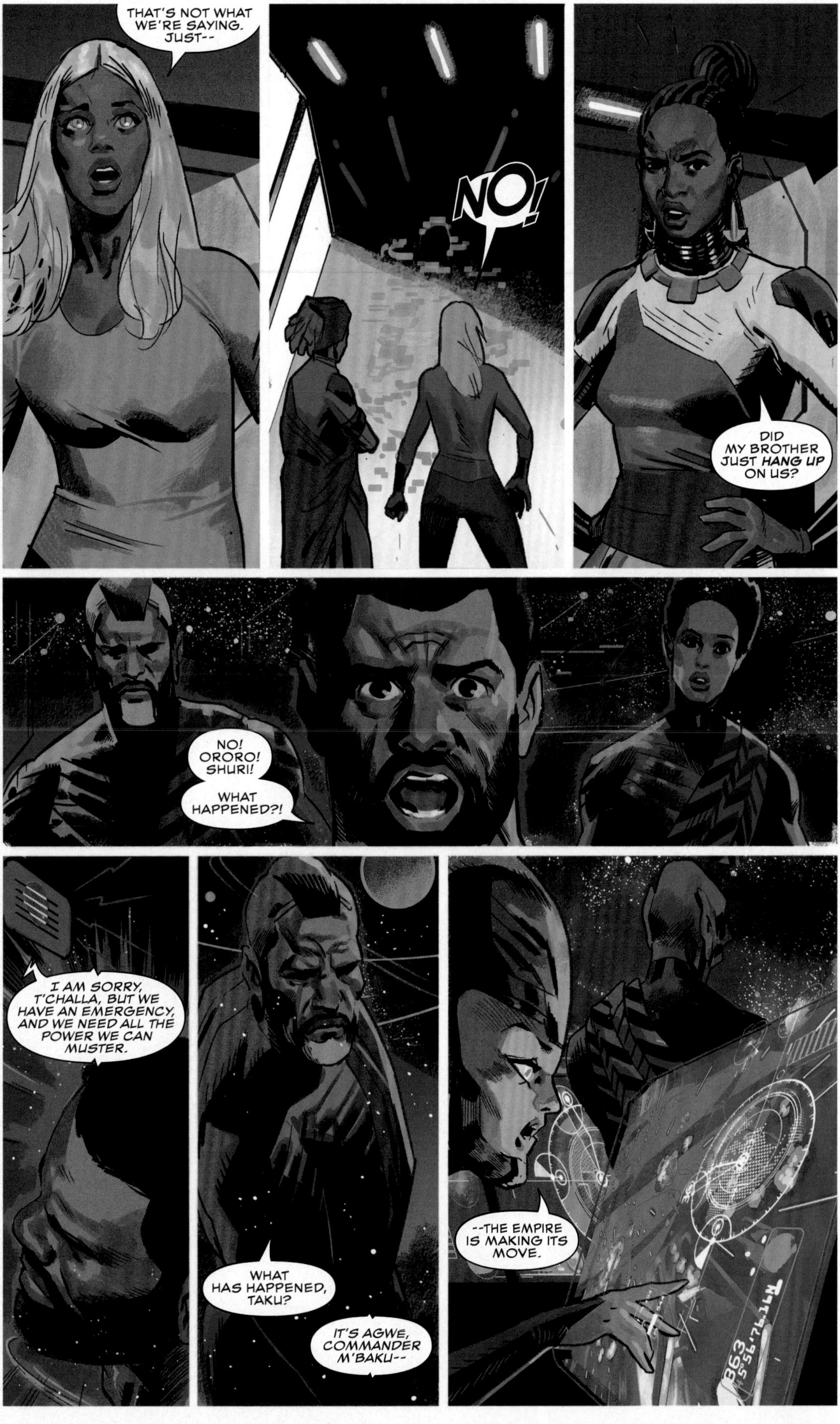
THAT'S NOT WHAT WE'RE SAYING. JUST--
NO!
DID MY BROTHER JUST HANG UP ON US?
NO! ORORO! SHURI!
WHAT HAPPENED?!
I AM SORRY, T'CHALLA, BUT WE HAVE AN EMERGENCY, AND WE NEED ALL THE POWER WE CAN MUSTER.
WHAT HAS HAPPENED, TAKU?
IT'S AGWE, COMMANDER M'BAKU--
--THE EMPIRE IS MAKING ITS MOVE.

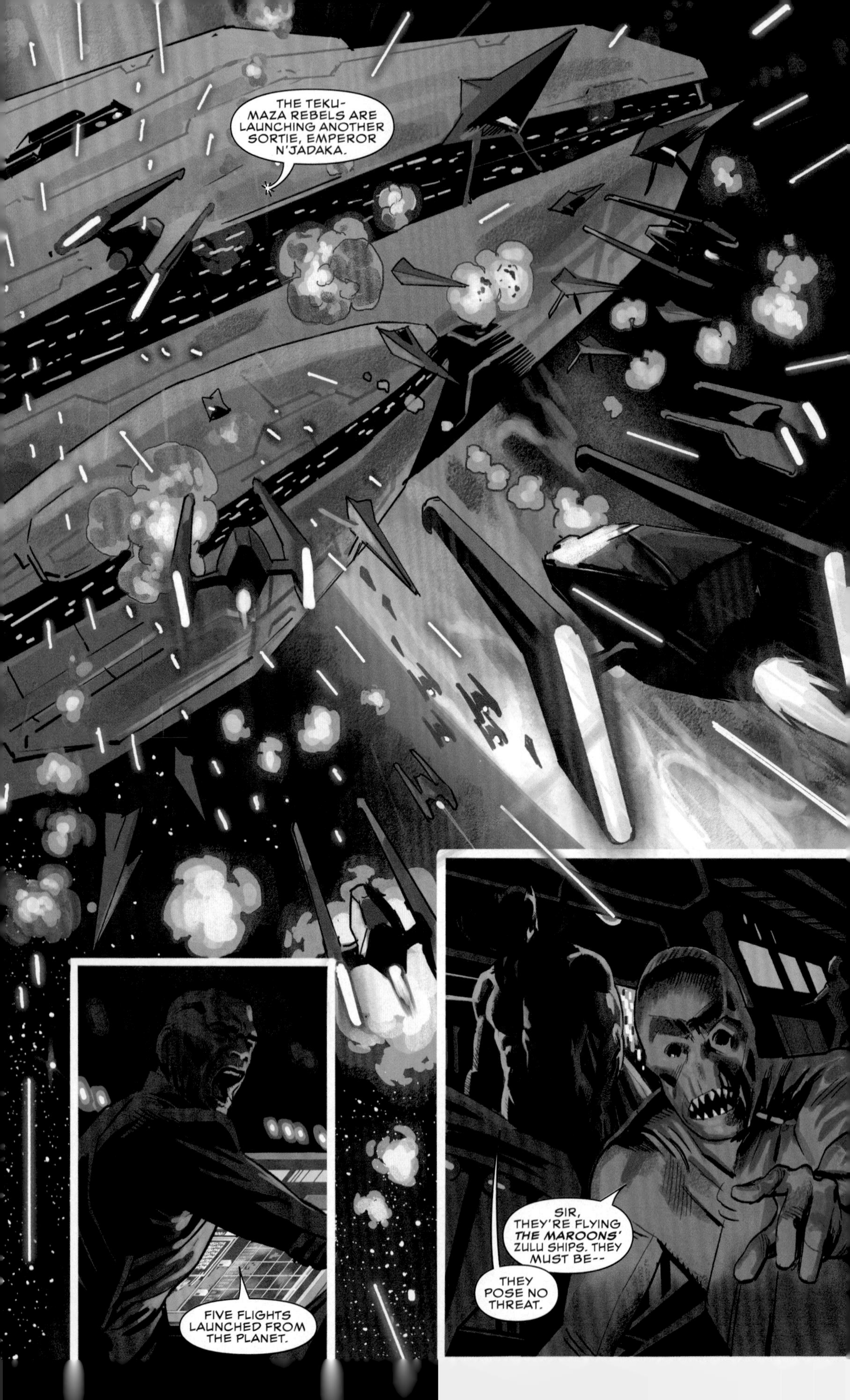
THE TEKU-MAZA REBELS ARE LAUNCHING ANOTHER SORTIE, EMPEROR N'JADAKA.
FIVE FLIGHTS LAUNCHED FROM THE PLANET.
SIR, THEY'RE FLYING *THE MAROONS'* ZULU SHIPS. THEY MUST BE--
THEY POSE NO THREAT.

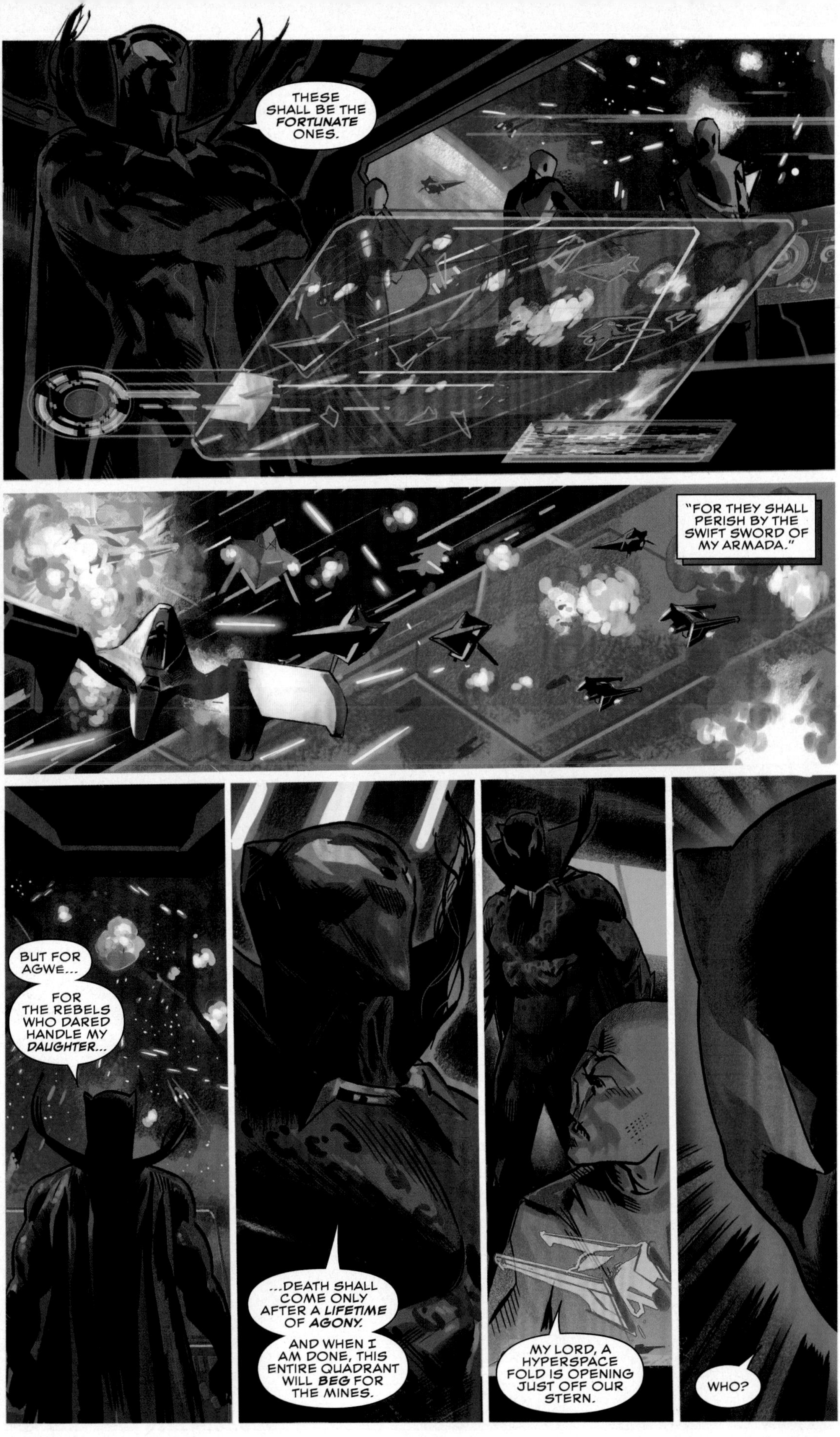
THESE SHALL BE THE FORTUNATE ONES.
"FOR THEY SHALL PERISH BY THE SWIFT SWORD OF MY ARMADA."
BUT FOR AGWE...
FOR THE REBELS WHO DARED HANDLE MY DAUGHTER...
...DEATH SHALL COME ONLY AFTER A LIFETIME OF AGONY.
AND WHEN I AM DONE, THIS ENTIRE QUADRANT WILL BEG FOR THE MINES.
MY LORD, A HYPERSPACE FOLD IS OPENING JUST OFF OUR STERN.
WHO?

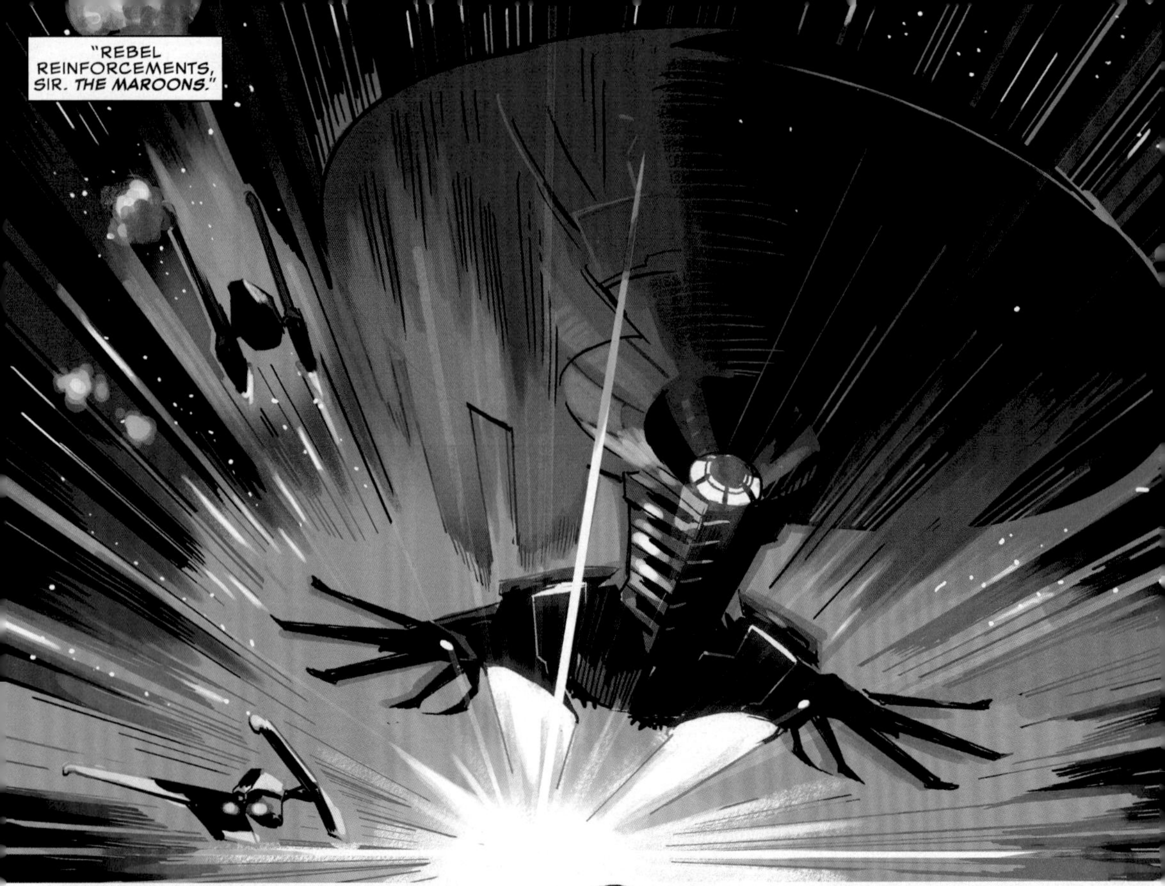
"REBEL REINFORCEMENTS, SIR. *THE MAROONS.*"

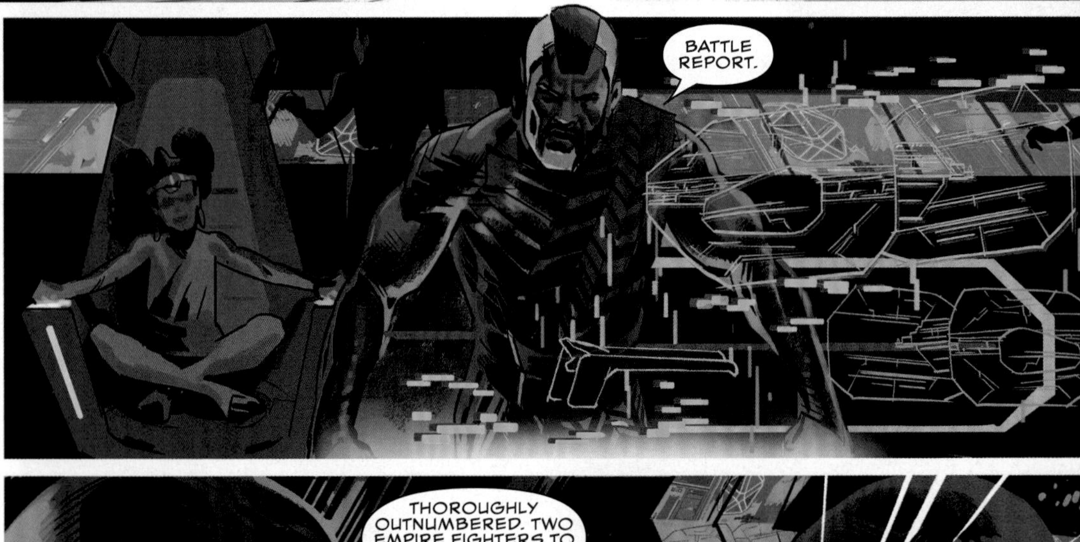
BATTLE REPORT.

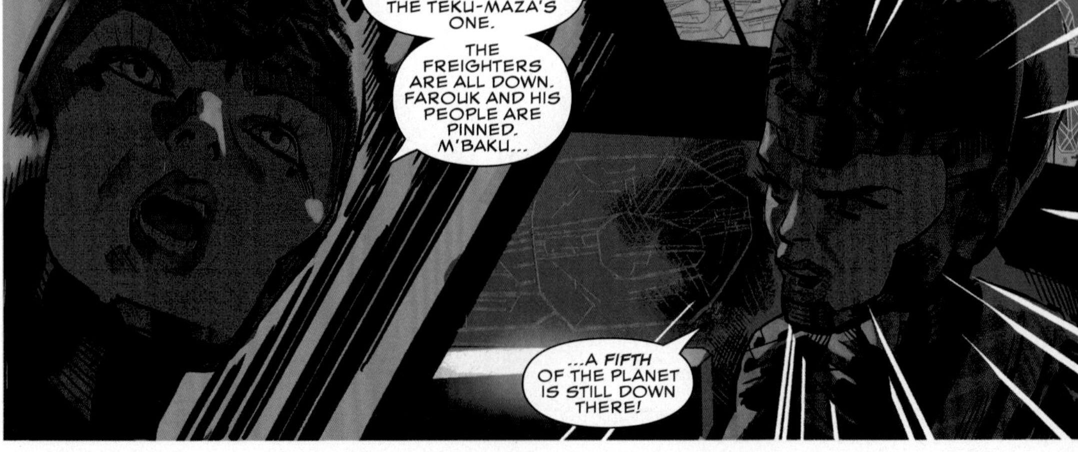
THOROUGHLY OUTNUMBERED. TWO EMPIRE FIGHTERS TO THE TEKU-MAZA'S ONE.
THE FREIGHTERS ARE ALL DOWN. FAROUK AND HIS PEOPLE ARE PINNED. M'BAKU...
...A *FIFTH* OF THE PLANET IS STILL DOWN THERE!

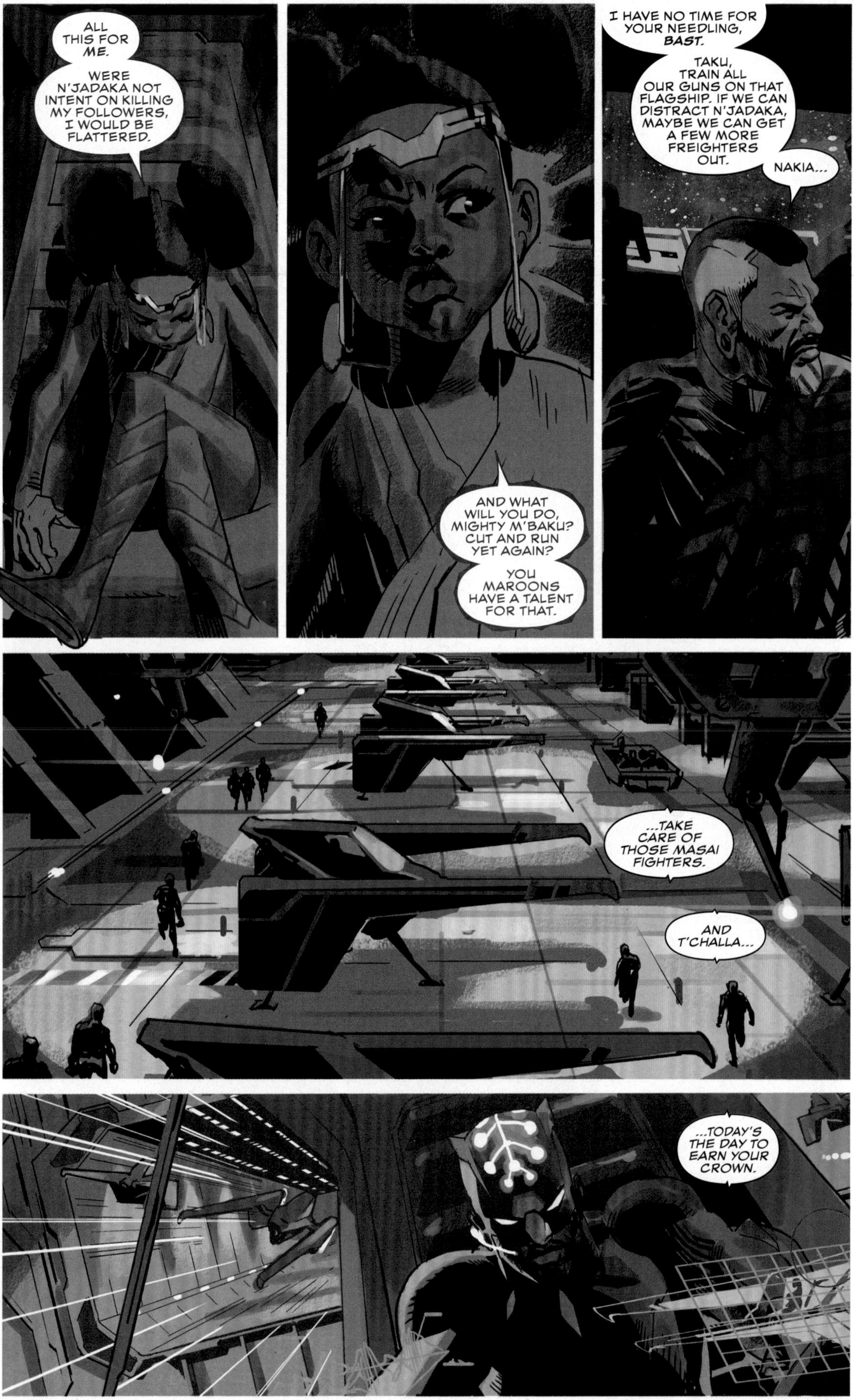
ALL THIS FOR *ME*.
WERE N'JADAKA NOT INTENT ON KILLING MY FOLLOWERS, I WOULD BE FLATTERED.
AND WHAT WILL YOU DO, MIGHTY M'BAKU? CUT AND RUN YET AGAIN?
YOU MAROONS HAVE A TALENT FOR THAT.
I HAVE NO TIME FOR YOUR NEEDLING, *BAST*.
TAKU, TRAIN ALL OUR GUNS ON THAT FLAGSHIP. IF WE CAN DISTRACT N'JADAKA, MAYBE WE CAN GET A FEW MORE FREIGHTERS OUT.
NAKIA...
...TAKE CARE OF THOSE MASAI FIGHTERS.
AND T'CHALLA...
...TODAY'S THE DAY TO EARN YOUR CROWN.

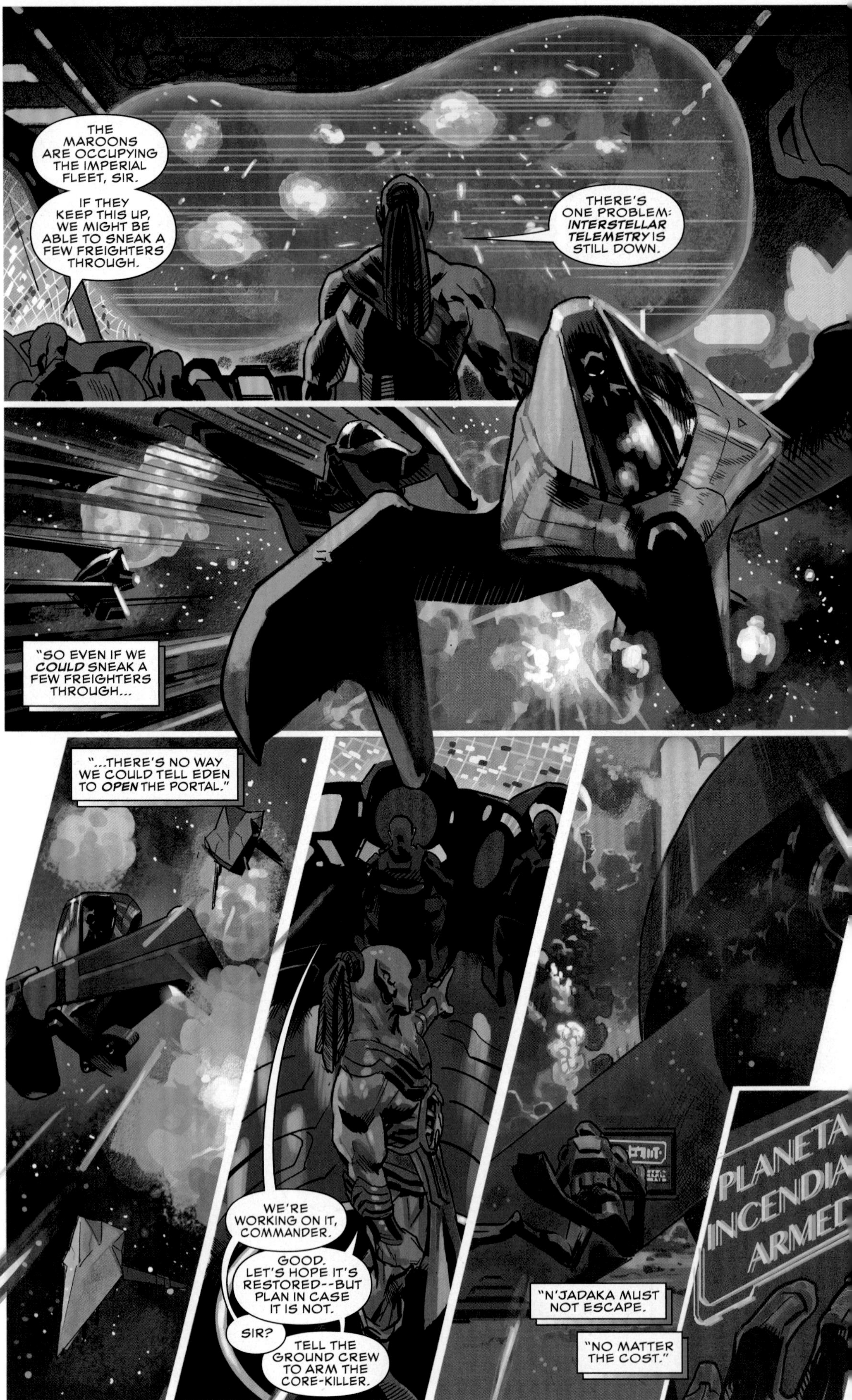
THE MAROONS ARE OCCUPYING THE IMPERIAL FLEET, SIR.
IF THEY KEEP THIS UP, WE MIGHT BE ABLE TO SNEAK A FEW FREIGHTERS THROUGH.
THERE'S ONE PROBLEM: INTERSTELLAR TELEMETRY IS STILL DOWN.
"SO EVEN IF WE COULD SNEAK A FEW FREIGHTERS THROUGH...
"...THERE'S NO WAY WE COULD TELL EDEN TO OPEN THE PORTAL."
WE'RE WORKING ON IT, COMMANDER.
GOOD. LET'S HOPE IT'S RESTORED--BUT PLAN IN CASE IT IS NOT.
SIR?
TELL THE GROUND CREW TO ARM THE CORE-KILLER.
"N'JADAKA MUST NOT ESCAPE.
"NO MATTER THE COST."
PLANETA
INCENDIA
ARMED

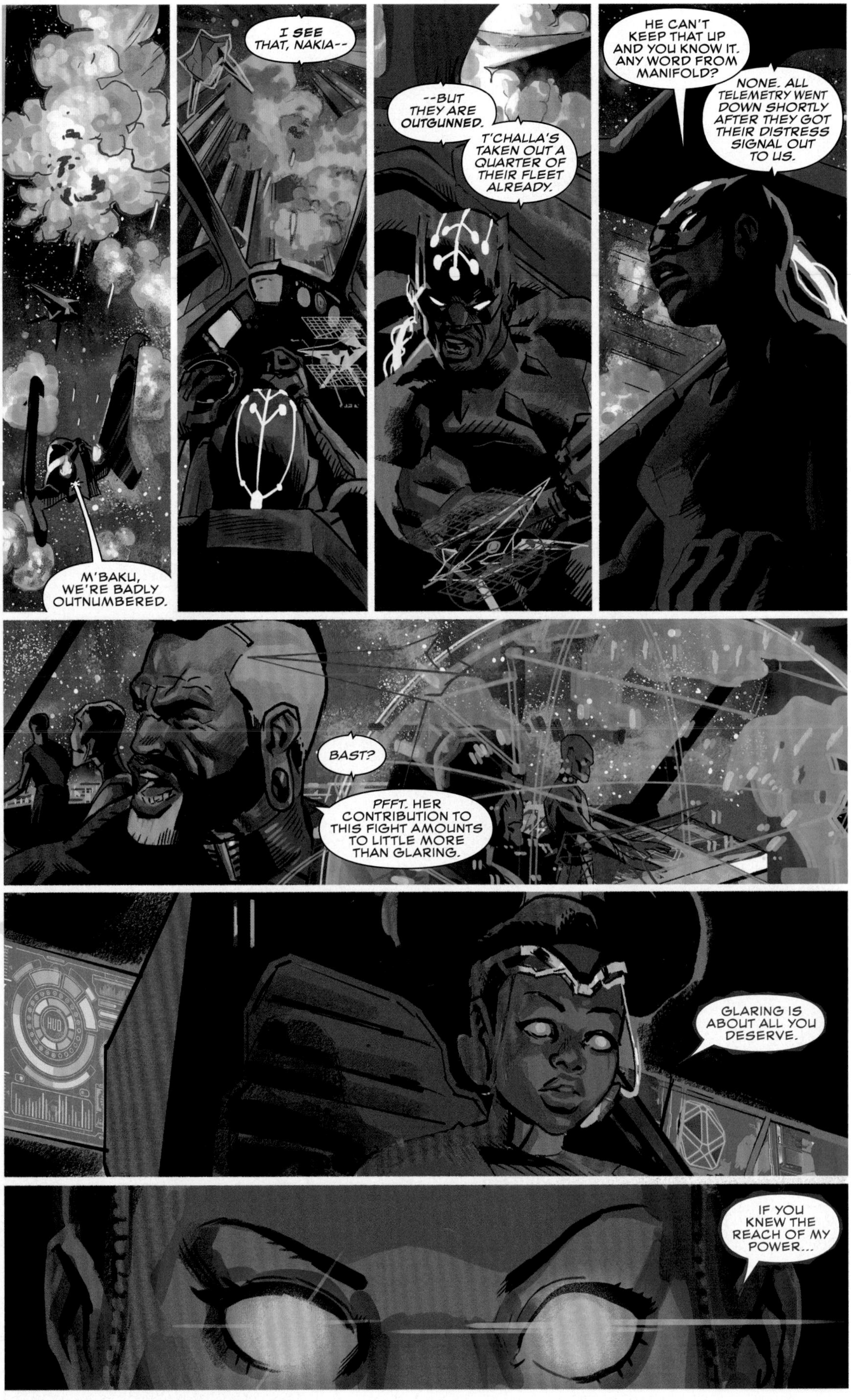
M'BAKU, WE'RE BADLY OUTNUMBERED.
I SEE THAT, NAKIA--
--BUT THEY ARE OUTGUNNED.
T'CHALLA'S TAKEN OUT A QUARTER OF THEIR FLEET ALREADY.
HE CAN'T KEEP THAT UP AND YOU KNOW IT. ANY WORD FROM MANIFOLD?
NONE. ALL TELEMETRY WENT DOWN SHORTLY AFTER THEY GOT THEIR DISTRESS SIGNAL OUT TO US.
BAST?
PFFT. HER CONTRIBUTION TO THIS FIGHT AMOUNTS TO LITTLE MORE THAN GLARING.
HUD
GLARING IS ABOUT ALL YOU DESERVE.
IF YOU KNEW THE REACH OF MY POWER...

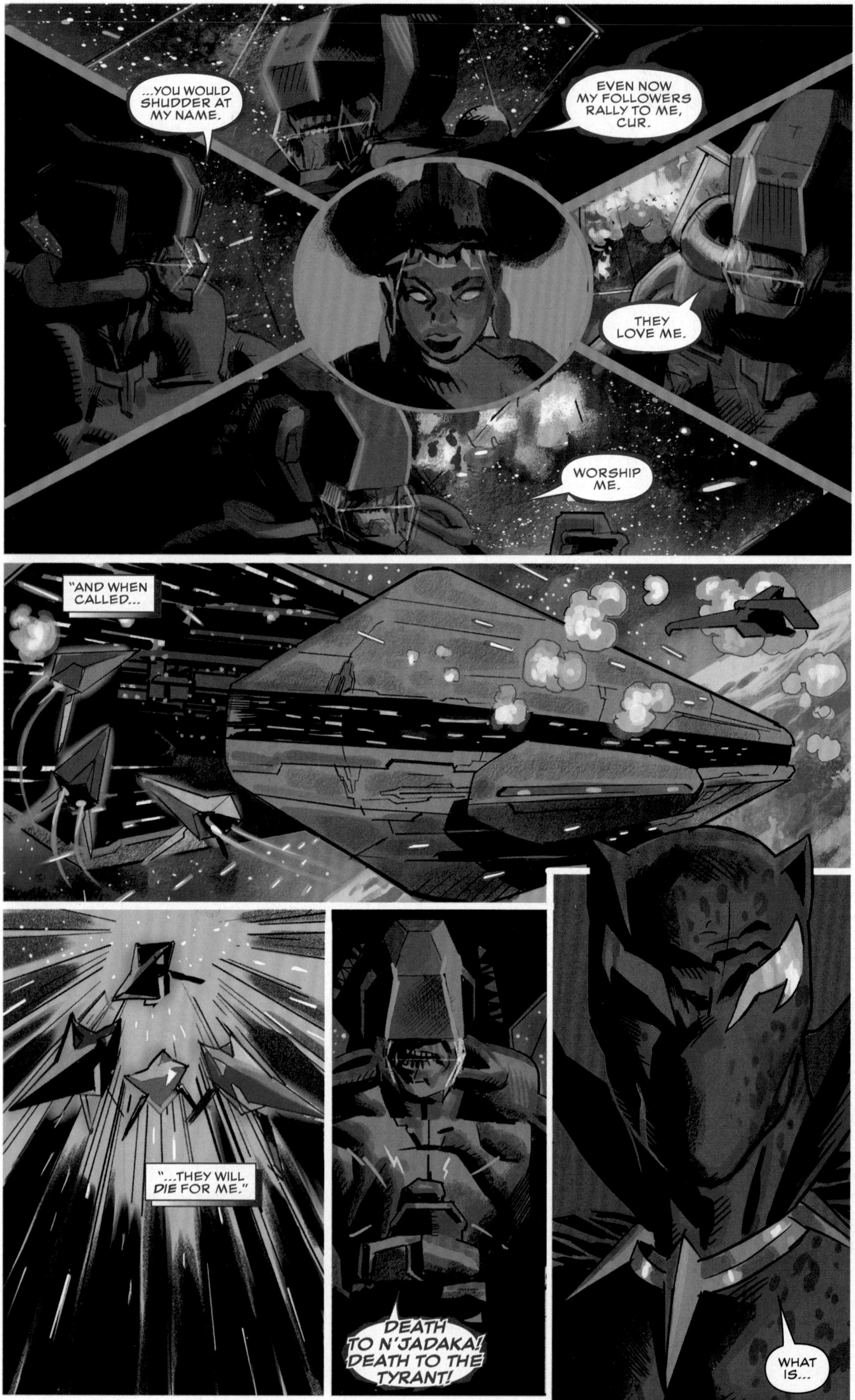
...YOU WOULD SHUDDER AT MY NAME.
EVEN NOW MY FOLLOWERS RALLY TO ME, CUR.
THEY LOVE ME.
WORSHIP ME.
"AND WHEN CALLED...
"...THEY WILL DIE FOR ME."
DEATH TO N'JADAKA! DEATH TO THE TYRANT!
WHAT IS...

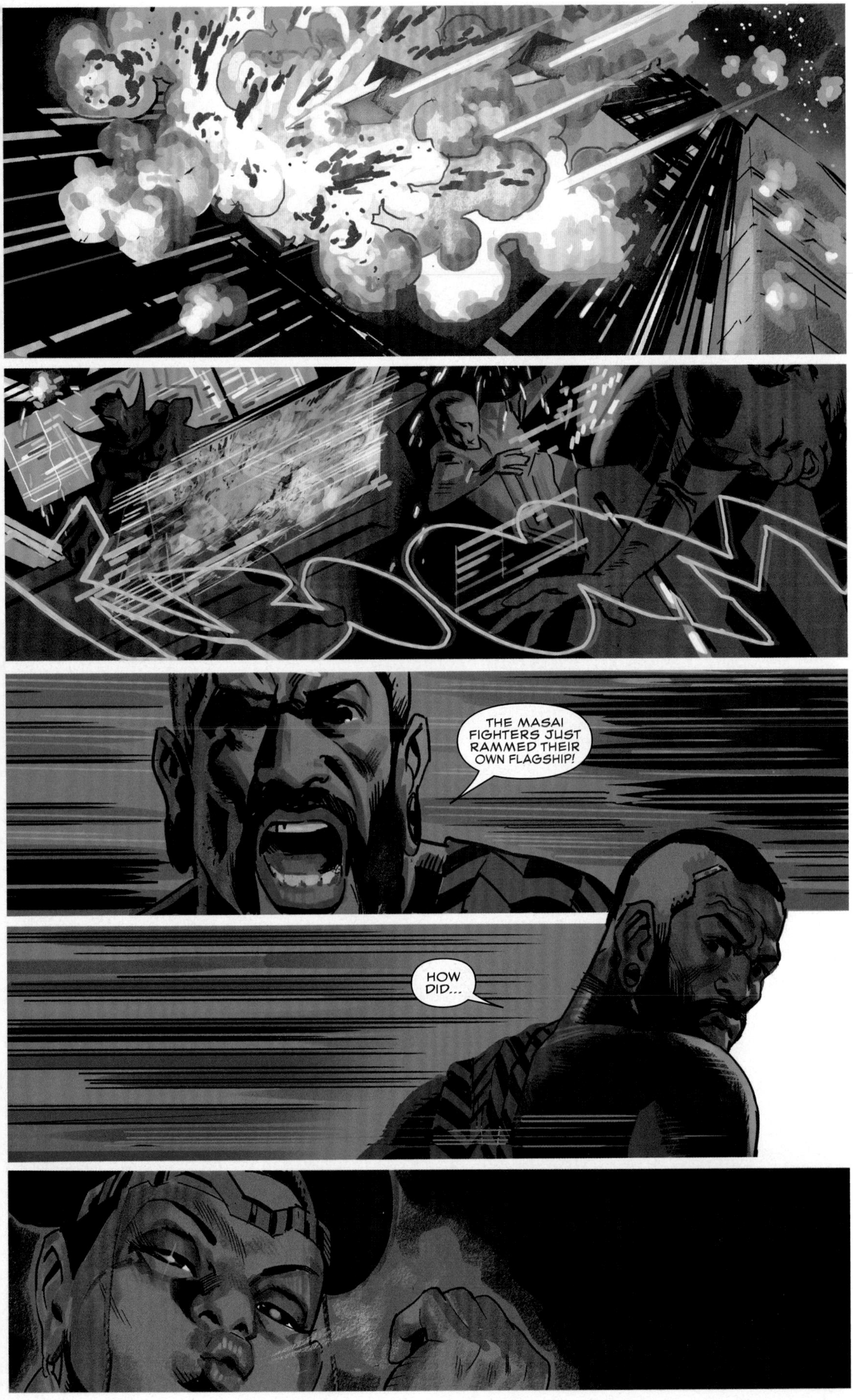
THE MASAI FIGHTERS JUST RAMMED THEIR OWN FLAGSHIP!
HOW DID...

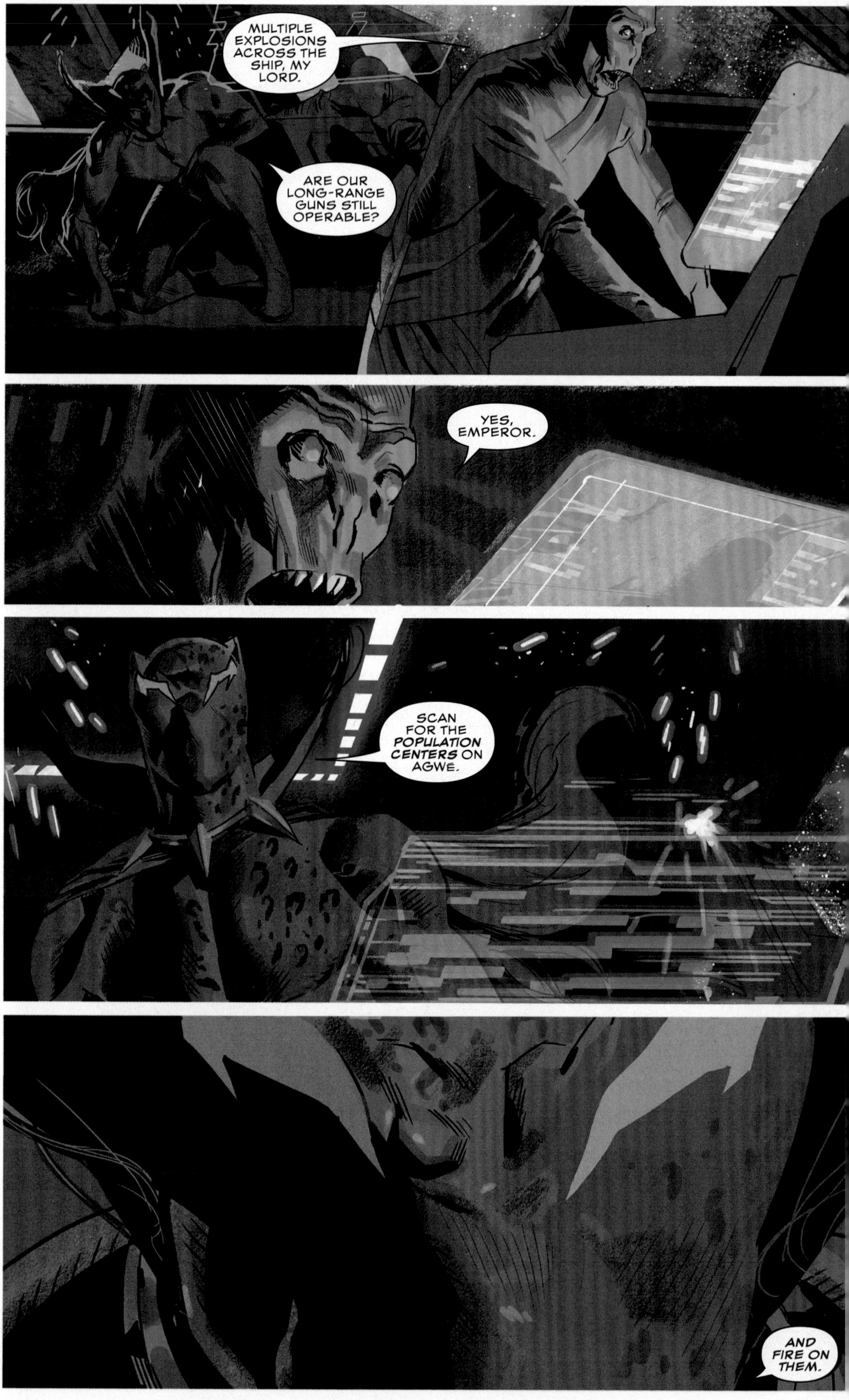
MULTIPLE EXPLOSIONS ACROSS THE SHIP, MY LORD.
ARE OUR LONG-RANGE GUNS STILL OPERABLE?
YES, EMPEROR.
SCAN FOR THE *POPULATION CENTERS* ON AGWE.
AND FIRE ON THEM.

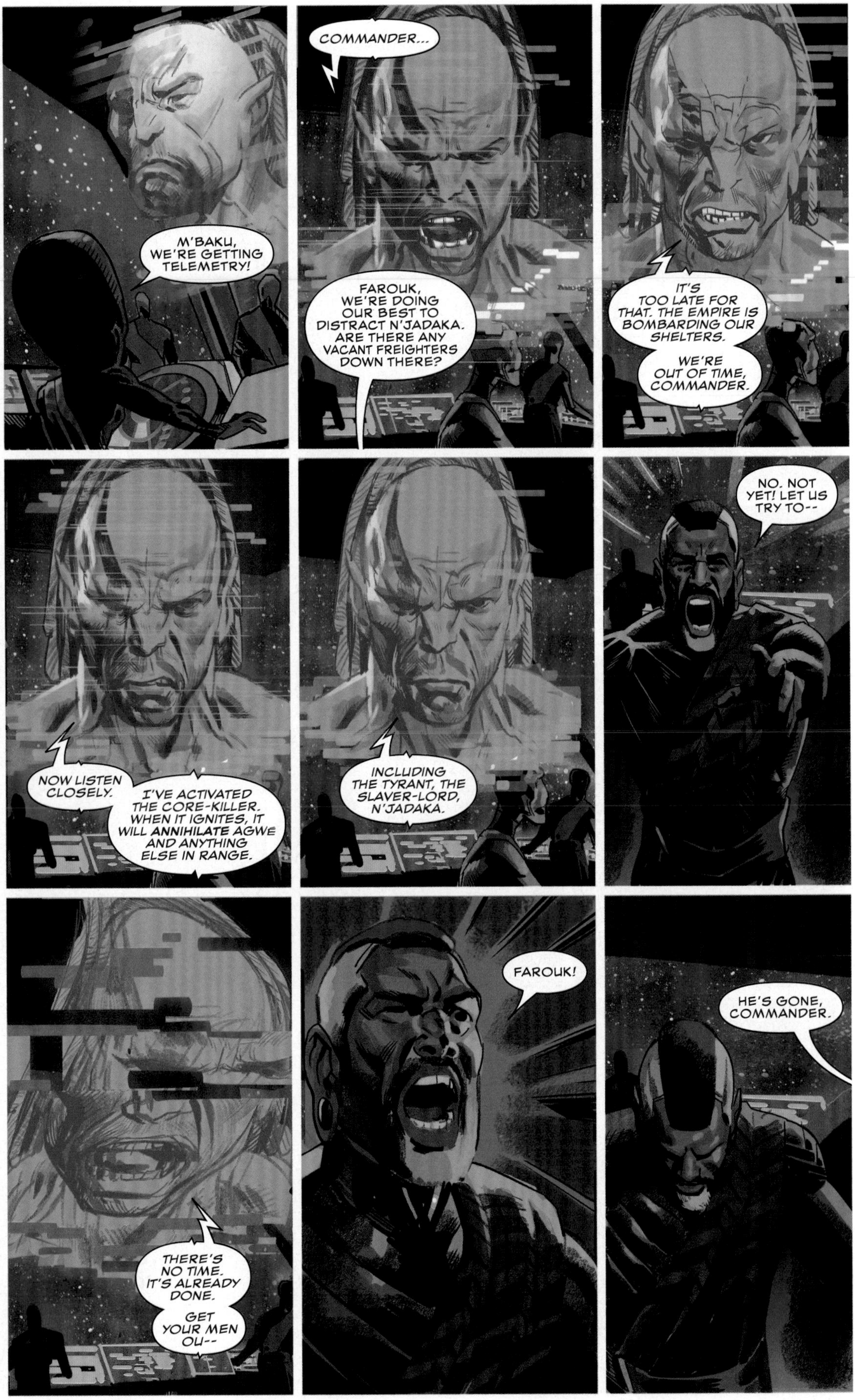
M'BAKU, WE'RE GETTING TELEMETRY!
COMMANDER...
FAROUK, WE'RE DOING OUR BEST TO DISTRACT N'JADAKA. ARE THERE ANY VACANT FREIGHTERS DOWN THERE?
IT'S TOO LATE FOR THAT. THE EMPIRE IS BOMBARDING OUR SHELTERS.
WE'RE OUT OF TIME, COMMANDER.
NOW LISTEN CLOSELY.
I'VE ACTIVATED THE CORE-KILLER. WHEN IT IGNITES, IT WILL ANNIHILATE AGWE AND ANYTHING ELSE IN RANGE.
INCLUDING THE TYRANT, THE SLAVER-LORD, N'JADAKA.
NO. NOT YET! LET US TRY TO--
THERE'S NO TIME. IT'S ALREADY DONE.
GET YOUR MEN OU--
FAROUK!
HE'S GONE, COMMANDER.

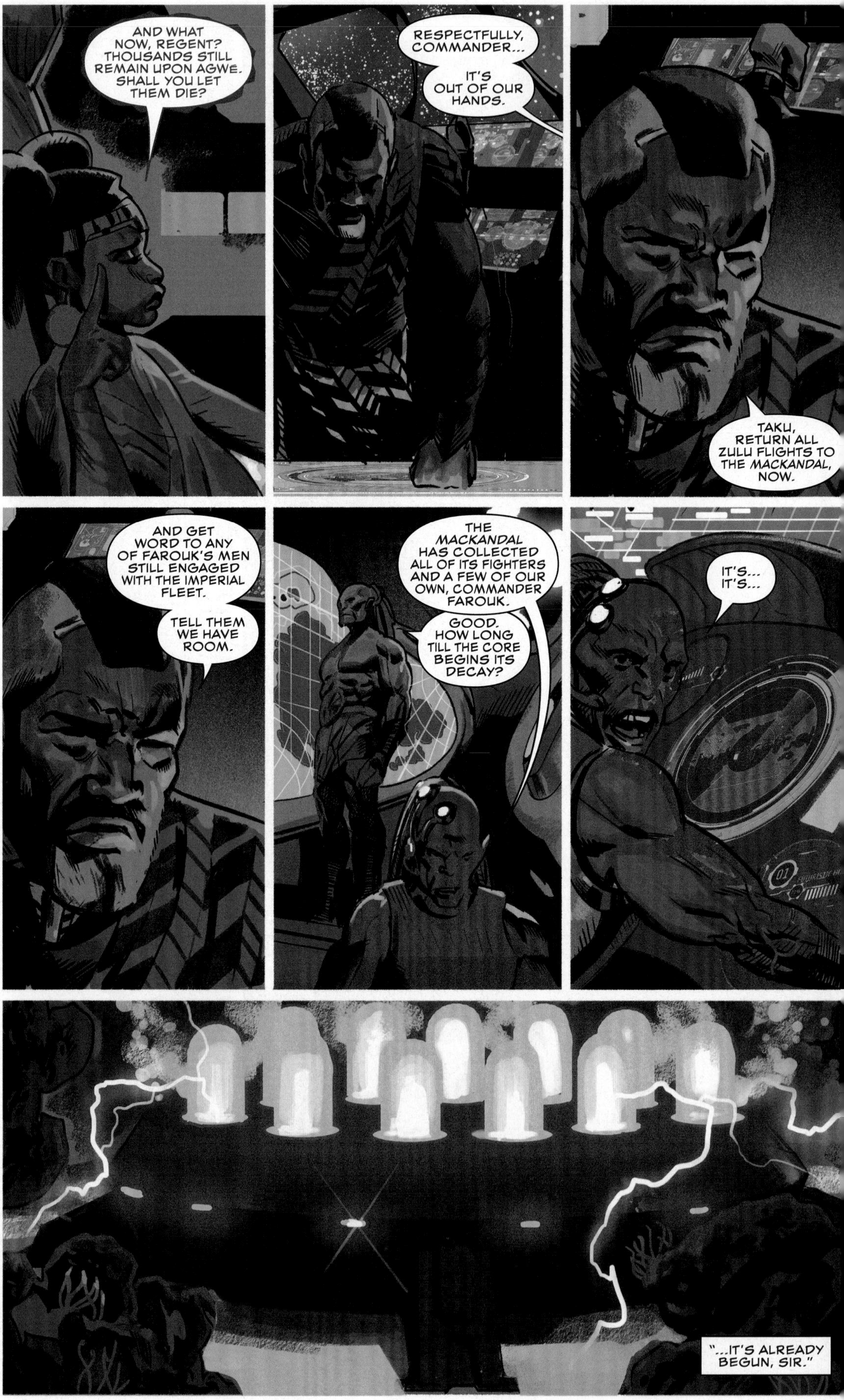
AND WHAT NOW, REGENT? THOUSANDS STILL REMAIN UPON AGWE. SHALL YOU LET THEM DIE?
RESPECTFULLY, COMMANDER...
IT'S OUT OF OUR HANDS.
TAKU, RETURN ALL ZULU FLIGHTS TO THE *MACKANDAL*, NOW.
AND GET WORD TO ANY OF FAROUK'S MEN STILL ENGAGED WITH THE IMPERIAL FLEET.
TELL THEM WE HAVE ROOM.
THE *MACKANDAL* HAS COLLECTED ALL OF ITS FIGHTERS AND A FEW OF OUR OWN, COMMANDER FAROUK.
GOOD. HOW LONG TILL THE CORE BEGINS ITS DECAY?
IT'S... IT'S...
"...IT'S ALREADY BEGUN, SIR."

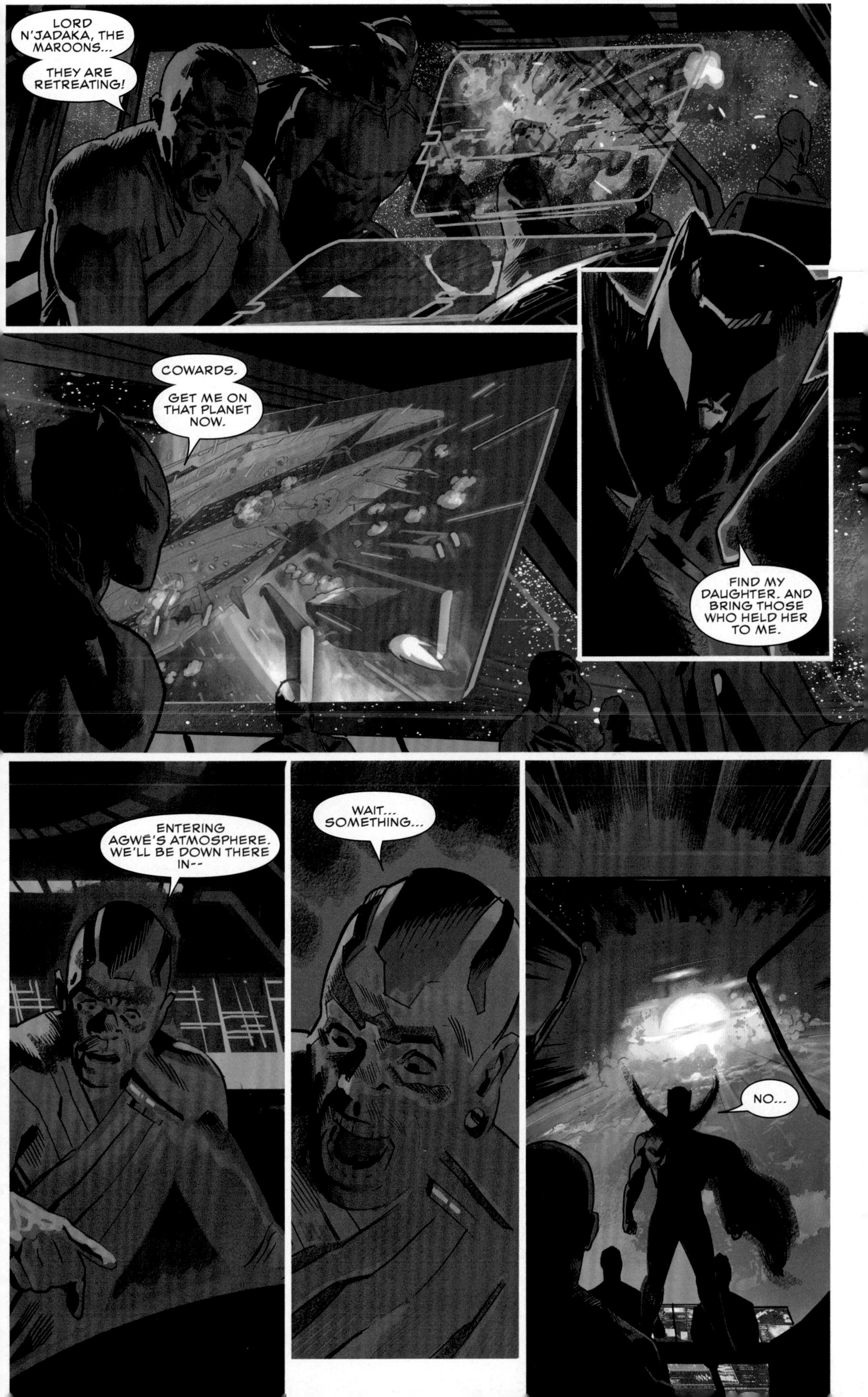
LORD N'JADAKA, THE MAROONS...
THEY ARE RETREATING!
COWARDS.
GET ME ON THAT PLANET NOW.
FIND MY DAUGHTER. AND BRING THOSE WHO HELD HER TO ME.
ENTERING AGWÉ'S ATMOSPHERE. WE'LL BE DOWN THERE IN--
WAIT... SOMETHING...
NO...

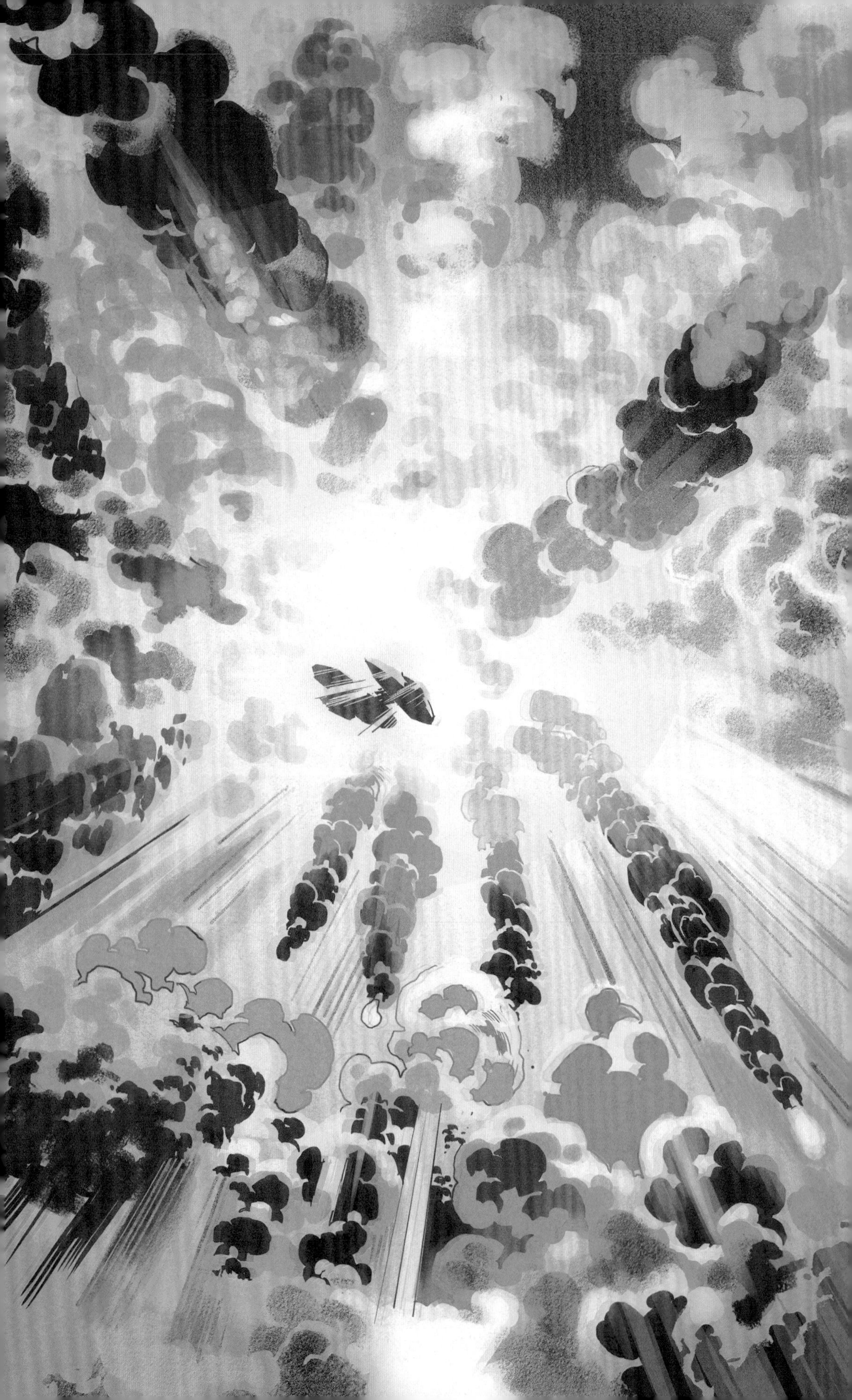

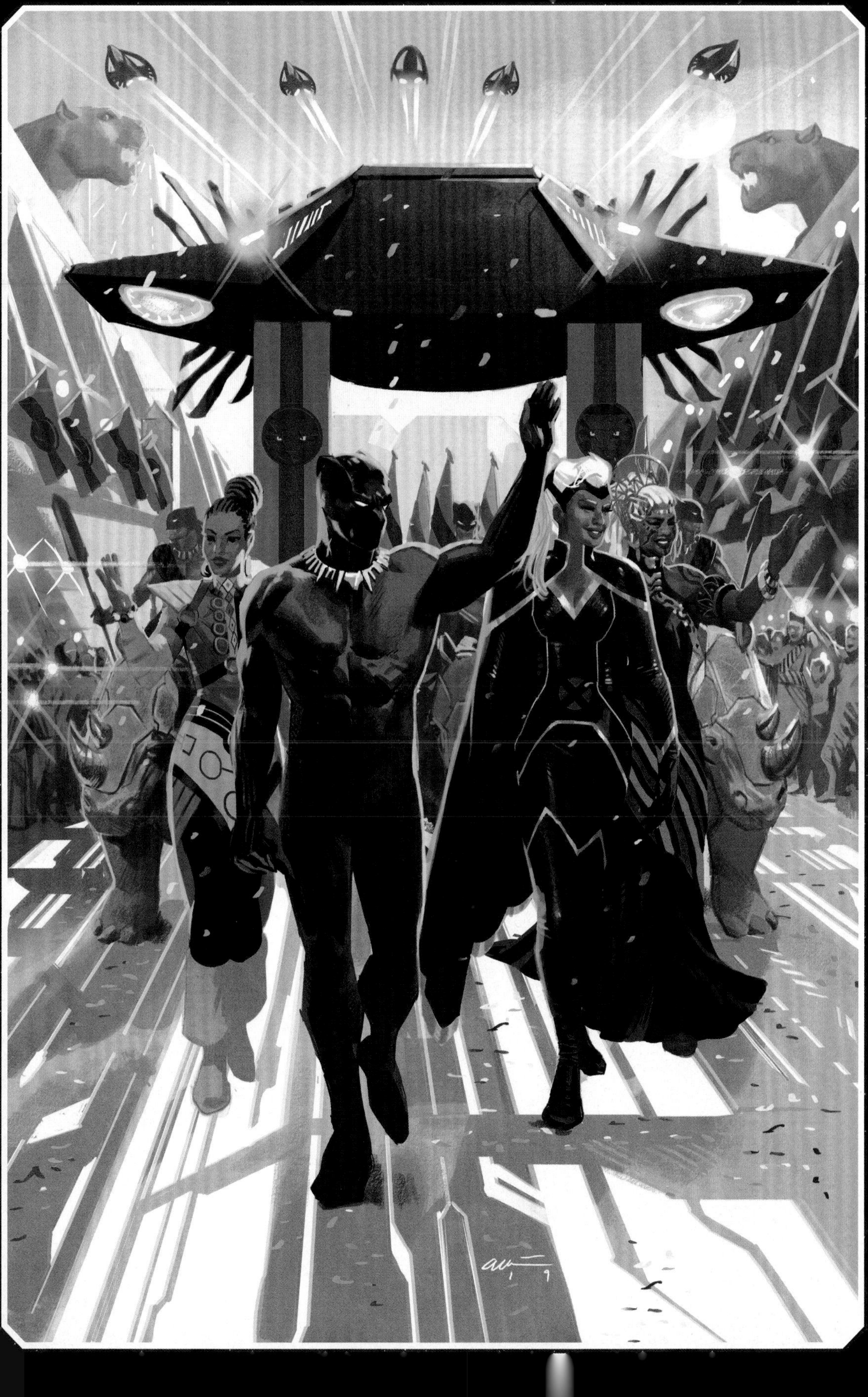

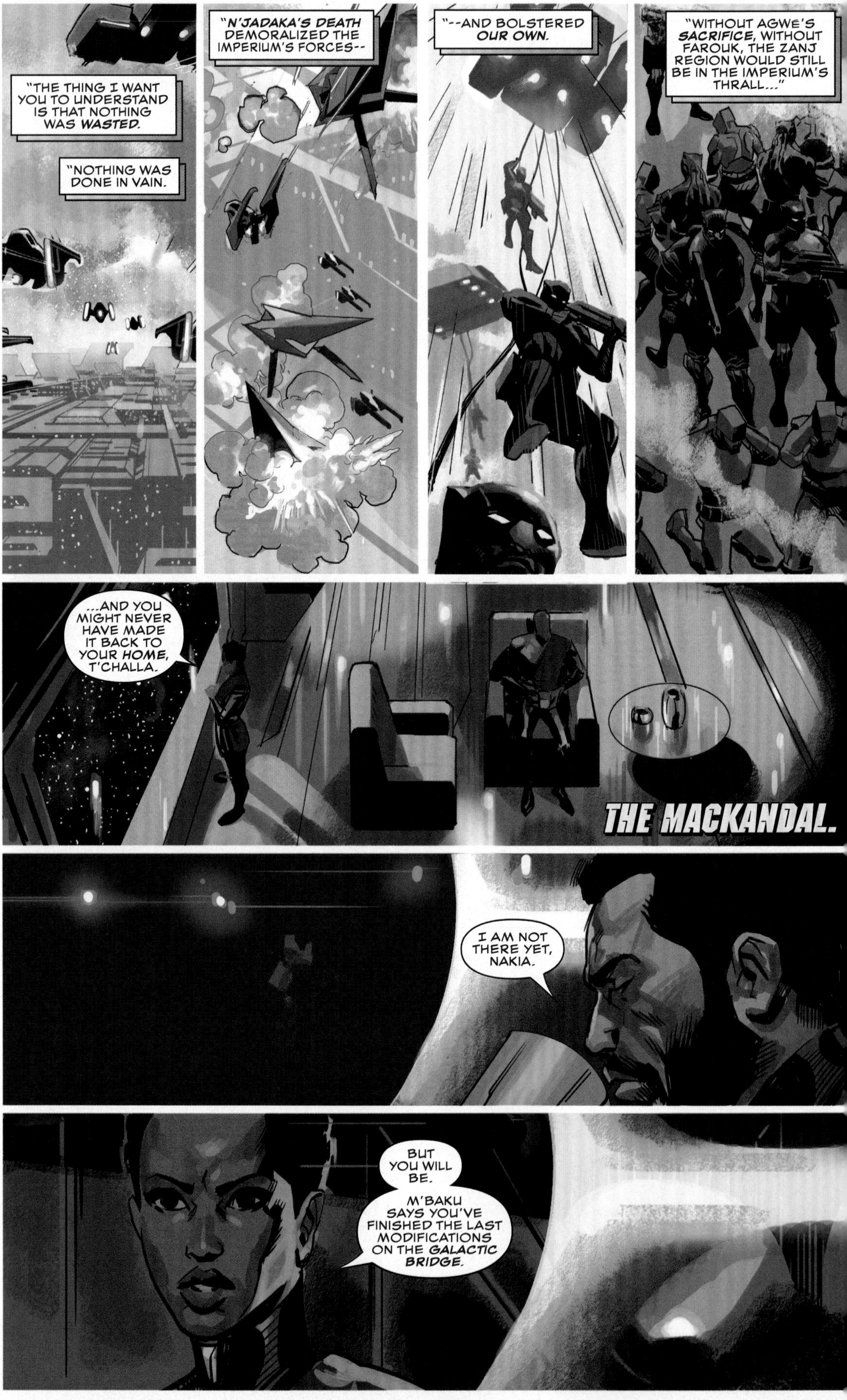
"THE THING I WANT YOU TO UNDERSTAND IS THAT NOTHING WAS WASTED.
"NOTHING WAS DONE IN VAIN.
"N'JADAKA'S DEATH DEMORALIZED THE IMPERIUM'S FORCES--
"--AND BOLSTERED OUR OWN.
"WITHOUT AGWE'S SACRIFICE, WITHOUT FAROUK, THE ZANJ REGION WOULD STILL BE IN THE IMPERIUM'S THRALL..."
...AND YOU MIGHT NEVER HAVE MADE IT BACK TO YOUR HOME, T'CHALLA.
THE MACKANDAL.
I AM NOT THERE YET, NAKIA.
BUT YOU WILL BE.
M'BAKU SAYS YOU'VE FINISHED THE LAST MODIFICATIONS ON THE GALACTIC BRIDGE.

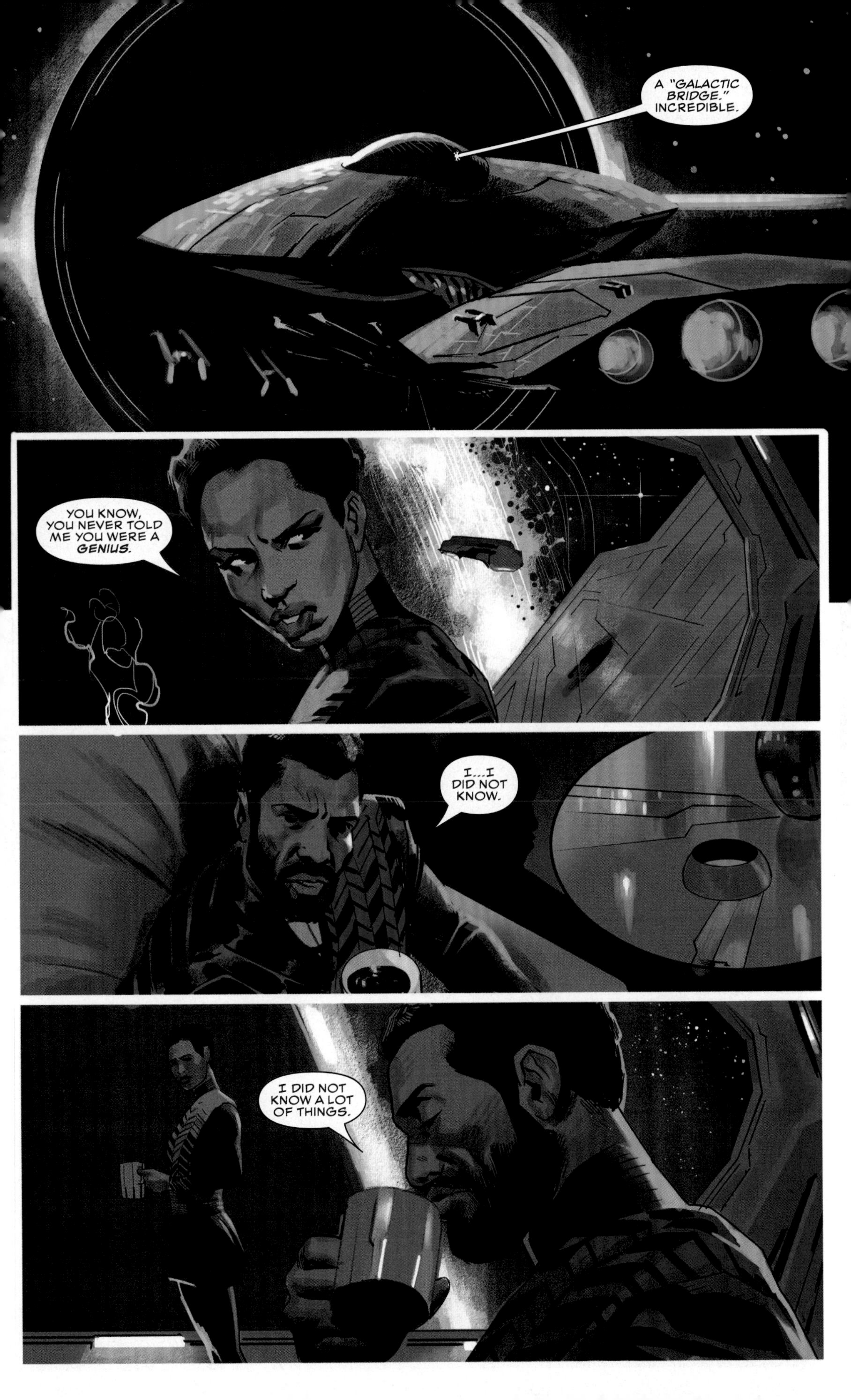
A "GALACTIC BRIDGE." INCREDIBLE.
YOU KNOW, YOU NEVER TOLD ME YOU WERE A GENIUS.
I...I DID NOT KNOW.
I DID NOT KNOW A LOT OF THINGS.

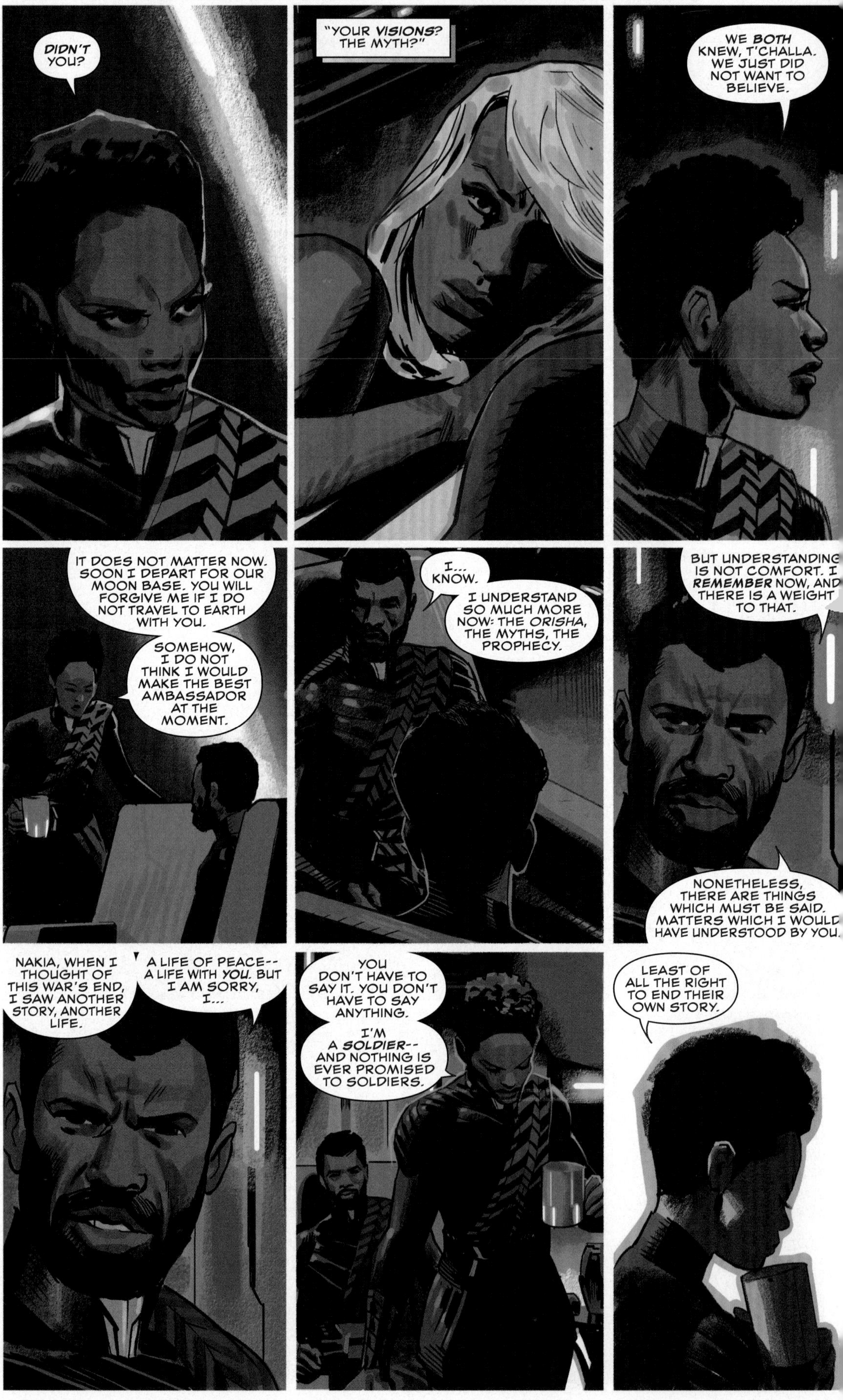
DIDN'T YOU?
"YOUR VISIONS? THE MYTH?"
WE BOTH KNEW, T'CHALLA. WE JUST DID NOT WANT TO BELIEVE.
IT DOES NOT MATTER NOW. SOON I DEPART FOR OUR MOON BASE. YOU WILL FORGIVE ME IF I DO NOT TRAVEL TO EARTH WITH YOU.
SOMEHOW, I DO NOT THINK I WOULD MAKE THE BEST AMBASSADOR AT THE MOMENT.
I... KNOW.
I UNDERSTAND SO MUCH MORE NOW: THE ORISHA, THE MYTHS, THE PROPHECY.
BUT UNDERSTANDING IS NOT COMFORT. I REMEMBER NOW, AND THERE IS A WEIGHT TO THAT.
NONETHELESS, THERE ARE THINGS WHICH MUST BE SAID. MATTERS WHICH I WOULD HAVE UNDERSTOOD BY YOU.
NAKIA, WHEN I THOUGHT OF THIS WAR'S END, I SAW ANOTHER STORY, ANOTHER LIFE.
A LIFE OF PEACE-- A LIFE WITH YOU. BUT I AM SORRY, I...
YOU DON'T HAVE TO SAY IT. YOU DON'T HAVE TO SAY ANYTHING.
I'M A SOLDIER-- AND NOTHING IS EVER PROMISED TO SOLDIERS.
LEAST OF ALL THE RIGHT TO END THEIR OWN STORY.

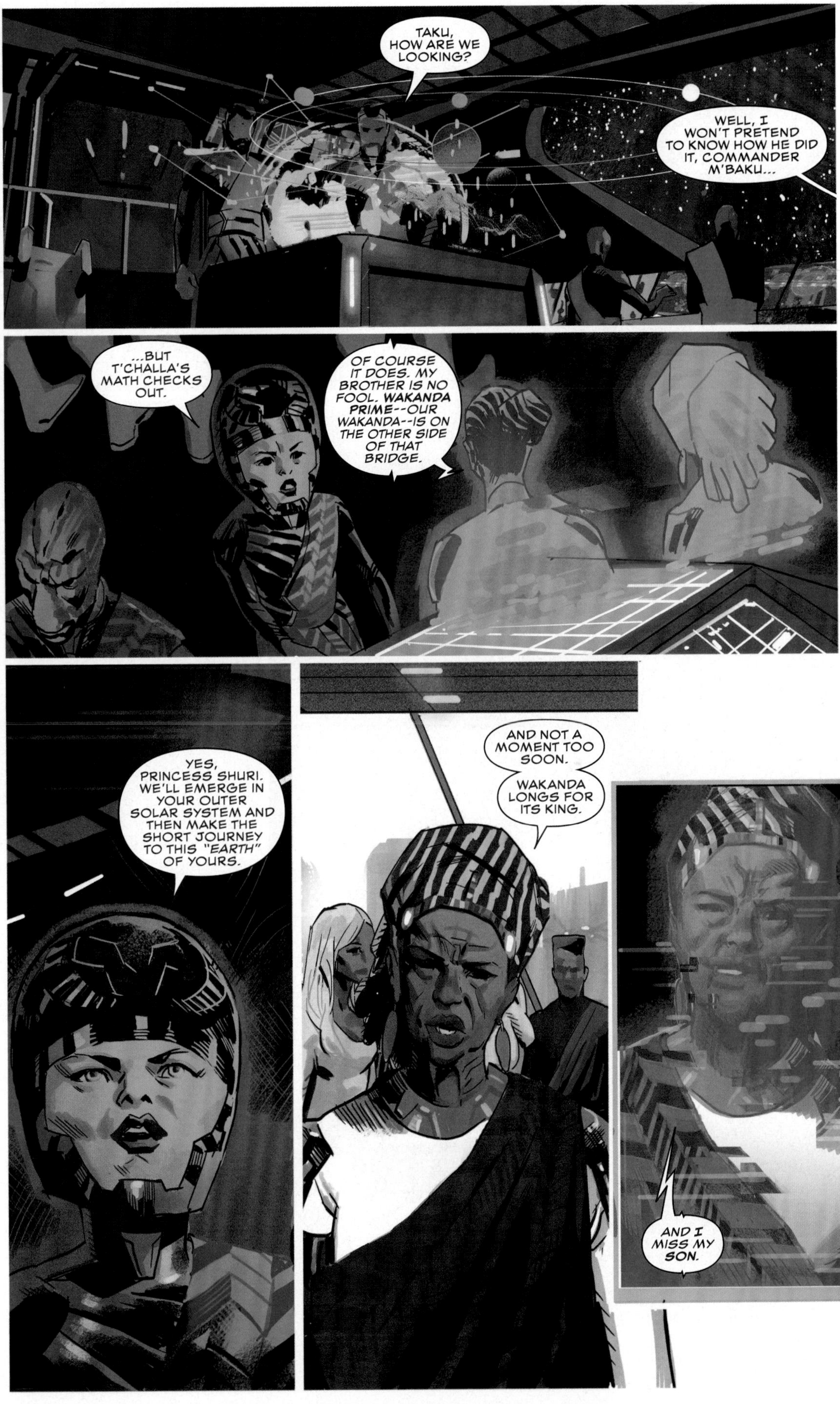
TAKU, HOW ARE WE LOOKING?
WELL, I WON'T PRETEND TO KNOW HOW HE DID IT, COMMANDER M'BAKU...
...BUT T'CHALLA'S MATH CHECKS OUT.
OF COURSE IT DOES. MY BROTHER IS NO FOOL. WAKANDA PRIME--OUR WAKANDA--IS ON THE OTHER SIDE OF THAT BRIDGE.
YES, PRINCESS SHURI. WE'LL EMERGE IN YOUR OUTER SOLAR SYSTEM AND THEN MAKE THE SHORT JOURNEY TO THIS "EARTH" OF YOURS.
AND NOT A MOMENT TOO SOON.
WAKANDA LONGS FOR ITS KING.
AND I MISS MY SON.

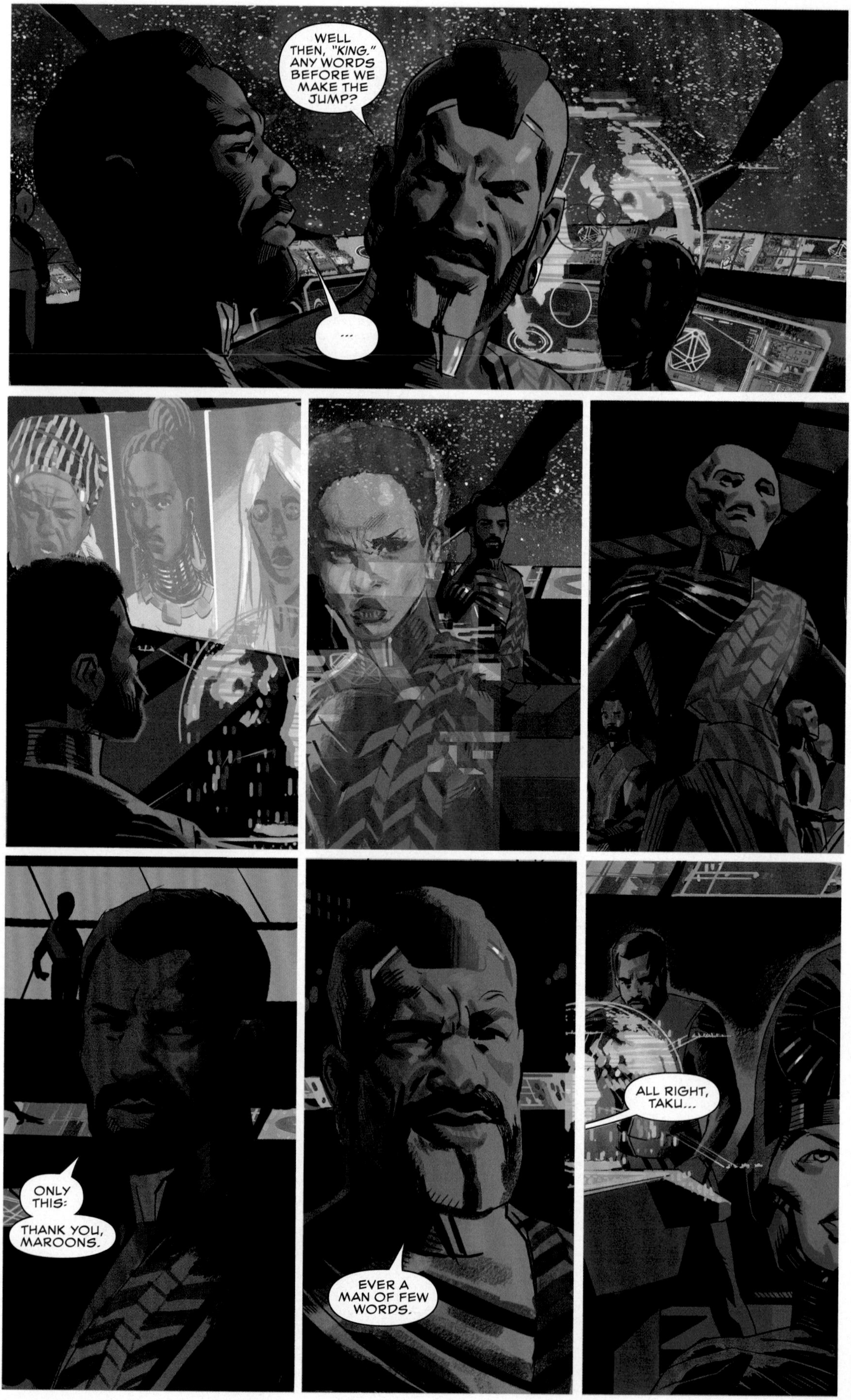
WELL THEN, "KING." ANY WORDS BEFORE WE MAKE THE JUMP?
...
ONLY THIS:
THANK YOU, MAROONS.
EVER A MAN OF FEW WORDS.
ALL RIGHT, TAKU...

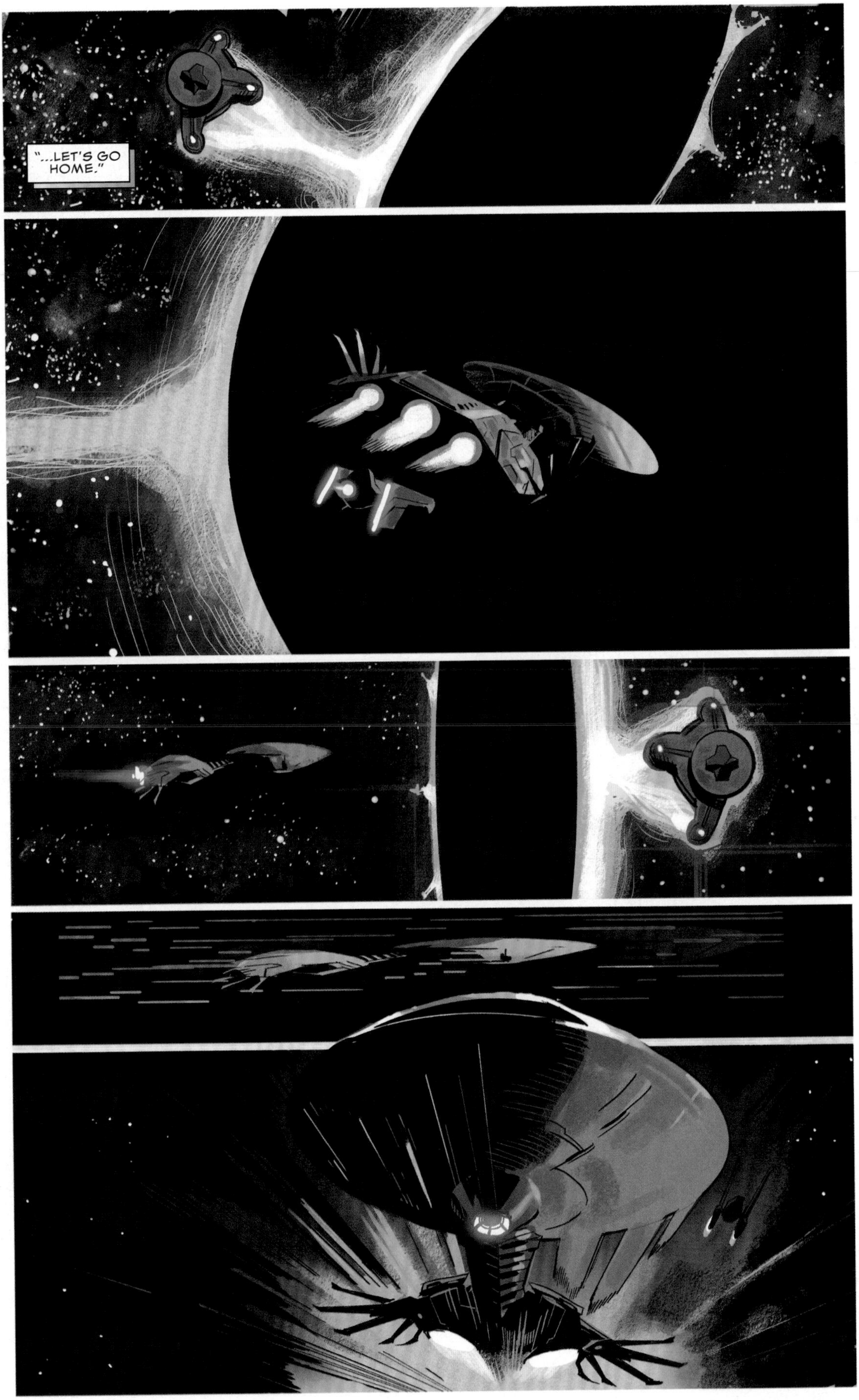
"...LET'S GO HOME."

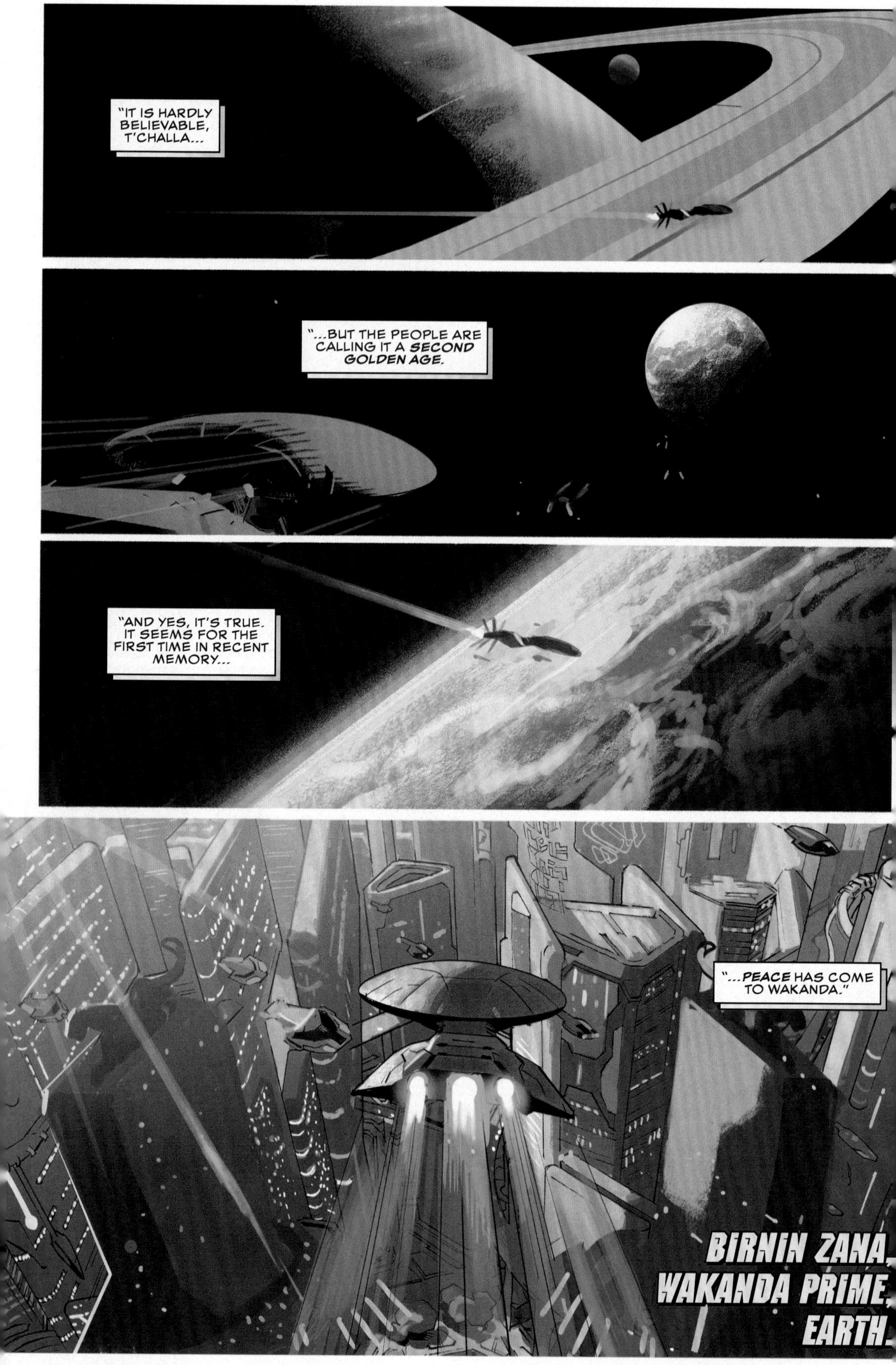
"IT IS HARDLY BELIEVABLE, T'CHALLA...
"...BUT THE PEOPLE ARE CALLING IT A SECOND GOLDEN AGE.
"AND YES, IT'S TRUE. IT SEEMS FOR THE FIRST TIME IN RECENT MEMORY...
"...PEACE HAS COME TO WAKANDA."
BIRNIN ZANA, WAKANDA PRIME, EARTH.

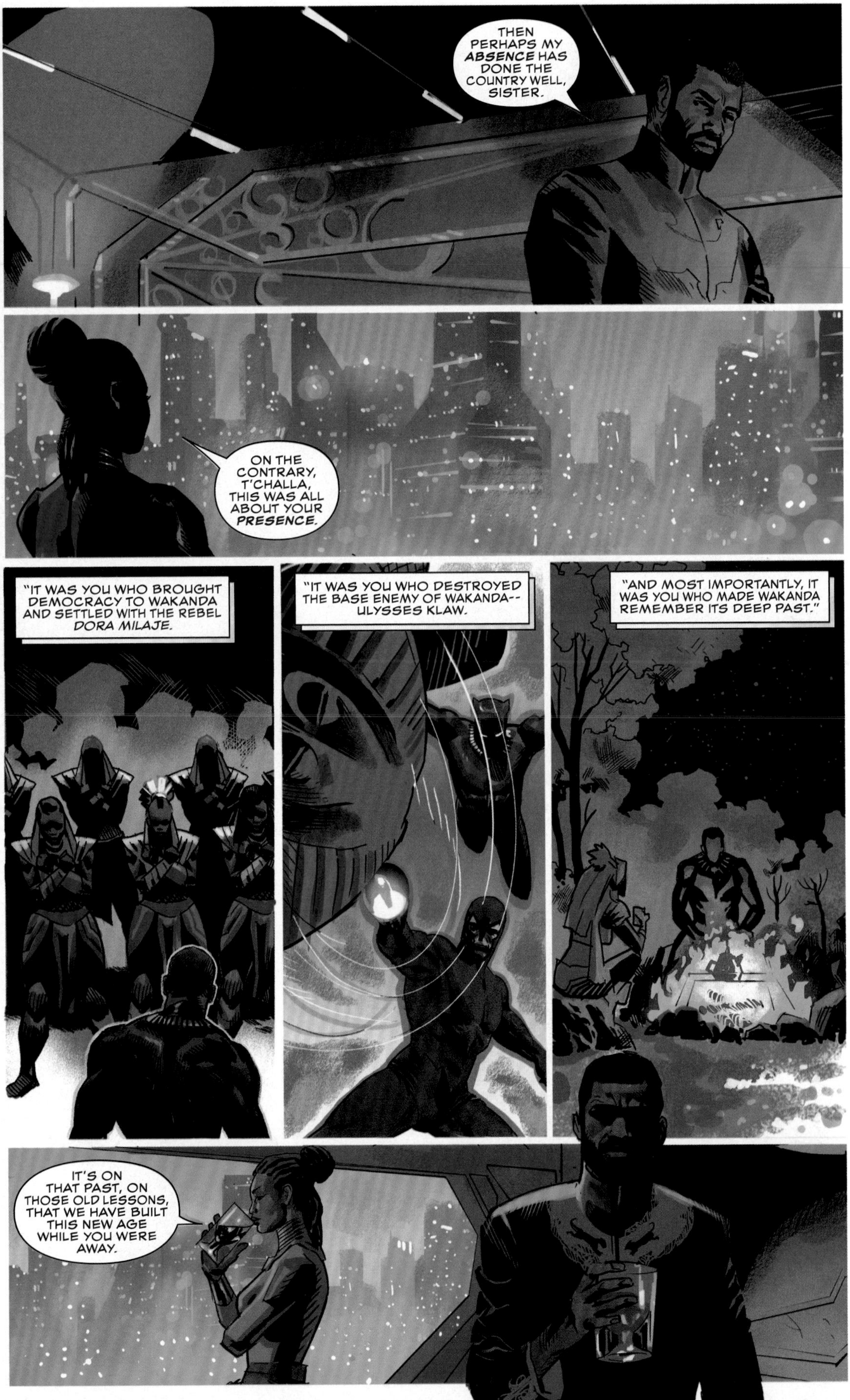
THEN PERHAPS MY ABSENCE HAS DONE THE COUNTRY WELL, SISTER.
ON THE CONTRARY, T'CHALLA, THIS WAS ALL ABOUT YOUR PRESENCE.
"IT WAS YOU WHO BROUGHT DEMOCRACY TO WAKANDA AND SETTLED WITH THE REBEL DORA MILAJE.
"IT WAS YOU WHO DESTROYED THE BASE ENEMY OF WAKANDA-- ULYSSES KLAW.
"AND MOST IMPORTANTLY, IT WAS YOU WHO MADE WAKANDA REMEMBER ITS DEEP PAST."
IT'S ON THAT PAST, ON THOSE OLD LESSONS, THAT WE HAVE BUILT THIS NEW AGE WHILE YOU WERE AWAY.

THE WORLD IS SO DANGEROUS. THE AMERICANS HAVE FALLEN UNDER THE SWAY OF VILLAINS AND THUGS.

WAKANDA COULD NO LONGER SAVE ITSELF AND LEAVE THE WORLD IN CHAOS-- FOR THE CHAOS WOULD SOON CONSUME US.

HYDRA TAUGHT US THAT.

IT IS THE MEMORY OF OUR *PAST* THAT TELLS US WHAT WE OWE TO OUR *FUTURE.*

AND WHAT WE OWE TO THE *WORLD.*

AND NOT JUST THE WORLD, SHURI...

I CANNOT BEGIN TO TELL YOU WHAT I SAW OUT THERE, HOW WAKANDA HAS GONE FROM A COUNTRY TO AN IDEA THAT SPANS GALAXIES.

YES. ANOTHER WAKANDA. PREMISED ON *SLAVERY* AND *TYRANNY.*

NO. IT'S *OUR* WAKANDA. THE WORMHOLE DISTORTED TIME, PULLING THOSE EXPLORERS I HAD SENT INTO THE PAST.

WE STARTED THE EMPIRE, SHURI. SO THEY ARE *US*-- JUST 2,000 YEARS AHEAD.

AND SO ATTRACTIVE WAS THEIR WAR-MAKING THAT OUR GODS *DESERTED* US FOR THEM.

IS THAT OUR FUTURE? IS THAT WHO WE ARE FATED TO BECOME?

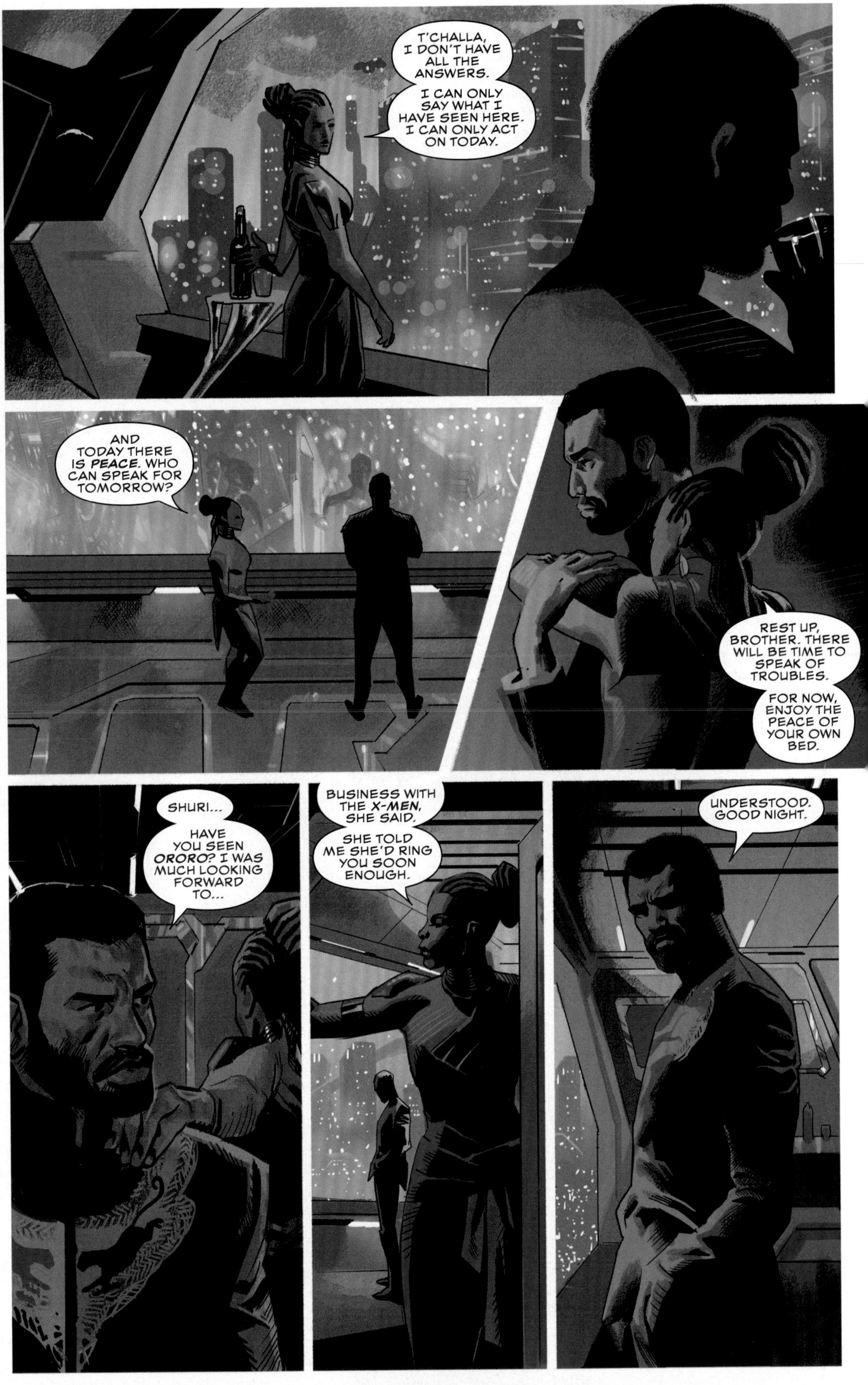
T'CHALLA, I DON'T HAVE ALL THE ANSWERS.
I CAN ONLY SAY WHAT I HAVE SEEN HERE. I CAN ONLY ACT ON TODAY.
AND TODAY THERE IS PEACE. WHO CAN SPEAK FOR TOMORROW?
REST UP, BROTHER. THERE WILL BE TIME TO SPEAK OF TROUBLES.
FOR NOW, ENJOY THE PEACE OF YOUR OWN BED.
SHURI...
HAVE YOU SEEN ORORO? I WAS MUCH LOOKING FORWARD TO...
BUSINESS WITH THE X-MEN, SHE SAID.
SHE TOLD ME SHE'D RING YOU SOON ENOUGH.
UNDERSTOOD. GOOD NIGHT.

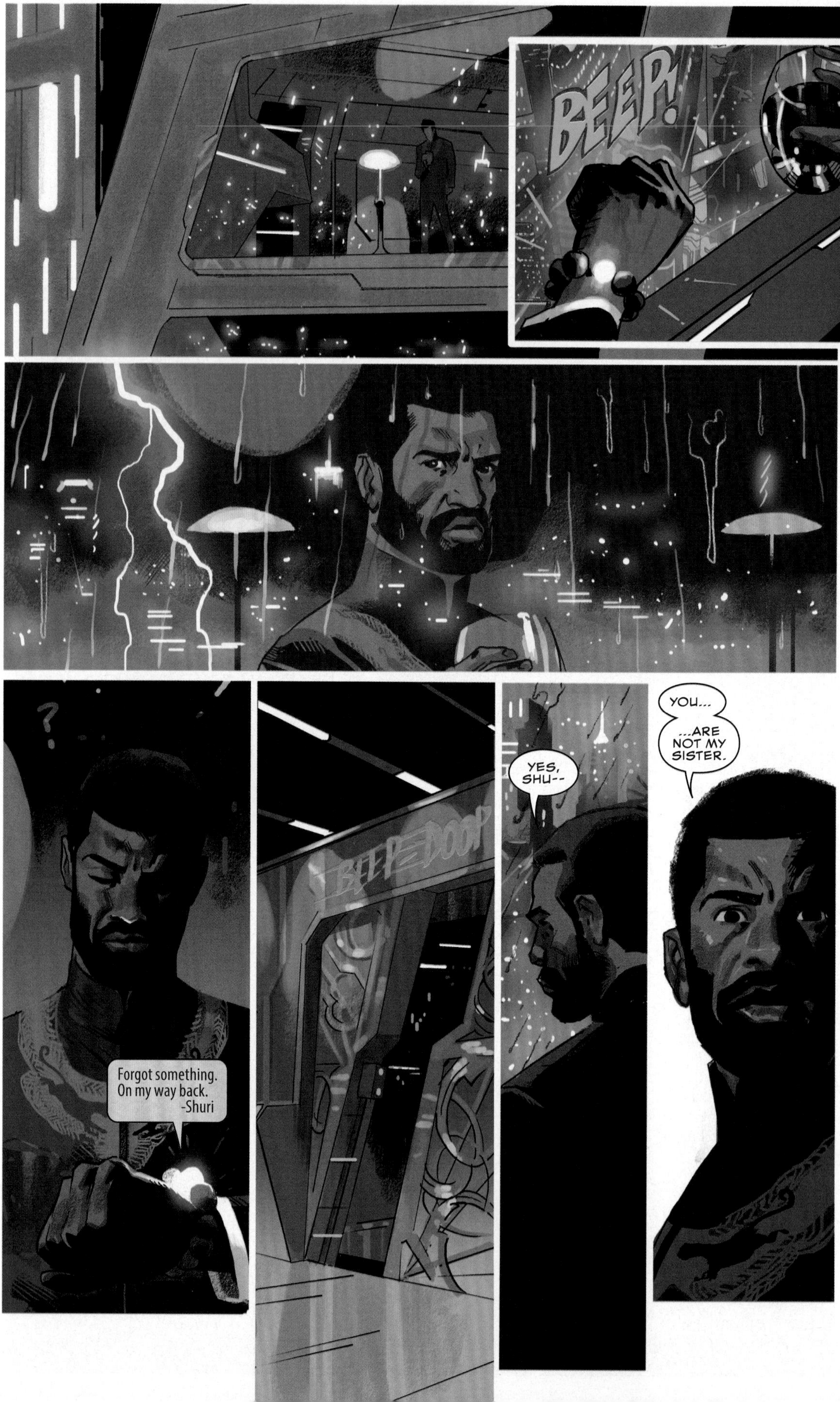
BEEP!
Forgot something.
On my way back.
-Shuri
BEEP DOOP
YES, SHU--
YOU...
...ARE NOT MY SISTER.

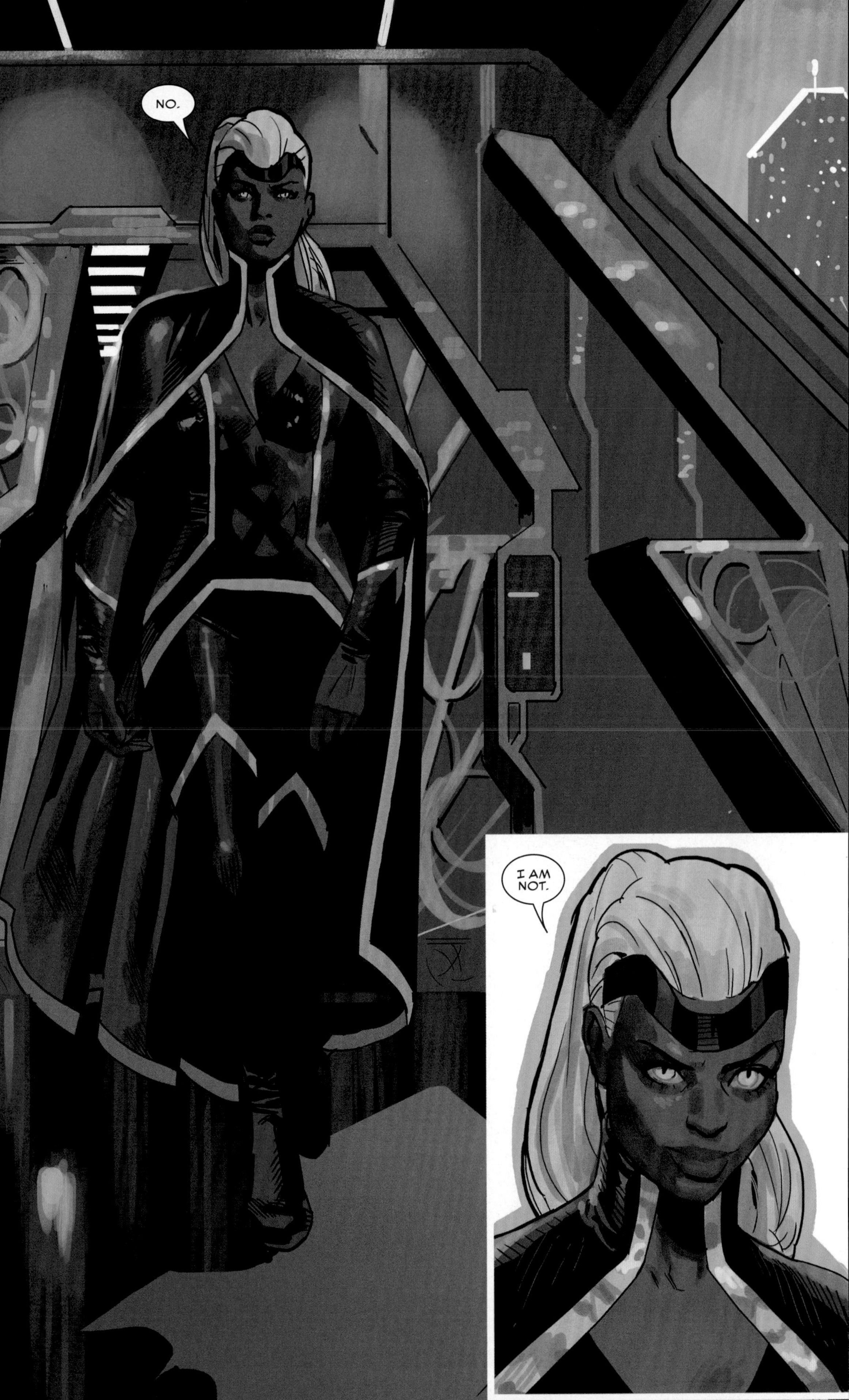
NO.
I AM NOT.

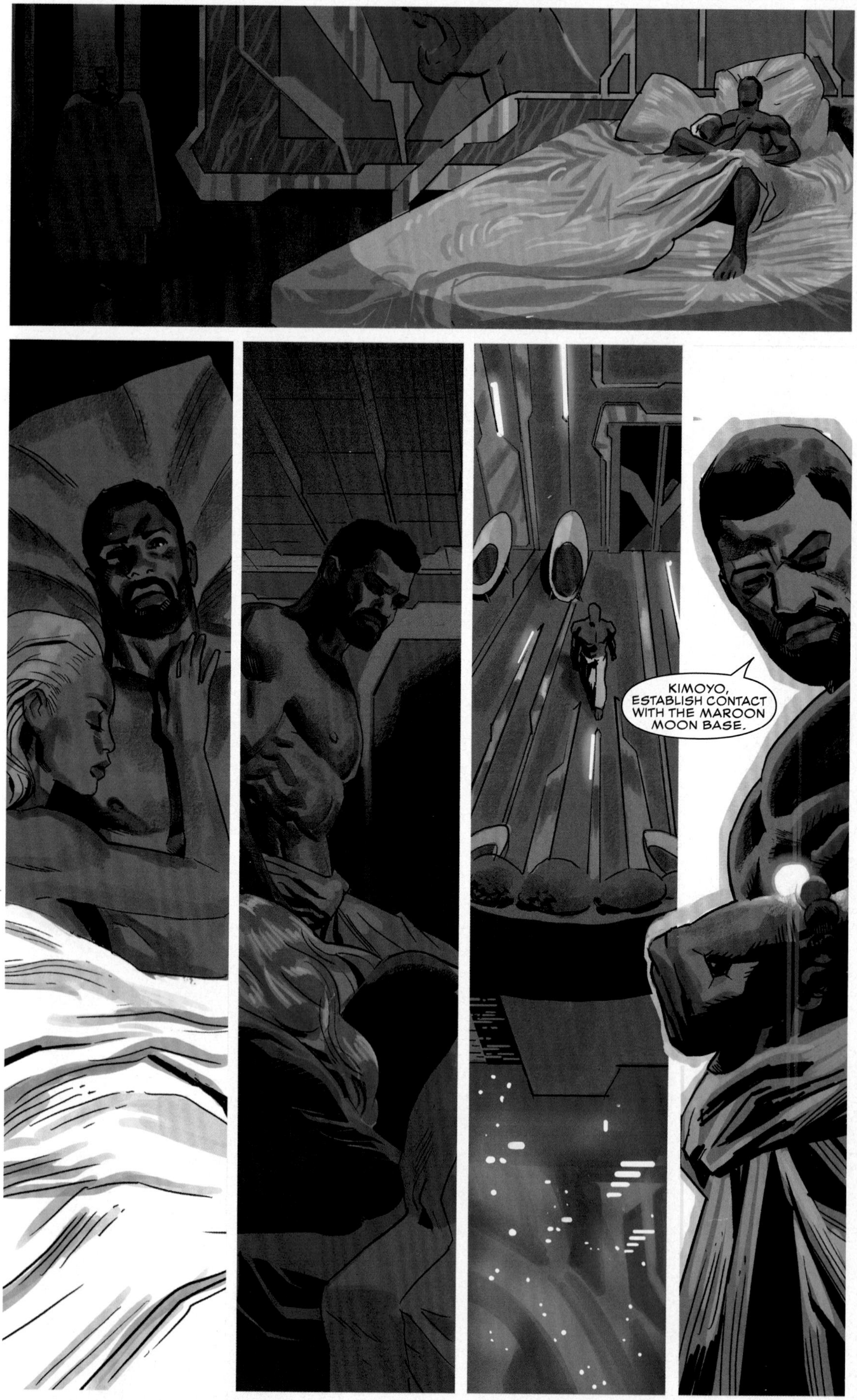
KIMOYO, ESTABLISH CONTACT WITH THE MAROON MOON BASE.

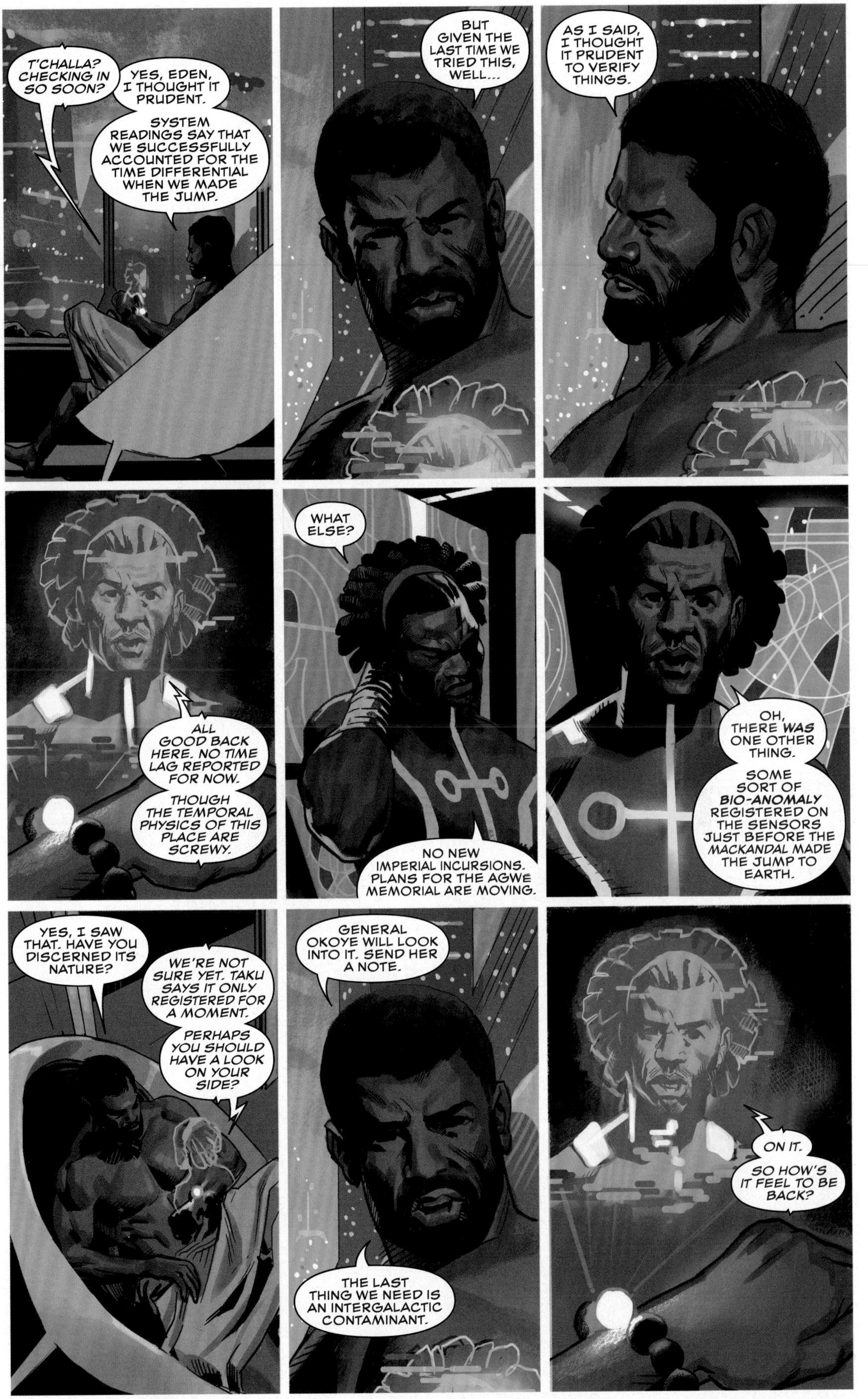
T'CHALLA? CHECKING IN SO SOON?
YES, EDEN, I THOUGHT IT PRUDENT.
SYSTEM READINGS SAY THAT WE SUCCESSFULLY ACCOUNTED FOR THE TIME DIFFERENTIAL WHEN WE MADE THE JUMP.
BUT GIVEN THE LAST TIME WE TRIED THIS, WELL...
AS I SAID, I THOUGHT IT PRUDENT TO VERIFY THINGS.
ALL GOOD BACK HERE. NO TIME LAG REPORTED FOR NOW.
THOUGH THE TEMPORAL PHYSICS OF THIS PLACE ARE SCREWY.
WHAT ELSE?
NO NEW IMPERIAL INCURSIONS. PLANS FOR THE AGWE MEMORIAL ARE MOVING.
OH, THERE WAS ONE OTHER THING.
SOME SORT OF BIO-ANOMALY REGISTERED ON THE SENSORS JUST BEFORE THE MACKANDAL MADE THE JUMP TO EARTH.
YES, I SAW THAT. HAVE YOU DISCERNED ITS NATURE?
WE'RE NOT SURE YET. TAKU SAYS IT ONLY REGISTERED FOR A MOMENT.
PERHAPS YOU SHOULD HAVE A LOOK ON YOUR SIDE?
GENERAL OKOYE WILL LOOK INTO IT. SEND HER A NOTE.
THE LAST THING WE NEED IS AN INTERGALACTIC CONTAMINANT.
ON IT.
SO HOW'S IT FEEL TO BE BACK?

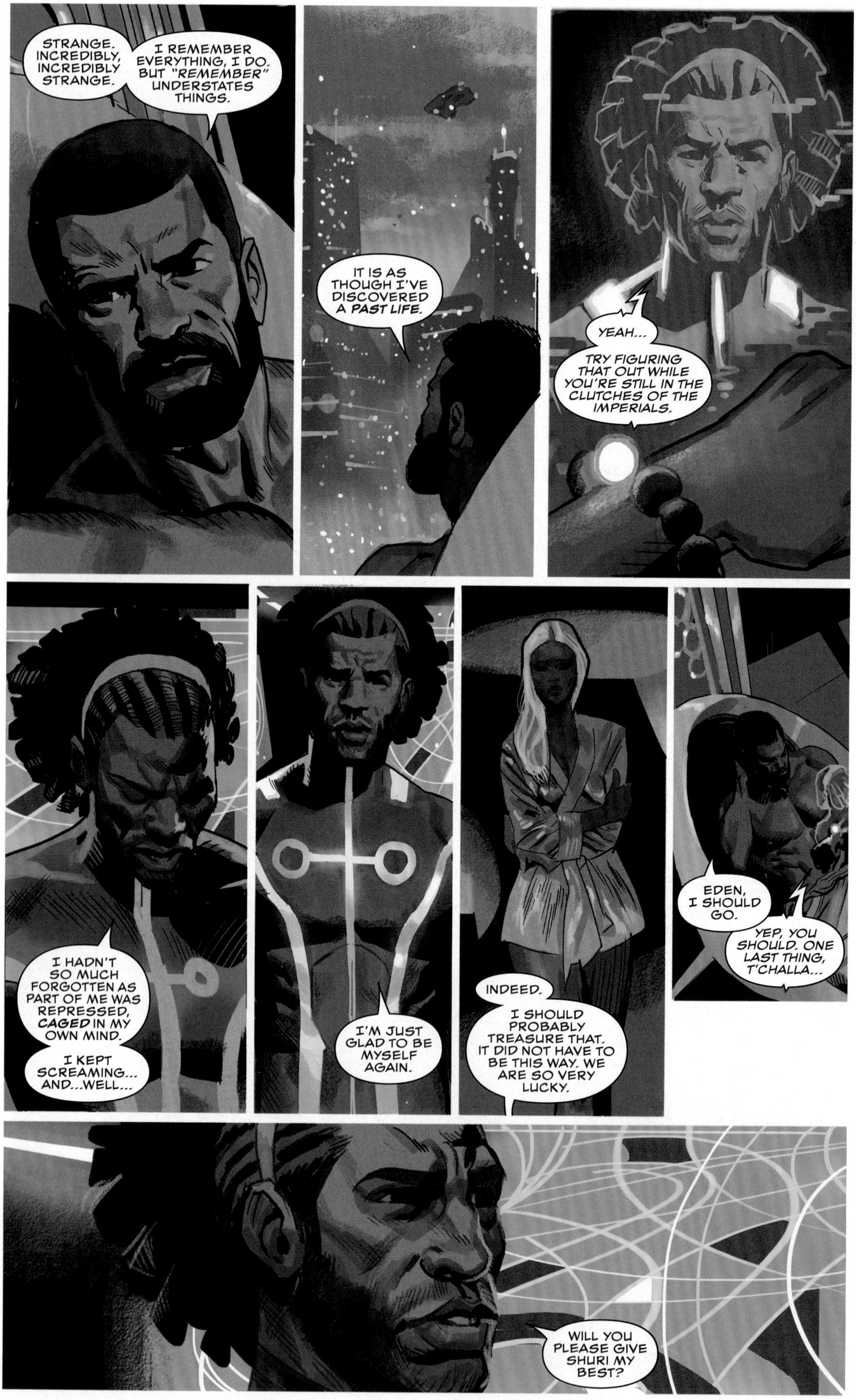
STRANGE. INCREDIBLY, INCREDIBLY STRANGE.
I REMEMBER EVERYTHING, I DO. BUT "REMEMBER" UNDERSTATES THINGS.
IT IS AS THOUGH I'VE DISCOVERED A PAST LIFE.
YEAH...
TRY FIGURING THAT OUT WHILE YOU'RE STILL IN THE CLUTCHES OF THE IMPERIALS.
I HADN'T SO MUCH FORGOTTEN AS PART OF ME WAS REPRESSED, CAGED IN MY OWN MIND.
I KEPT SCREAMING... AND...WELL...
I'M JUST GLAD TO BE MYSELF AGAIN.
INDEED.
I SHOULD PROBABLY TREASURE THAT. IT DID NOT HAVE TO BE THIS WAY. WE ARE SO VERY LUCKY.
EDEN, I SHOULD GO.
YEP, YOU SHOULD. ONE LAST THING, T'CHALLA...
WILL YOU PLEASE GIVE SHURI MY BEST?

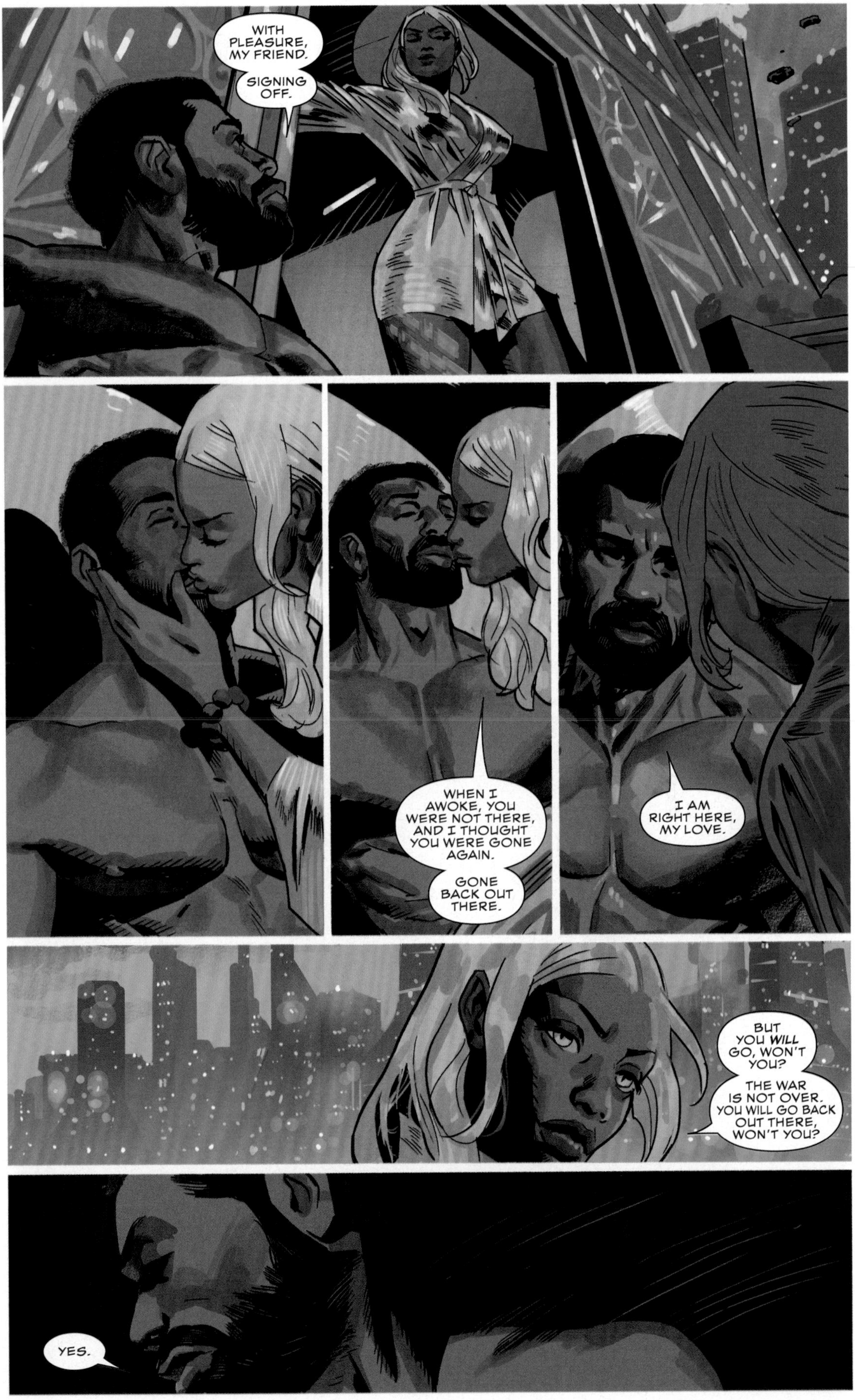
WITH PLEASURE, MY FRIEND.
SIGNING OFF.
WHEN I AWOKE, YOU WERE NOT THERE, AND I THOUGHT YOU WERE GONE AGAIN.
GONE BACK OUT THERE.
I AM RIGHT HERE, MY LOVE.
BUT YOU WILL GO, WON'T YOU?
THE WAR IS NOT OVER. YOU WILL GO BACK OUT THERE, WON'T YOU?
YES.

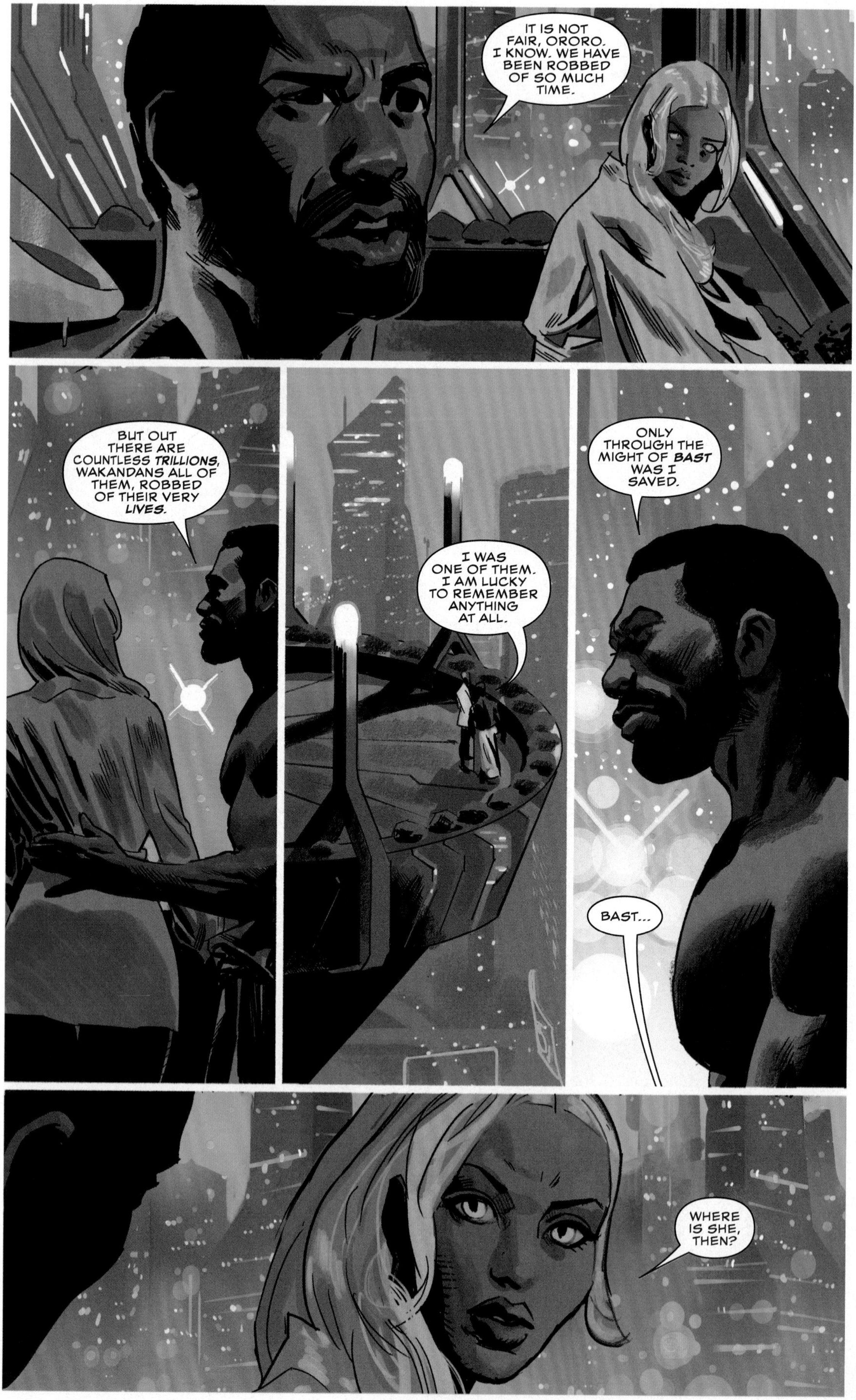
IT IS NOT FAIR, ORORO. I KNOW. WE HAVE BEEN ROBBED OF SO MUCH TIME.
BUT OUT THERE ARE COUNTLESS TRILLIONS, WAKANDANS ALL OF THEM, ROBBED OF THEIR VERY LIVES.
I WAS ONE OF THEM. I AM LUCKY TO REMEMBER ANYTHING AT ALL.
ONLY THROUGH THE MIGHT OF BAST WAS I SAVED.
BAST...
WHERE IS SHE, THEN?

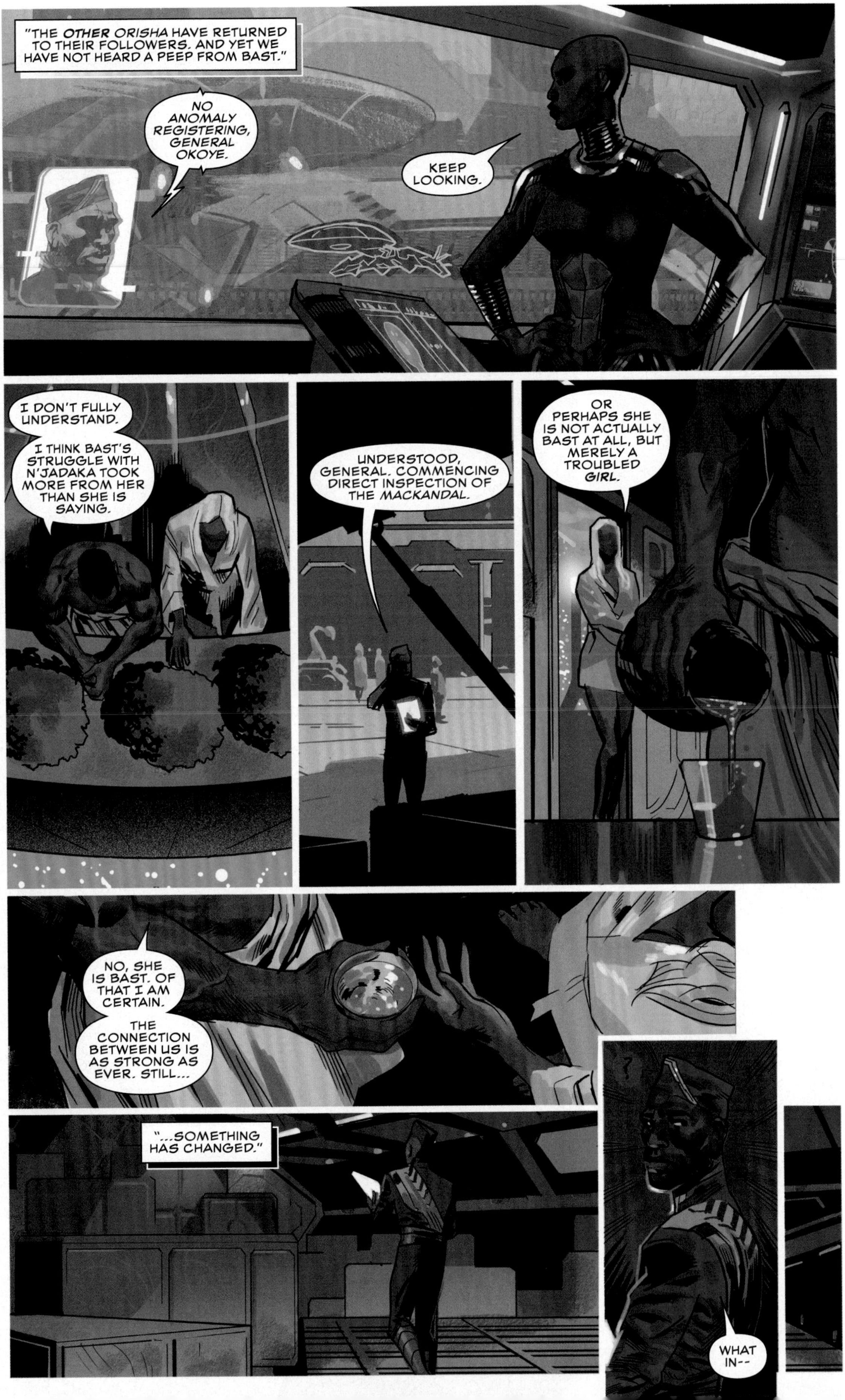
"THE OTHER ORISHA HAVE RETURNED TO THEIR FOLLOWERS. AND YET WE HAVE NOT HEARD A PEEP FROM BAST."
NO ANOMALY REGISTERING, GENERAL OKOYE.
KEEP LOOKING.
I DON'T FULLY UNDERSTAND.
I THINK BAST'S STRUGGLE WITH N'JADAKA TOOK MORE FROM HER THAN SHE IS SAYING.
UNDERSTOOD, GENERAL. COMMENCING DIRECT INSPECTION OF THE MACKANDAL.
OR PERHAPS SHE IS NOT ACTUALLY BAST AT ALL, BUT MERELY A TROUBLED GIRL.
NO, SHE IS BAST. OF THAT I AM CERTAIN.
THE CONNECTION BETWEEN US IS AS STRONG AS EVER. STILL...
"...SOMETHING HAS CHANGED."
WHAT IN--

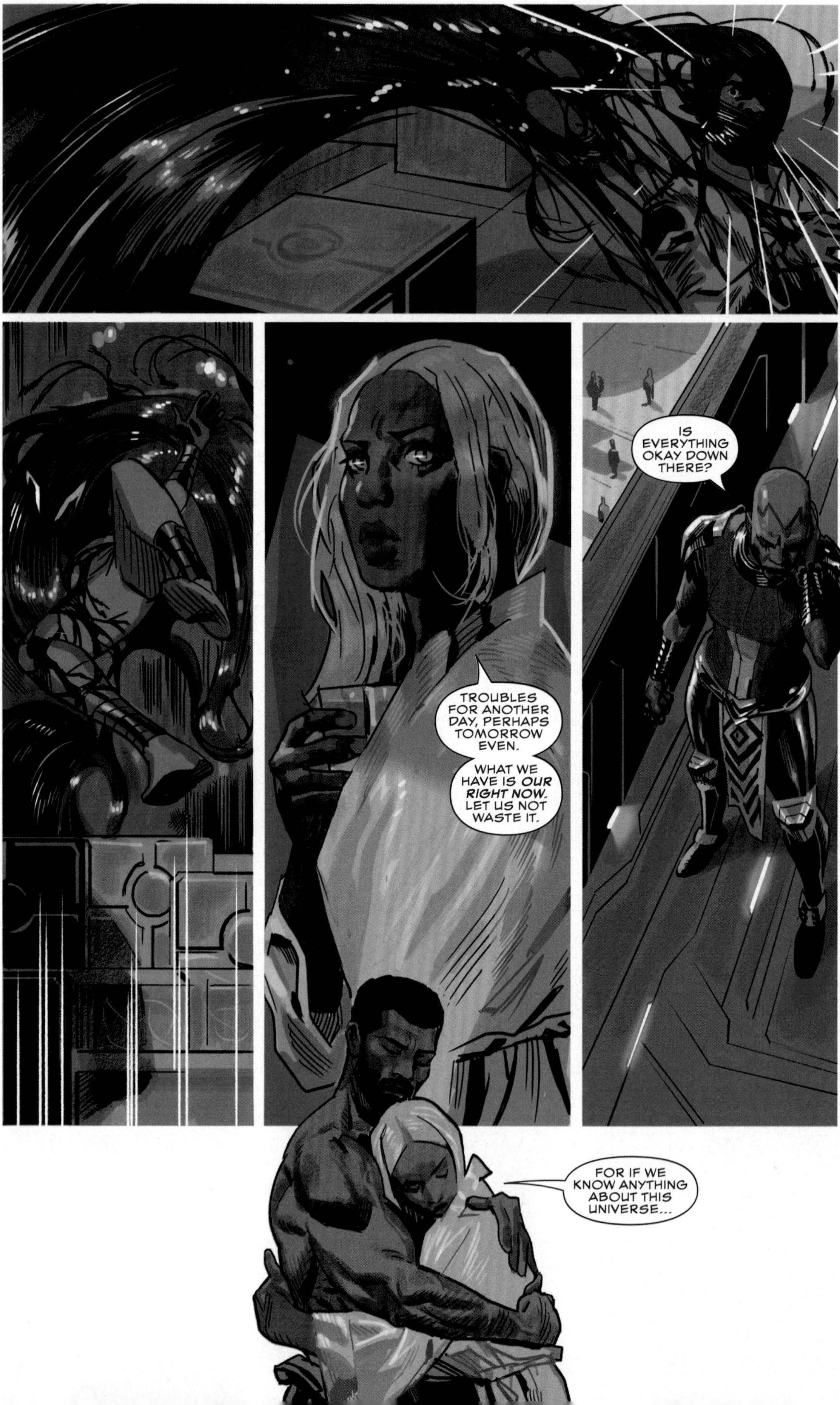
IS EVERYTHING OKAY DOWN THERE?
TROUBLES FOR ANOTHER DAY, PERHAPS TOMORROW EVEN.
WHAT WE HAVE IS OUR RIGHT NOW. LET US NOT WASTE IT.
FOR IF WE KNOW ANYTHING ABOUT THIS UNIVERSE...

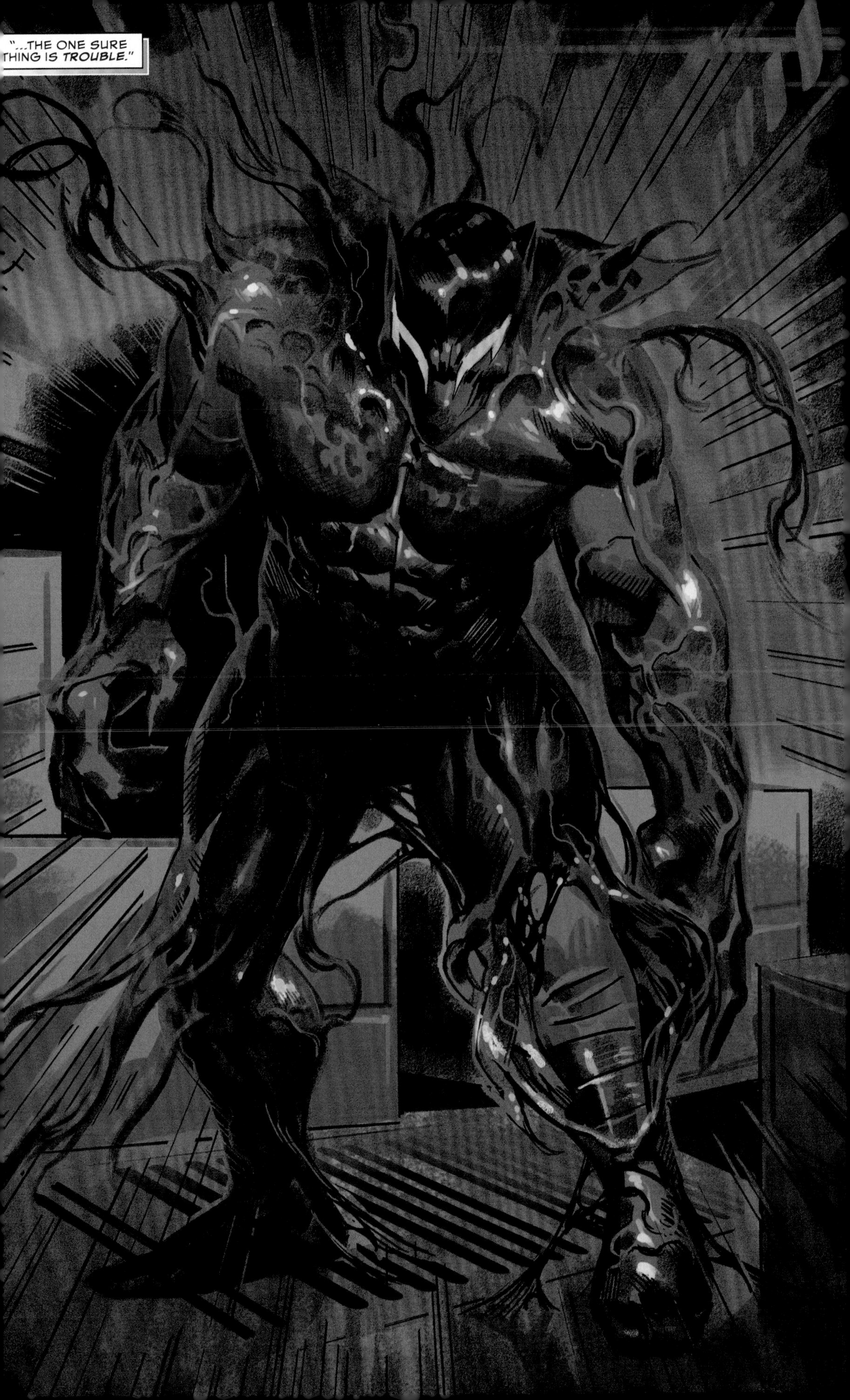
"...THE ONE SURE THING IS TROUBLE."

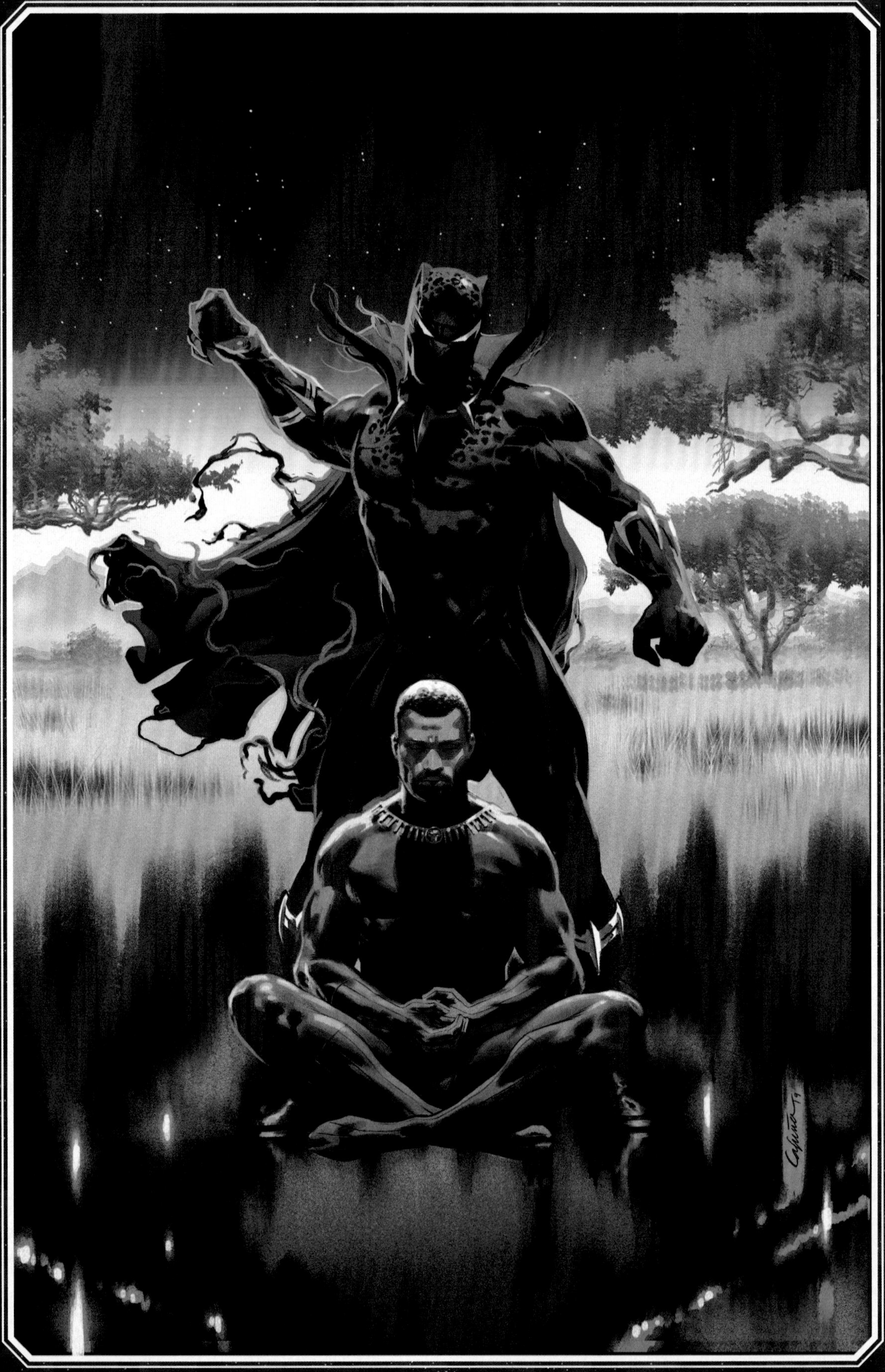

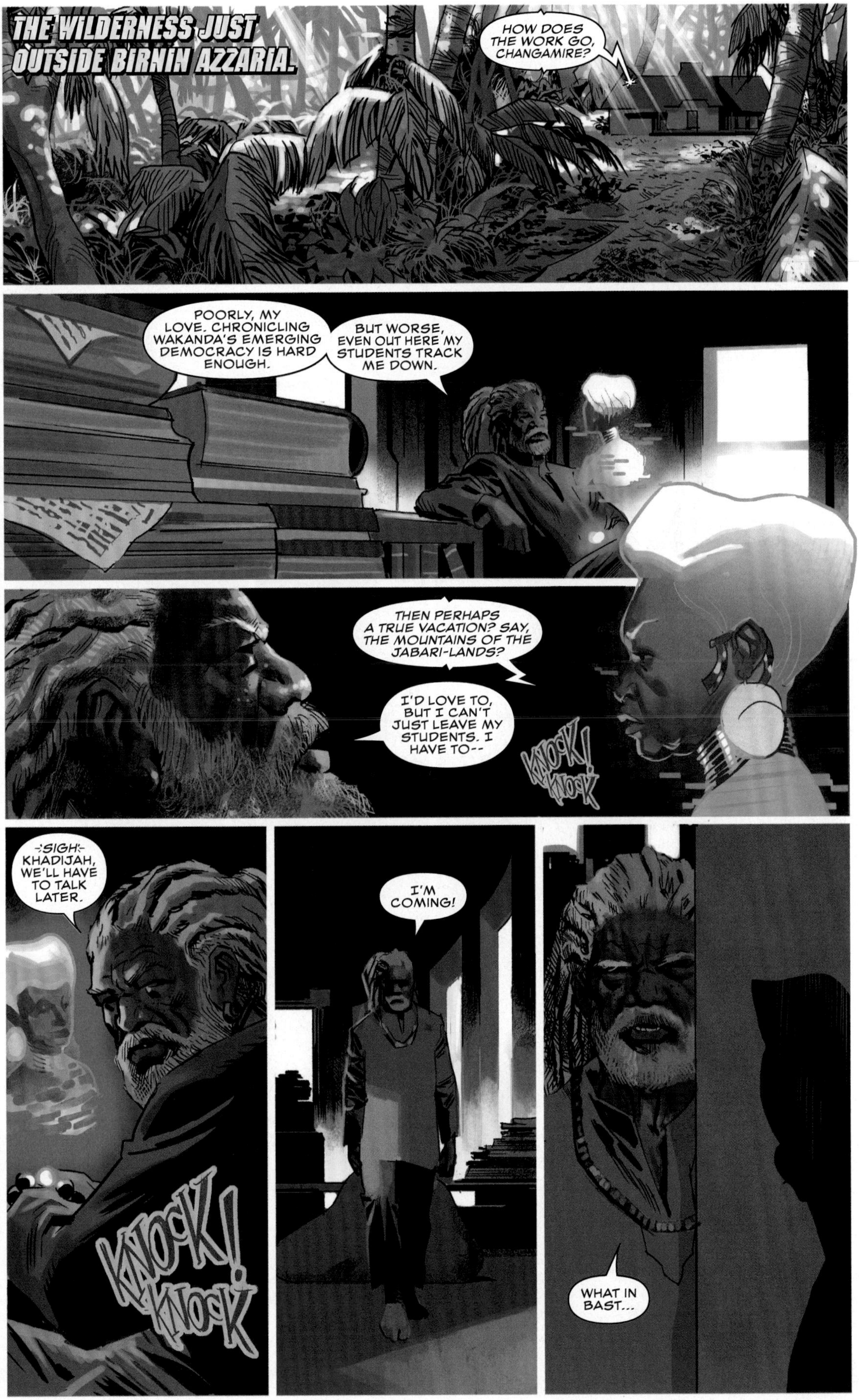
THE WILDERNESS JUST OUTSIDE BIRNIN AZZARIA.
HOW DOES THE WORK GO, CHANGAMIRE?
POORLY, MY LOVE. CHRONICLING WAKANDA'S EMERGING DEMOCRACY IS HARD ENOUGH.
BUT WORSE, EVEN OUT HERE MY STUDENTS TRACK ME DOWN.
THEN PERHAPS A TRUE VACATION? SAY, THE MOUNTAINS OF THE JABARI-LANDS?
I'D LOVE TO, BUT I CAN'T JUST LEAVE MY STUDENTS. I HAVE TO--
KNOCK! KNOCK
-SIGH- KHADIJAH, WE'LL HAVE TO TALK LATER.
KNOCK! KNOCK
I'M COMING!
WHAT IN BAST...

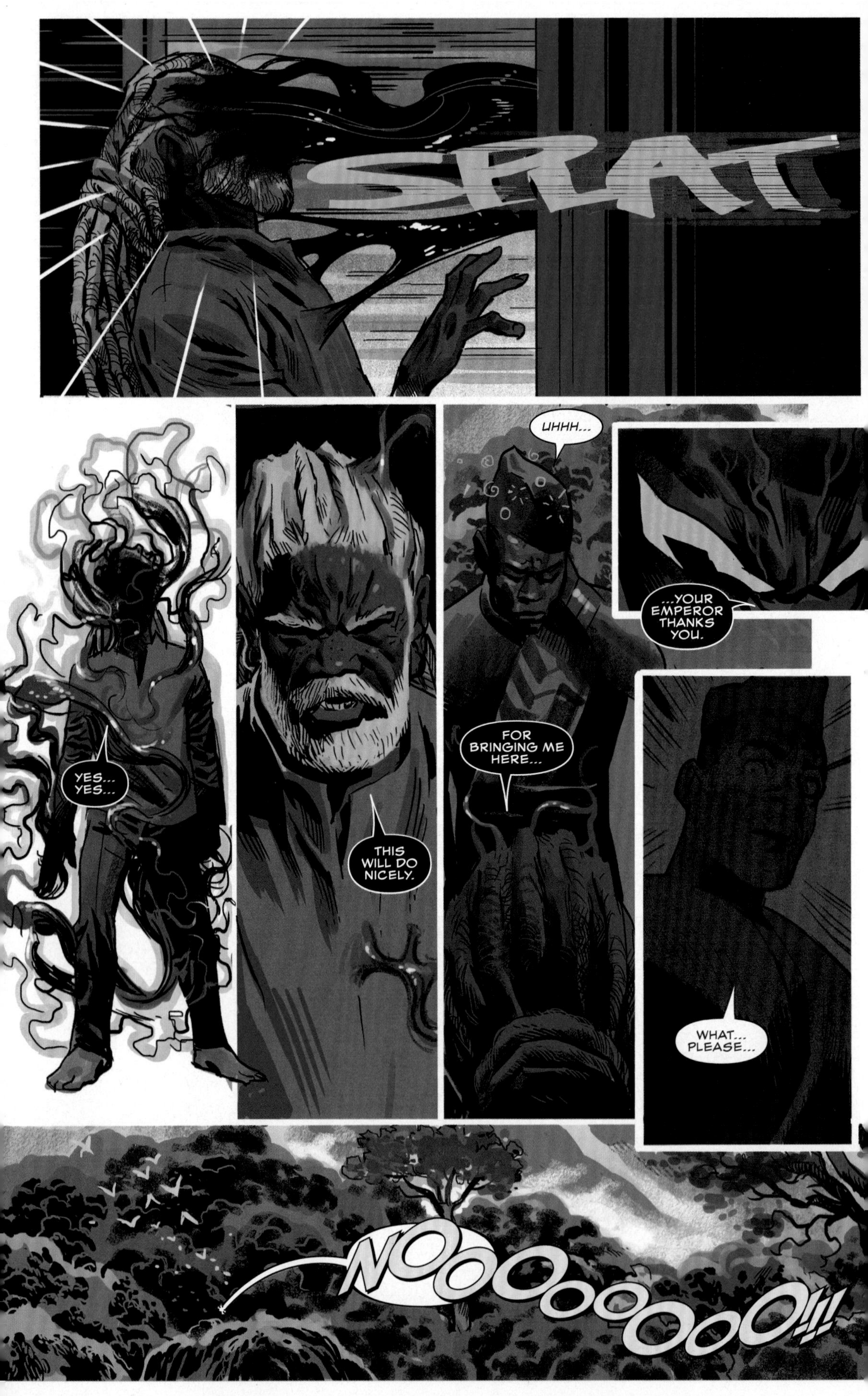
SPLAT
YES... YES...
THIS WILL DO NICELY.
UHHH...
FOR BRINGING ME HERE...
...YOUR EMPEROR THANKS YOU.
WHAT... PLEASE...
NOOOOOOOOOO!!!

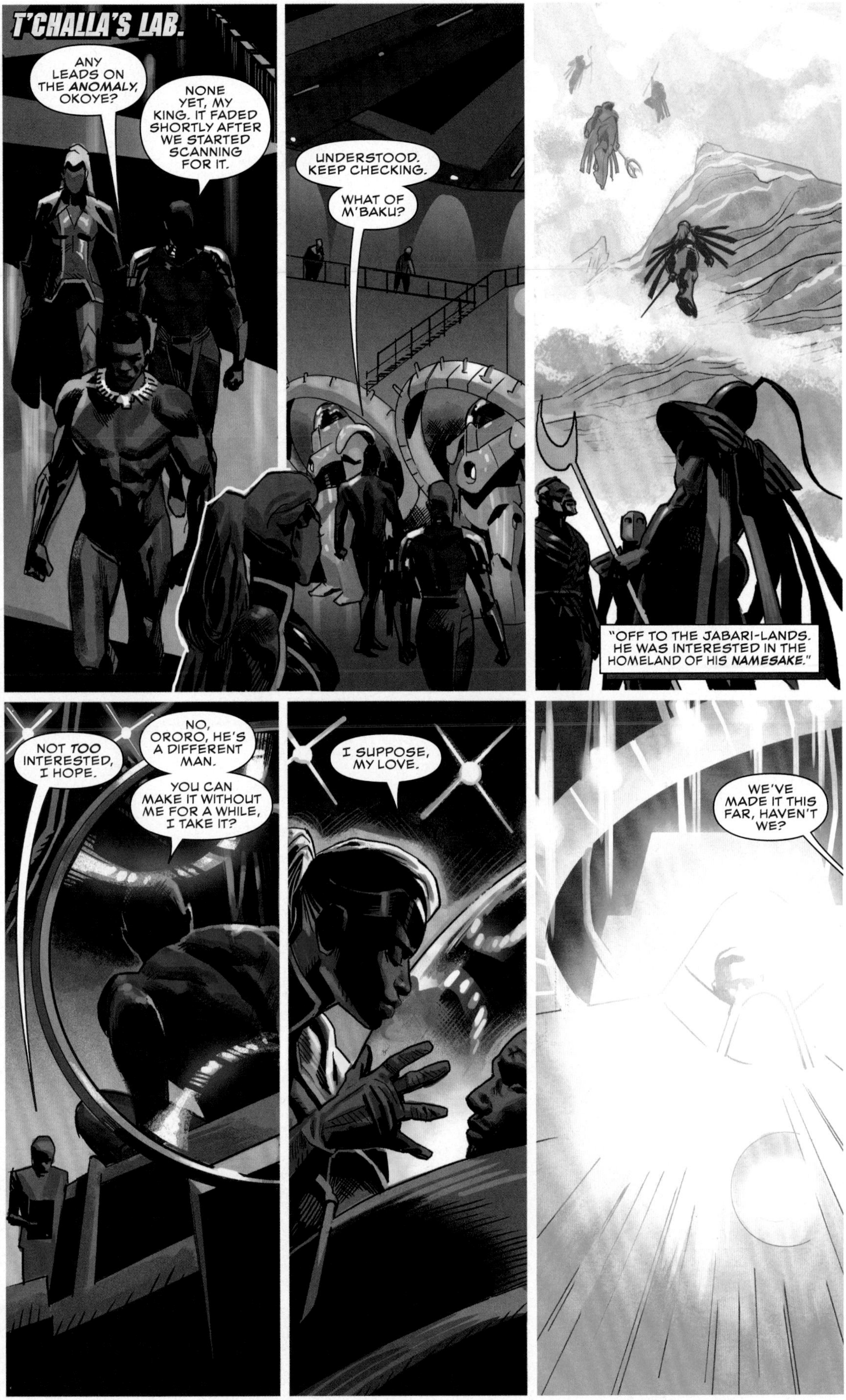
T'CHALLA'S LAB.
ANY LEADS ON THE *ANOMALY*, OKOYE?
NONE YET, MY KING. IT FADED SHORTLY AFTER WE STARTED SCANNING FOR IT.
UNDERSTOOD. KEEP CHECKING.
WHAT OF M'BAKU?
"OFF TO THE JABARI-LANDS. HE WAS INTERESTED IN THE HOMELAND OF HIS *NAMESAKE*."
NOT *TOO* INTERESTED, I HOPE.
NO, ORORO, HE'S A DIFFERENT MAN.
YOU CAN MAKE IT WITHOUT ME FOR A WHILE, I TAKE IT?
I SUPPOSE, MY LOVE.
WE'VE MADE IT THIS FAR, HAVEN'T WE?

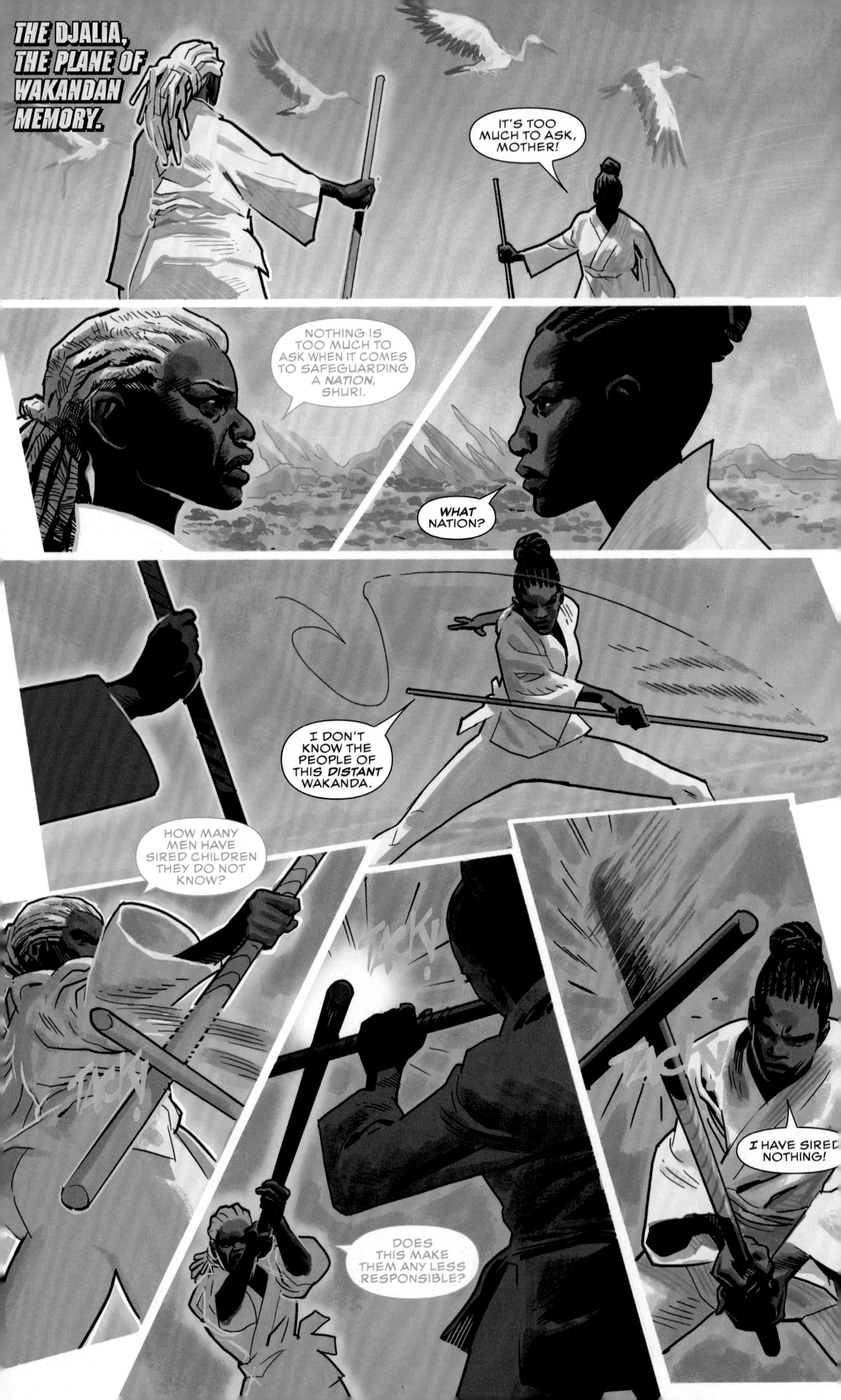
THE DJALIA, THE PLANE OF WAKANDAN MEMORY.
IT'S TOO MUCH TO ASK, MOTHER!
NOTHING IS TOO MUCH TO ASK WHEN IT COMES TO SAFEGUARDING A NATION, SHURI.
WHAT NATION?
I DON'T KNOW THE PEOPLE OF THIS DISTANT WAKANDA.
HOW MANY MEN HAVE SIRED CHILDREN THEY DO NOT KNOW?
TACK!
TACK!
DOES THIS MAKE THEM ANY LESS RESPONSIBLE?
TACK!
I HAVE SIRED NOTHING!

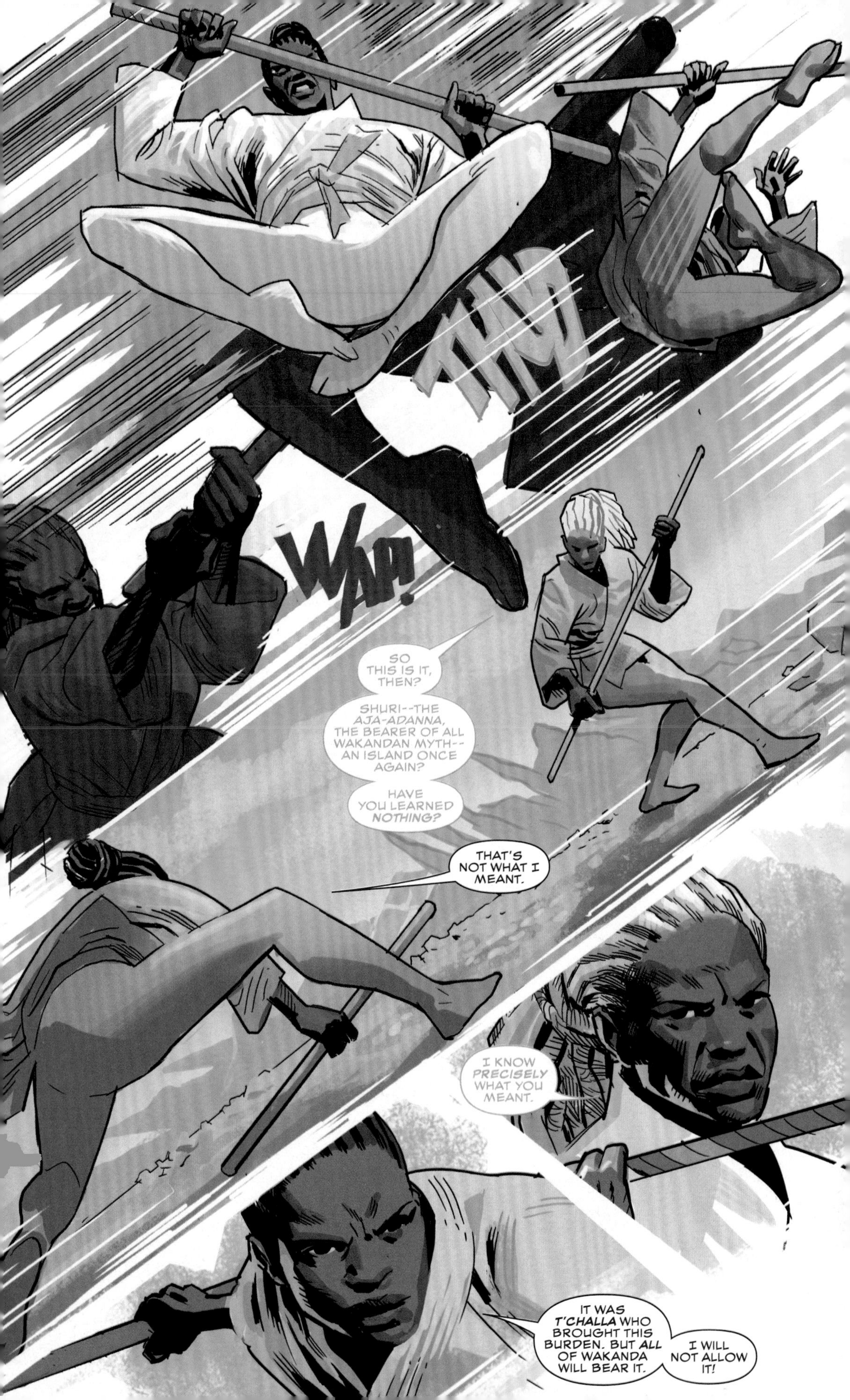
THUD
WAP!
SO THIS IS IT, THEN?
SHURI--THE AJA-ADANNA, THE BEARER OF ALL WAKANDAN MYTH--AN ISLAND ONCE AGAIN?
HAVE YOU LEARNED NOTHING?
THAT'S NOT WHAT I MEANT.
I KNOW PRECISELY WHAT YOU MEANT.
IT WAS T'CHALLA WHO BROUGHT THIS BURDEN. BUT ALL OF WAKANDA WILL BEAR IT.
I WILL NOT ALLOW IT!

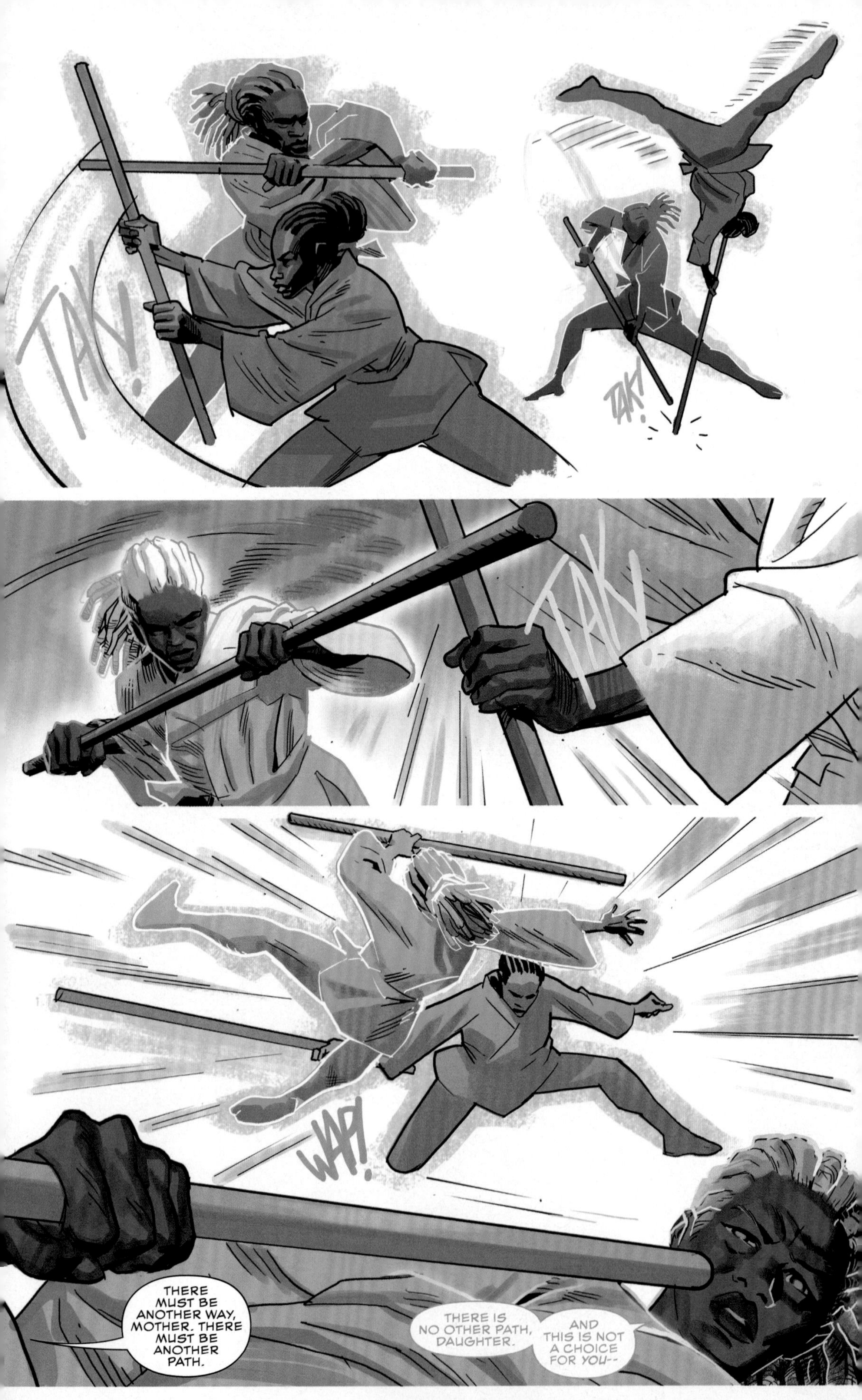
TAK!
TAK!
TAK!
WAP!
THERE MUST BE ANOTHER WAY, MOTHER. THERE MUST BE ANOTHER PATH.
THERE IS NO OTHER PATH, DAUGHTER.
AND THIS IS NOT A CHOICE FOR YOU--

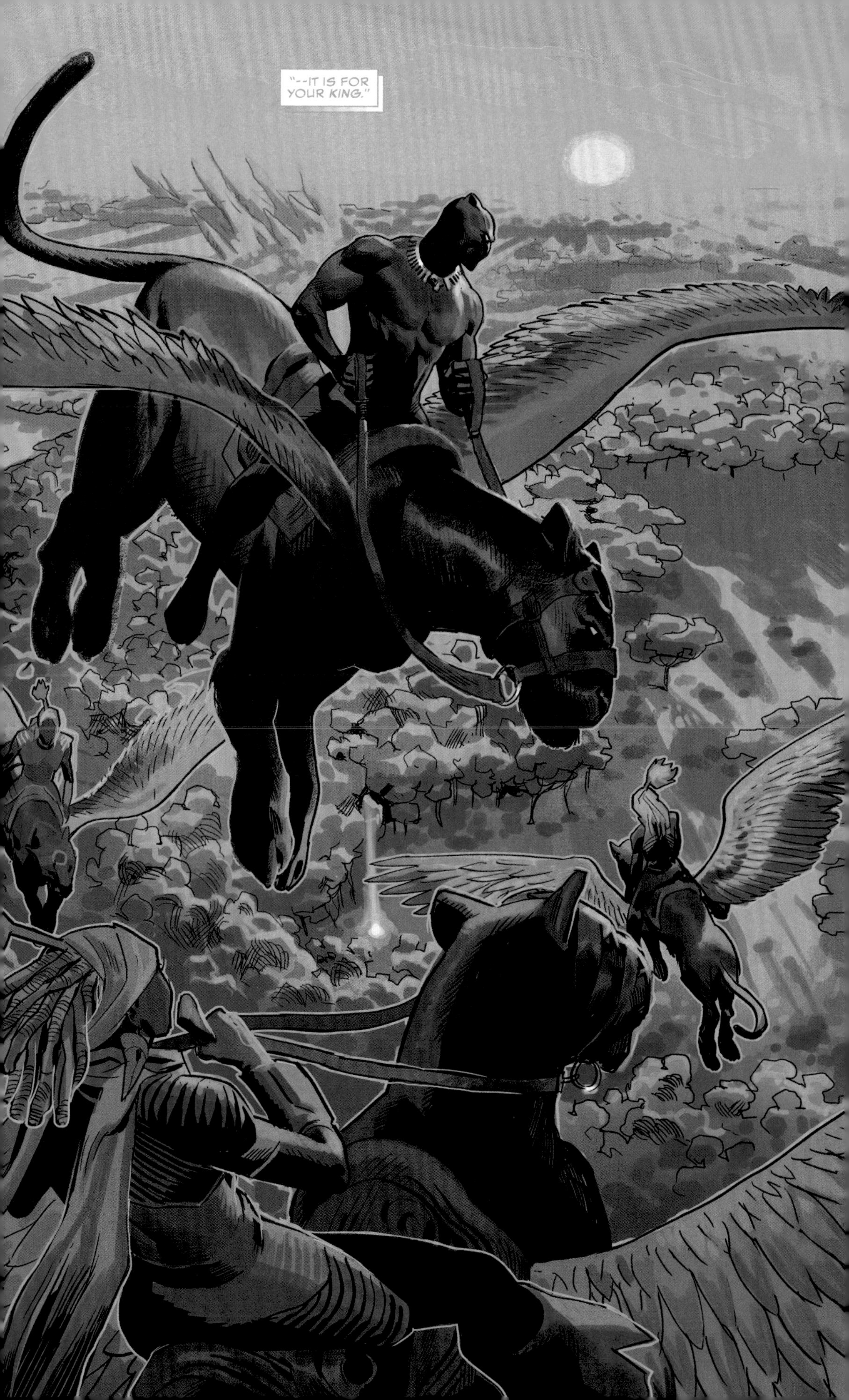
"--IT IS FOR YOUR KING."

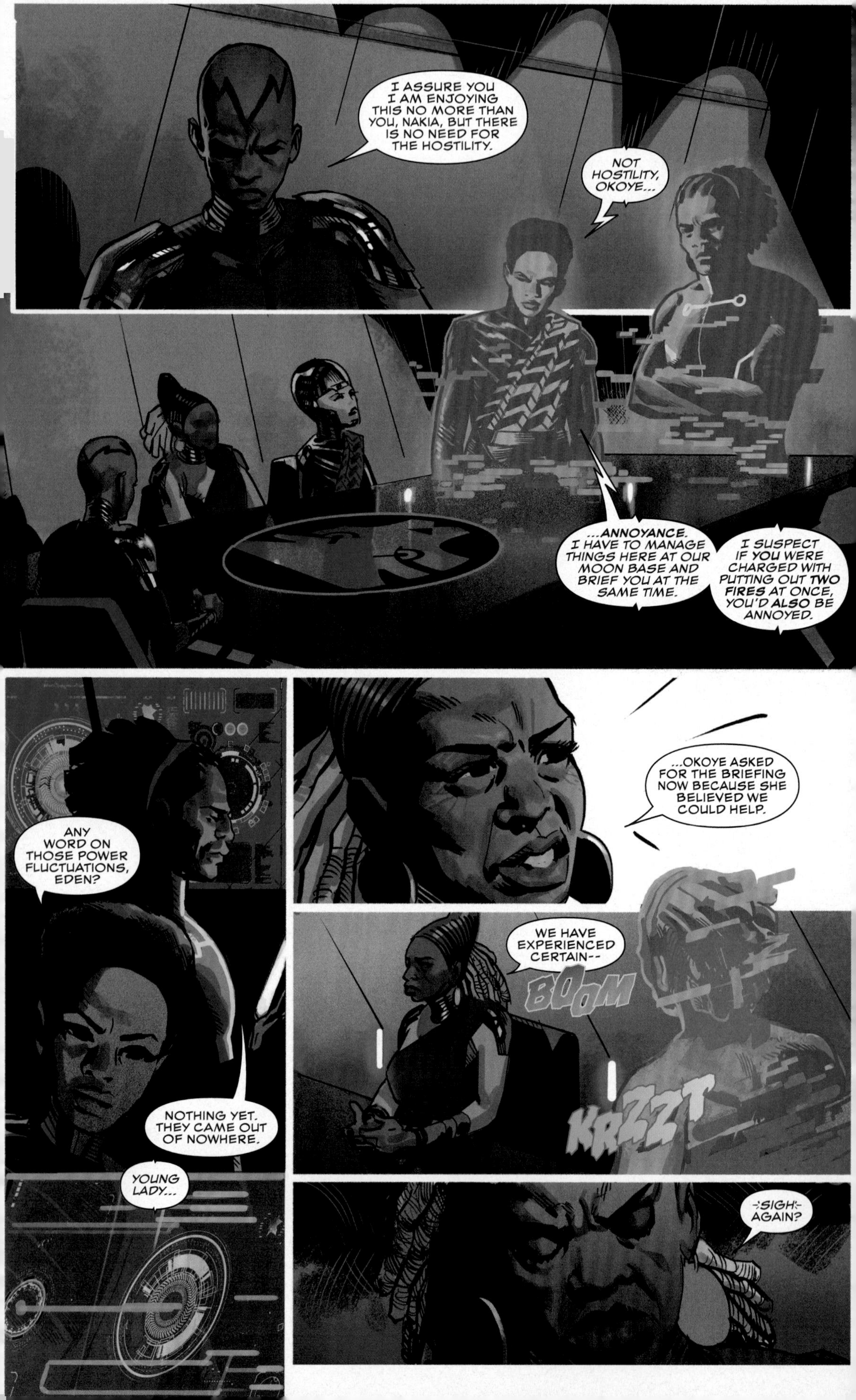
I ASSURE YOU I AM ENJOYING THIS NO MORE THAN YOU, NAKIA, BUT THERE IS NO NEED FOR THE HOSTILITY.
NOT HOSTILITY, OKOYE...
...ANNOYANCE. I HAVE TO MANAGE THINGS HERE AT OUR MOON BASE AND BRIEF YOU AT THE SAME TIME.
I SUSPECT IF YOU WERE CHARGED WITH PUTTING OUT TWO FIRES AT ONCE, YOU'D ALSO BE ANNOYED.
ANY WORD ON THOSE POWER FLUCTUATIONS, EDEN?
NOTHING YET. THEY CAME OUT OF NOWHERE.
YOUNG LADY...
...OKOYE ASKED FOR THE BRIEFING NOW BECAUSE SHE BELIEVED WE COULD HELP.
WE HAVE EXPERIENCED CERTAIN--
BOOM
KRZZT
-SIGH- AGAIN?

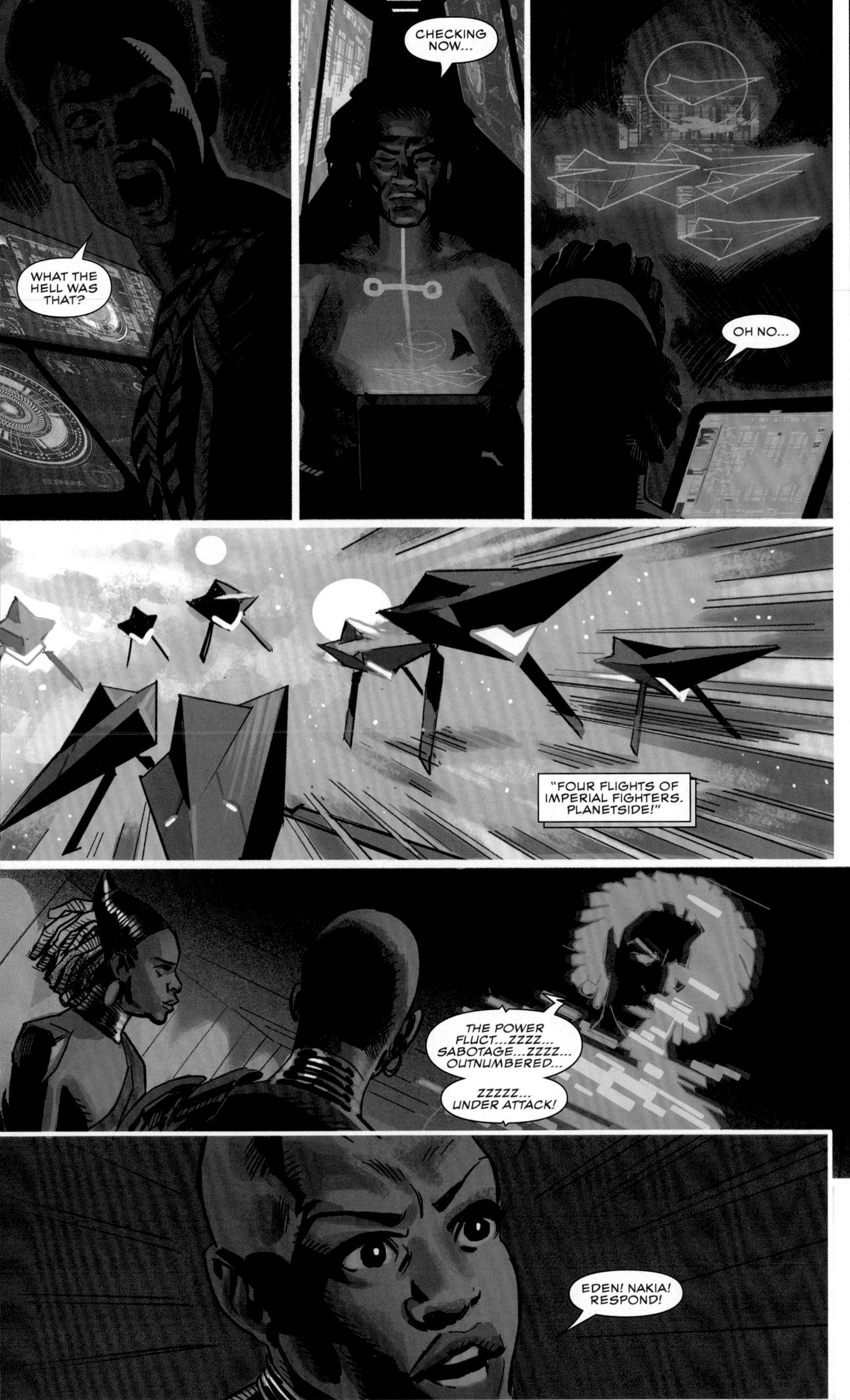
WHAT THE HELL WAS THAT?
CHECKING NOW...
OH NO...
"FOUR FLIGHTS OF IMPERIAL FIGHTERS. PLANETSIDE!"
THE POWER FLUCT...ZZZZ... SABOTAGE...ZZZZ... OUTNUMBERED...
ZZZZZ... UNDER ATTACK!
EDEN! NAKIA! RESPOND!

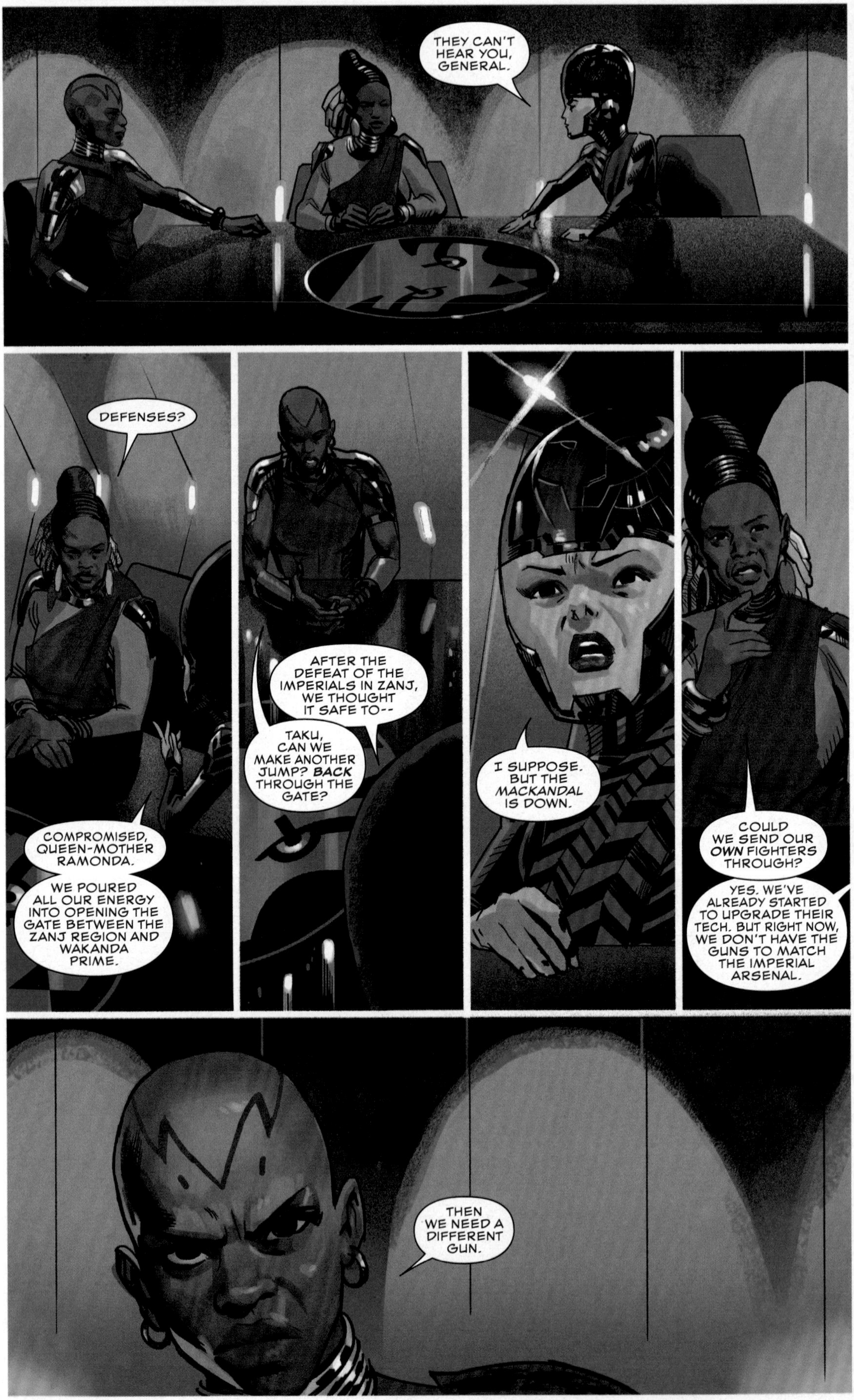
THEY CAN'T HEAR YOU, GENERAL.
DEFENSES?
COMPROMISED, QUEEN-MOTHER RAMONDA.
WE POURED ALL OUR ENERGY INTO OPENING THE GATE BETWEEN THE ZANJ REGION AND WAKANDA PRIME.
AFTER THE DEFEAT OF THE IMPERIALS IN ZANJ, WE THOUGHT IT SAFE TO--
TAKU, CAN WE MAKE ANOTHER JUMP? BACK THROUGH THE GATE?
I SUPPOSE. BUT THE MACKANDAL IS DOWN.
COULD WE SEND OUR OWN FIGHTERS THROUGH?
YES. WE'VE ALREADY STARTED TO UPGRADE THEIR TECH. BUT RIGHT NOW, WE DON'T HAVE THE GUNS TO MATCH THE IMPERIAL ARSENAL.
THEN WE NEED A DIFFERENT GUN.

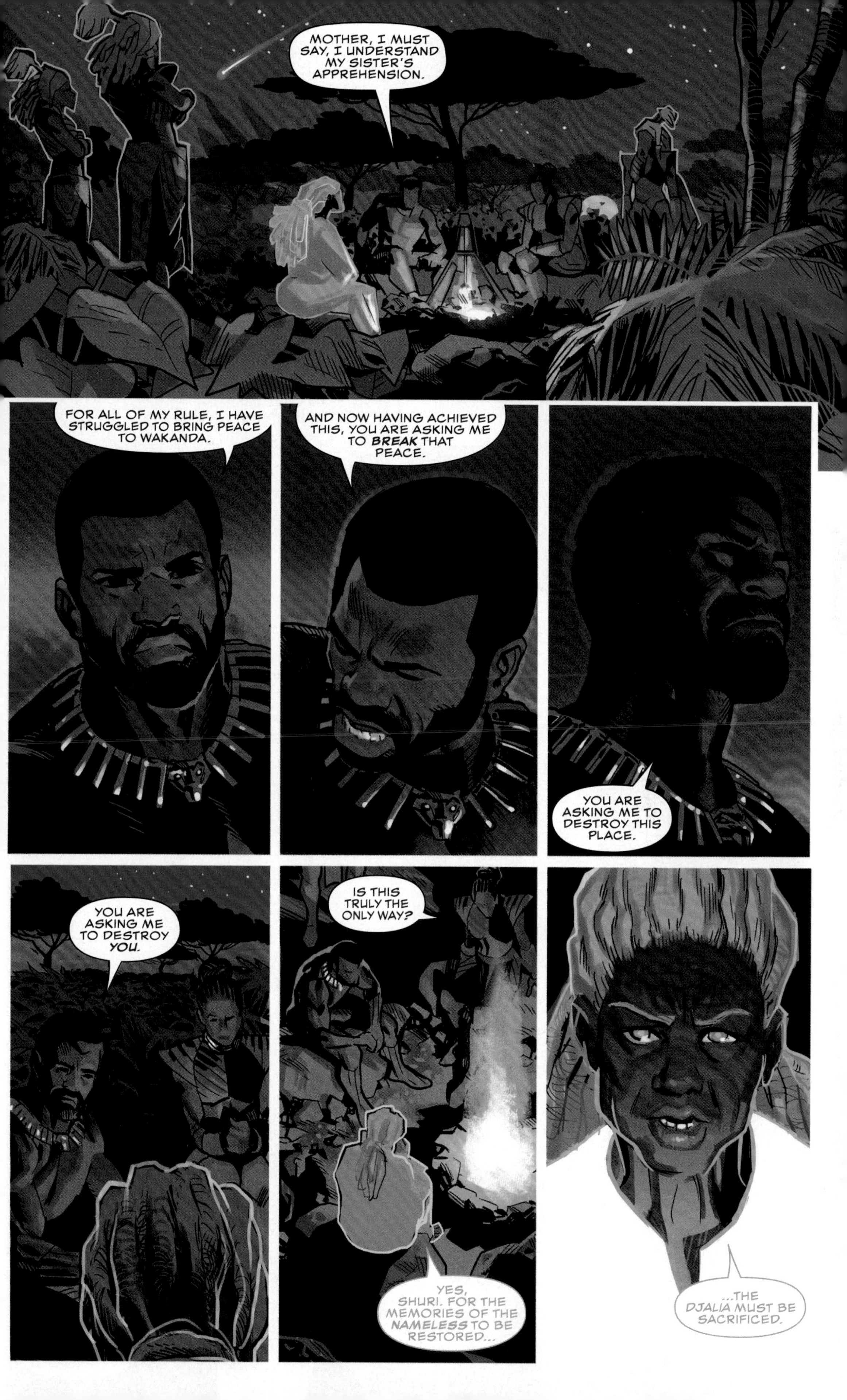
MOTHER, I MUST SAY, I UNDERSTAND MY SISTER'S APPREHENSION.
FOR ALL OF MY RULE, I HAVE STRUGGLED TO BRING PEACE TO WAKANDA.
AND NOW HAVING ACHIEVED THIS, YOU ARE ASKING ME TO *BREAK* THAT PEACE.
YOU ARE ASKING ME TO DESTROY THIS PLACE.
YOU ARE ASKING ME TO DESTROY *YOU.*
IS THIS TRULY THE ONLY WAY?
YES, SHURI. FOR THE MEMORIES OF THE *NAMELESS* TO BE RESTORED...
...THE *DJALIA* MUST BE SACRIFICED.

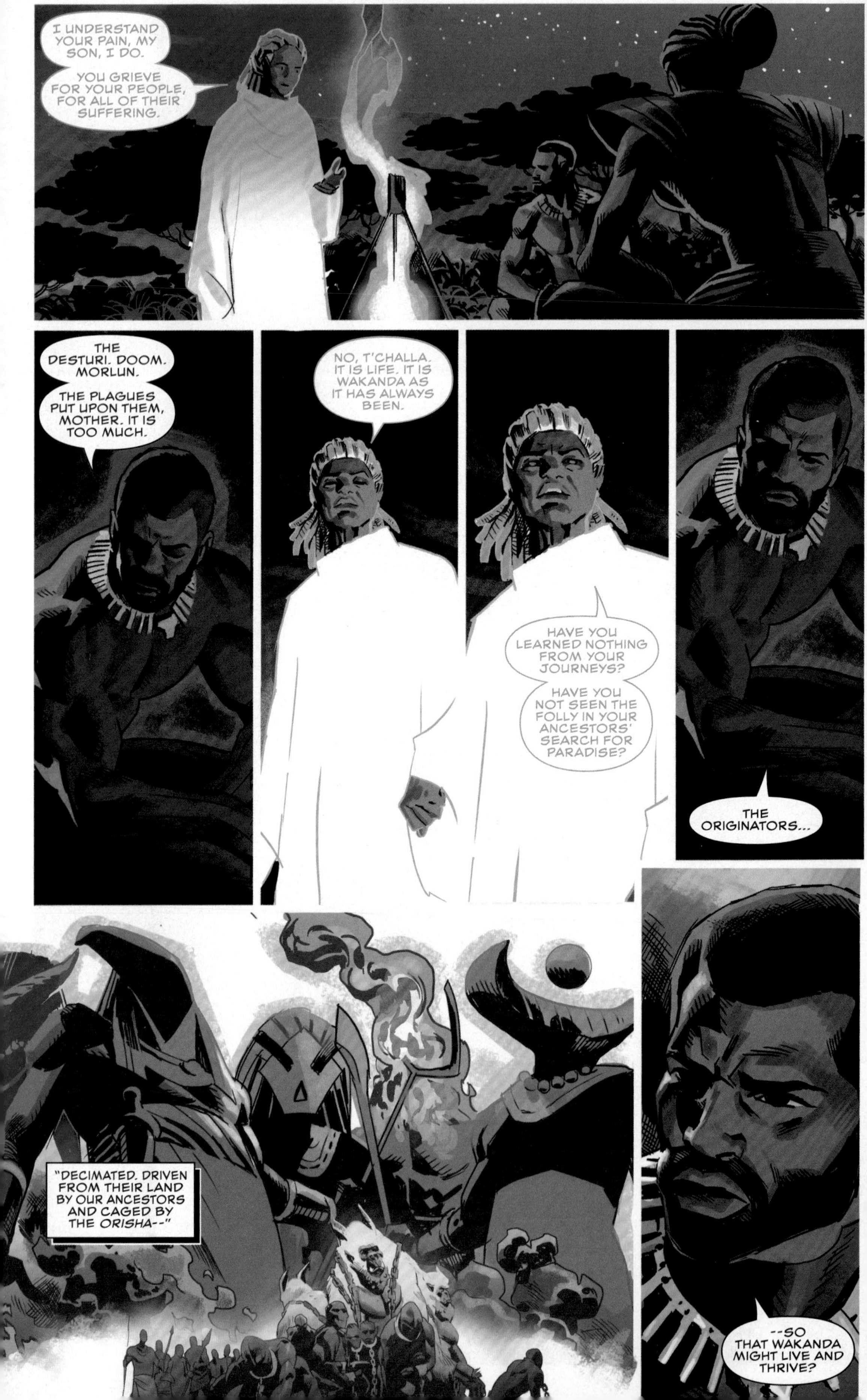
I UNDERSTAND YOUR PAIN, MY SON, I DO.
YOU GRIEVE FOR YOUR PEOPLE, FOR ALL OF THEIR SUFFERING.
THE DESTURI. DOOM. MORLUN.
THE PLAGUES PUT UPON THEM, MOTHER. IT IS TOO MUCH.
NO, T'CHALLA. IT IS LIFE. IT IS WAKANDA AS IT HAS ALWAYS BEEN.
HAVE YOU LEARNED NOTHING FROM YOUR JOURNEYS?
HAVE YOU NOT SEEN THE FOLLY IN YOUR ANCESTORS' SEARCH FOR PARADISE?
THE ORIGINATORS...
"DECIMATED. DRIVEN FROM THEIR LAND BY OUR ANCESTORS AND CAGED BY THE ORISHA--"
--SO THAT WAKANDA MIGHT LIVE AND THRIVE?

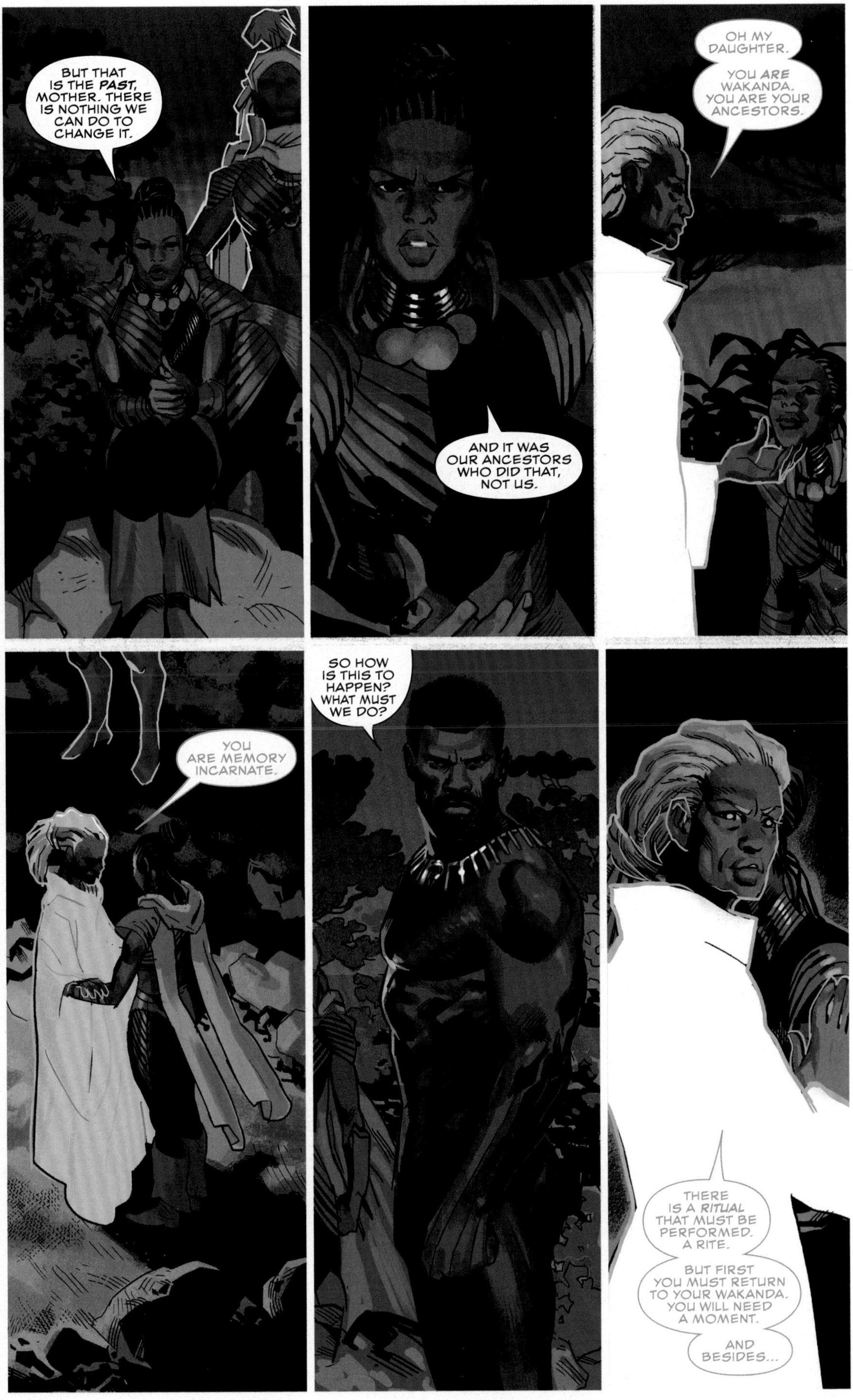
BUT THAT IS THE PAST, MOTHER. THERE IS NOTHING WE CAN DO TO CHANGE IT.
AND IT WAS OUR ANCESTORS WHO DID THAT, NOT US.
OH MY DAUGHTER.
YOU ARE WAKANDA. YOU ARE YOUR ANCESTORS.
YOU ARE MEMORY INCARNATE.
SO HOW IS THIS TO HAPPEN? WHAT MUST WE DO?
THERE IS A RITUAL THAT MUST BE PERFORMED. A RITE.
BUT FIRST YOU MUST RETURN TO YOUR WAKANDA. YOU WILL NEED A MOMENT.
AND BESIDES...

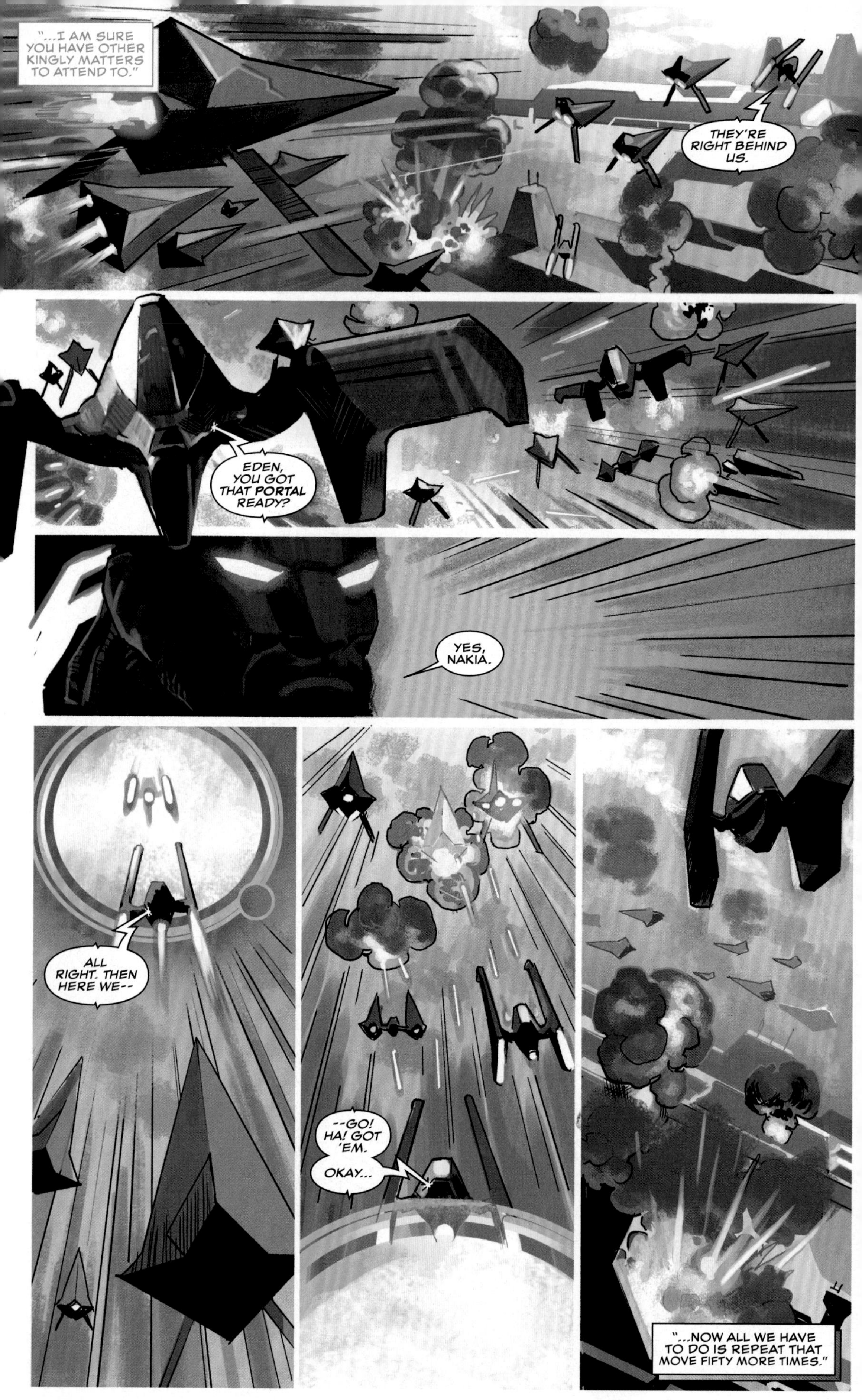
"...I AM SURE YOU HAVE OTHER KINGLY MATTERS TO ATTEND TO."
THEY'RE RIGHT BEHIND US.
EDEN, YOU GOT THAT PORTAL READY?
YES, NAKIA.
ALL RIGHT. THEN HERE WE--
--GO! HA! GOT 'EM.
OKAY...
"...NOW ALL WE HAVE TO DO IS REPEAT THAT MOVE FIFTY MORE TIMES."

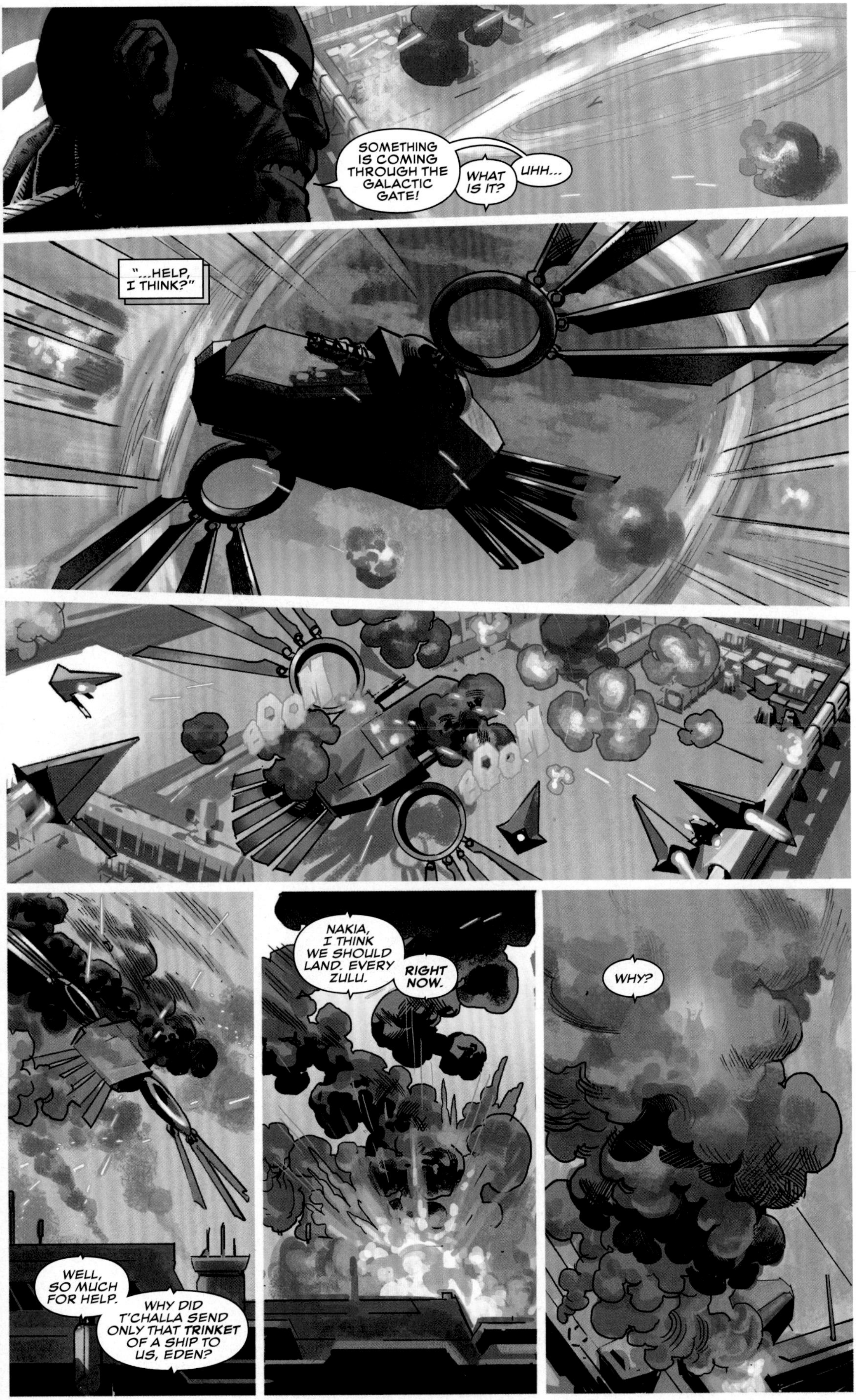
SOMETHING IS COMING THROUGH THE GALACTIC GATE!
WHAT IS IT?
UHH...
"...HELP, I THINK?"
BOOM
BOOM
WELL, SO MUCH FOR HELP.
WHY DID T'CHALLA SEND ONLY THAT TRINKET OF A SHIP TO US, EDEN?
NAKIA, I THINK WE SHOULD LAND. EVERY ZULU.
RIGHT NOW.
WHY?

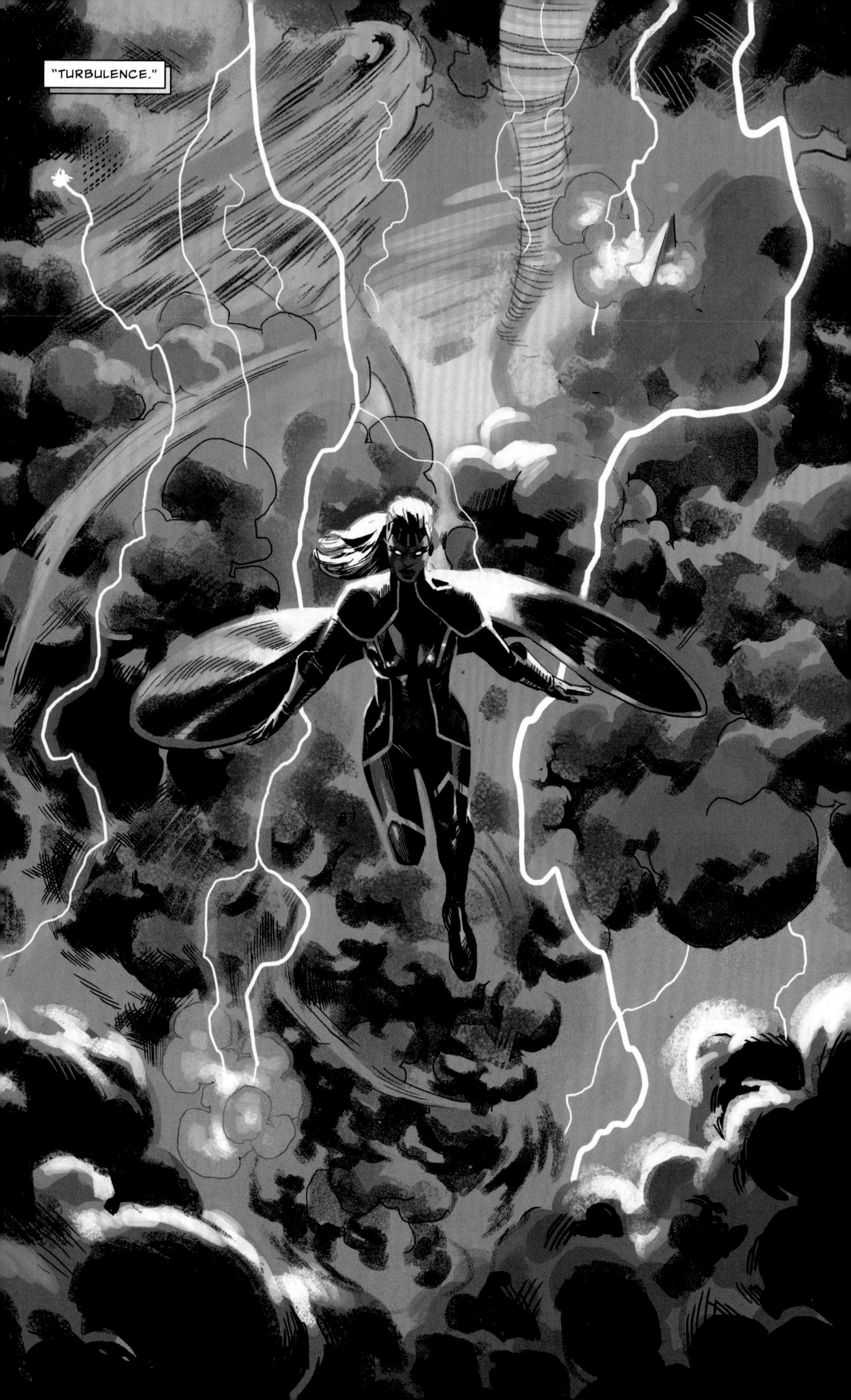
"TURBULENCE."

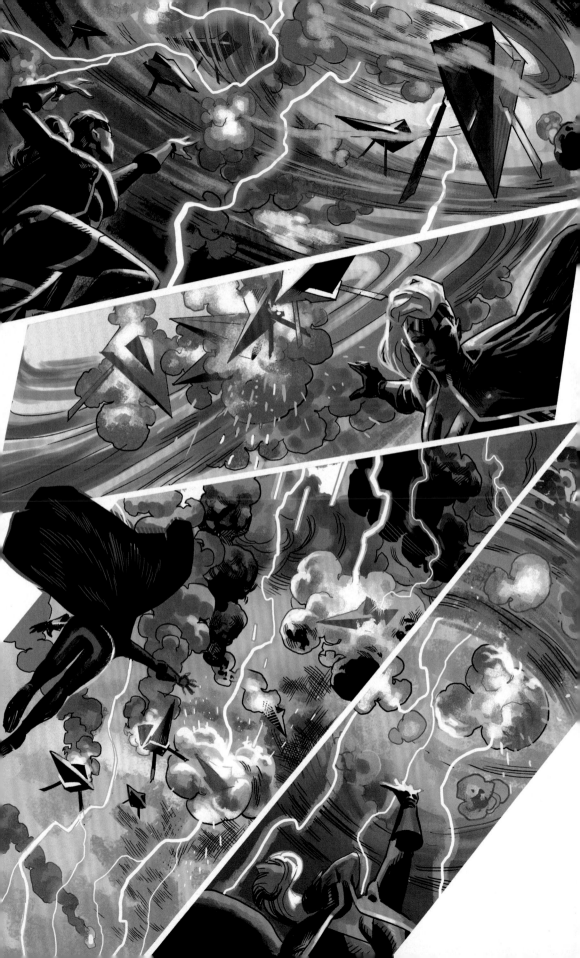

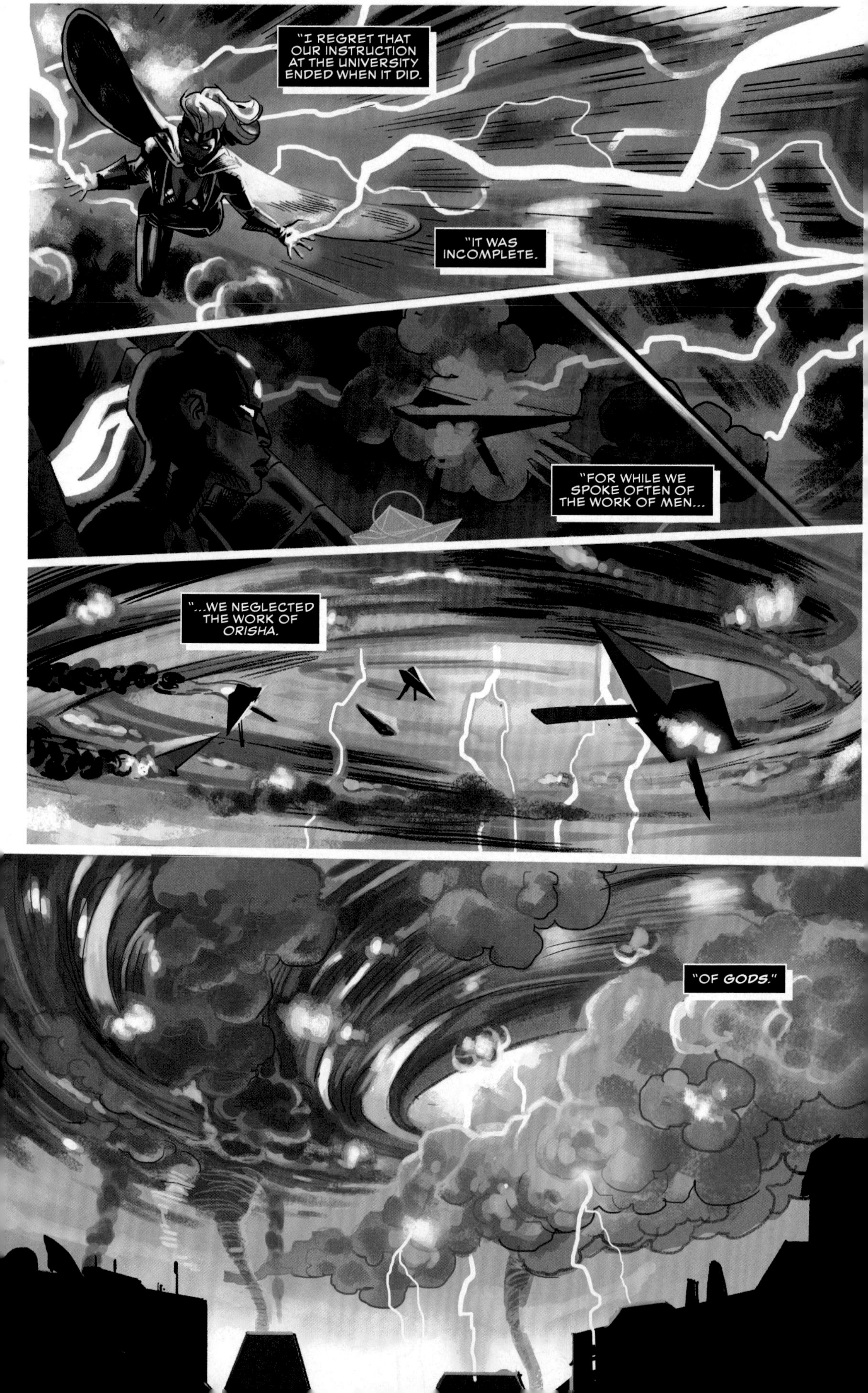
"I REGRET THAT OUR INSTRUCTION AT THE UNIVERSITY ENDED WHEN IT DID.
"IT WAS INCOMPLETE.
"FOR WHILE WE SPOKE OFTEN OF THE WORK OF MEN...
"...WE NEGLECTED THE WORK OF ORISHA.
"OF GODS."

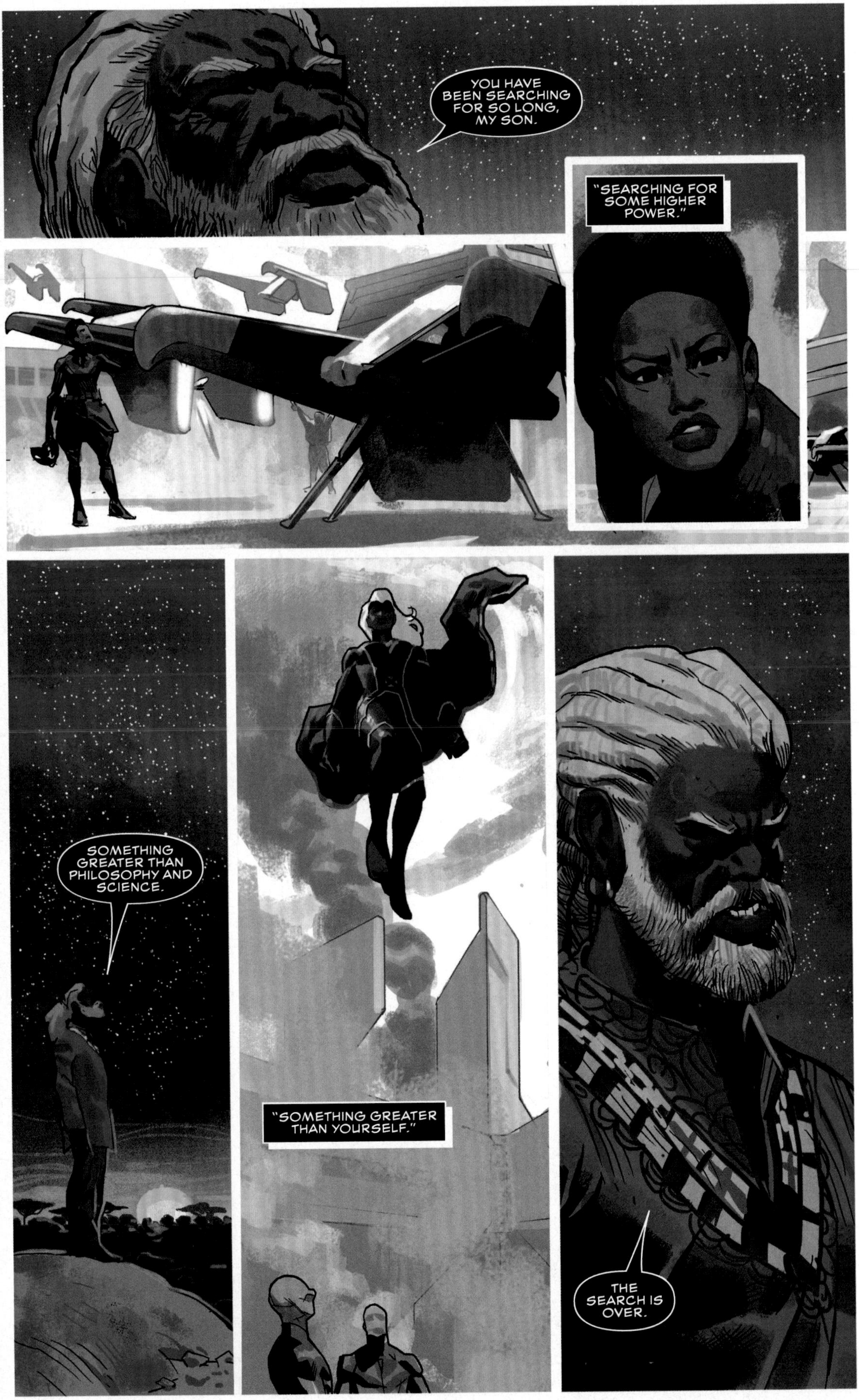
YOU HAVE BEEN SEARCHING FOR SO LONG, MY SON.
"SEARCHING FOR SOME HIGHER POWER."
SOMETHING GREATER THAN PHILOSOPHY AND SCIENCE.
"SOMETHING GREATER THAN YOURSELF."
THE SEARCH IS OVER.

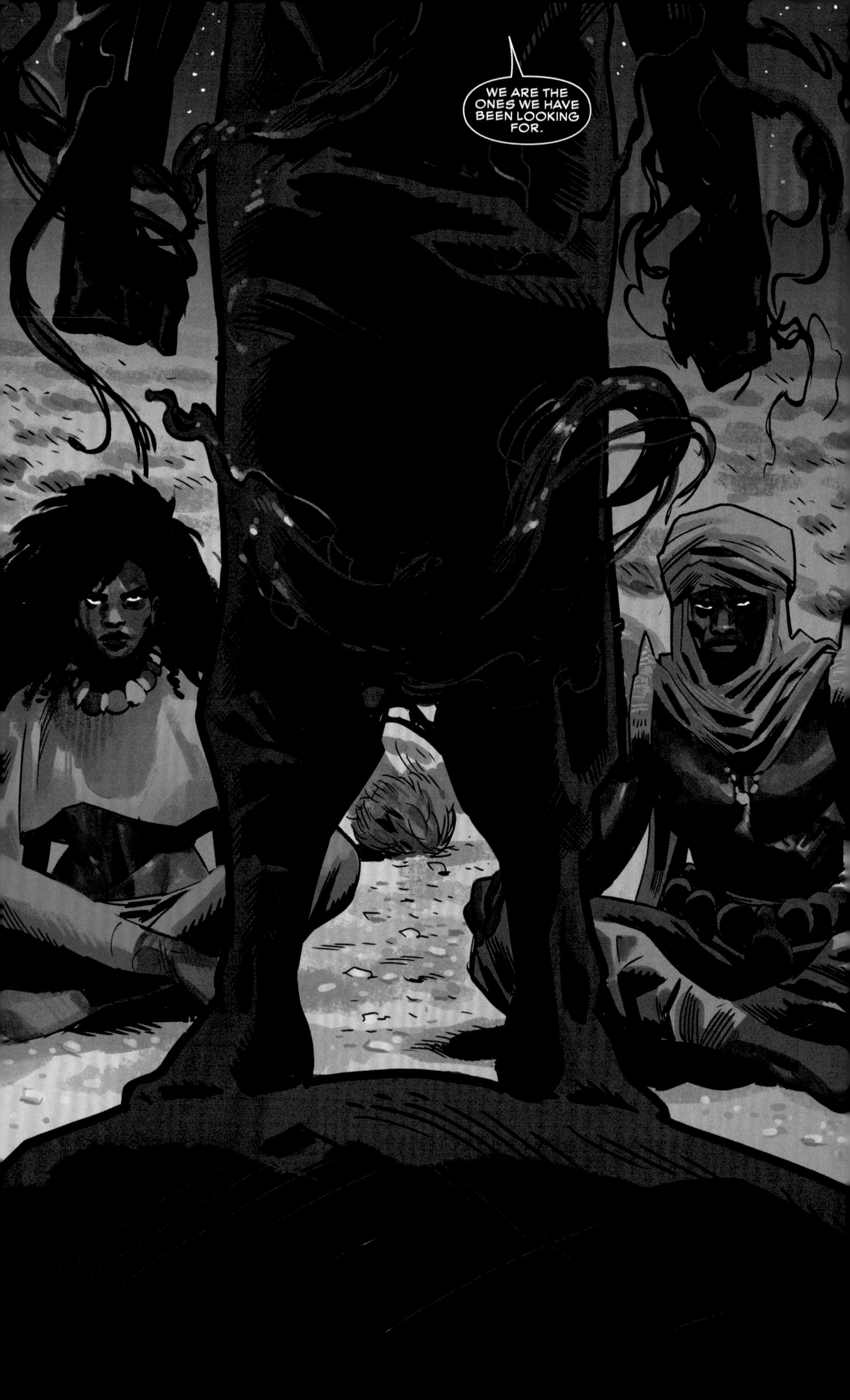
WE ARE THE ONES WE HAVE BEEN LOOKING FOR.

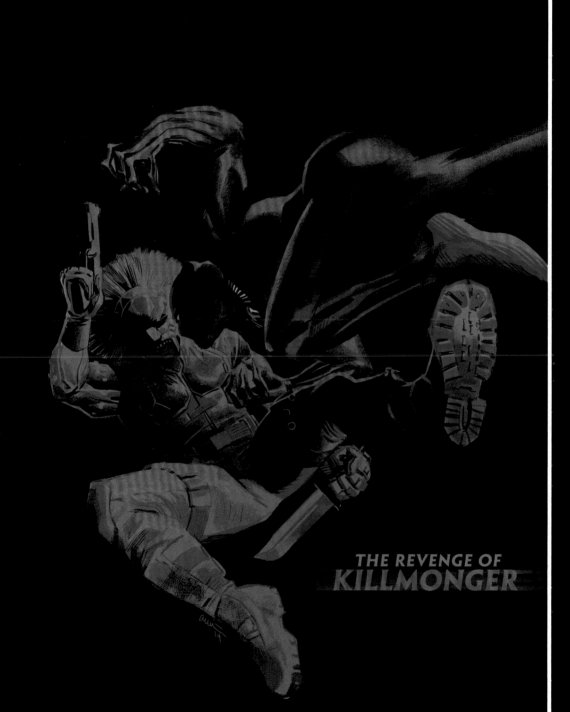

THE REVENGE OF
KILLMONGER

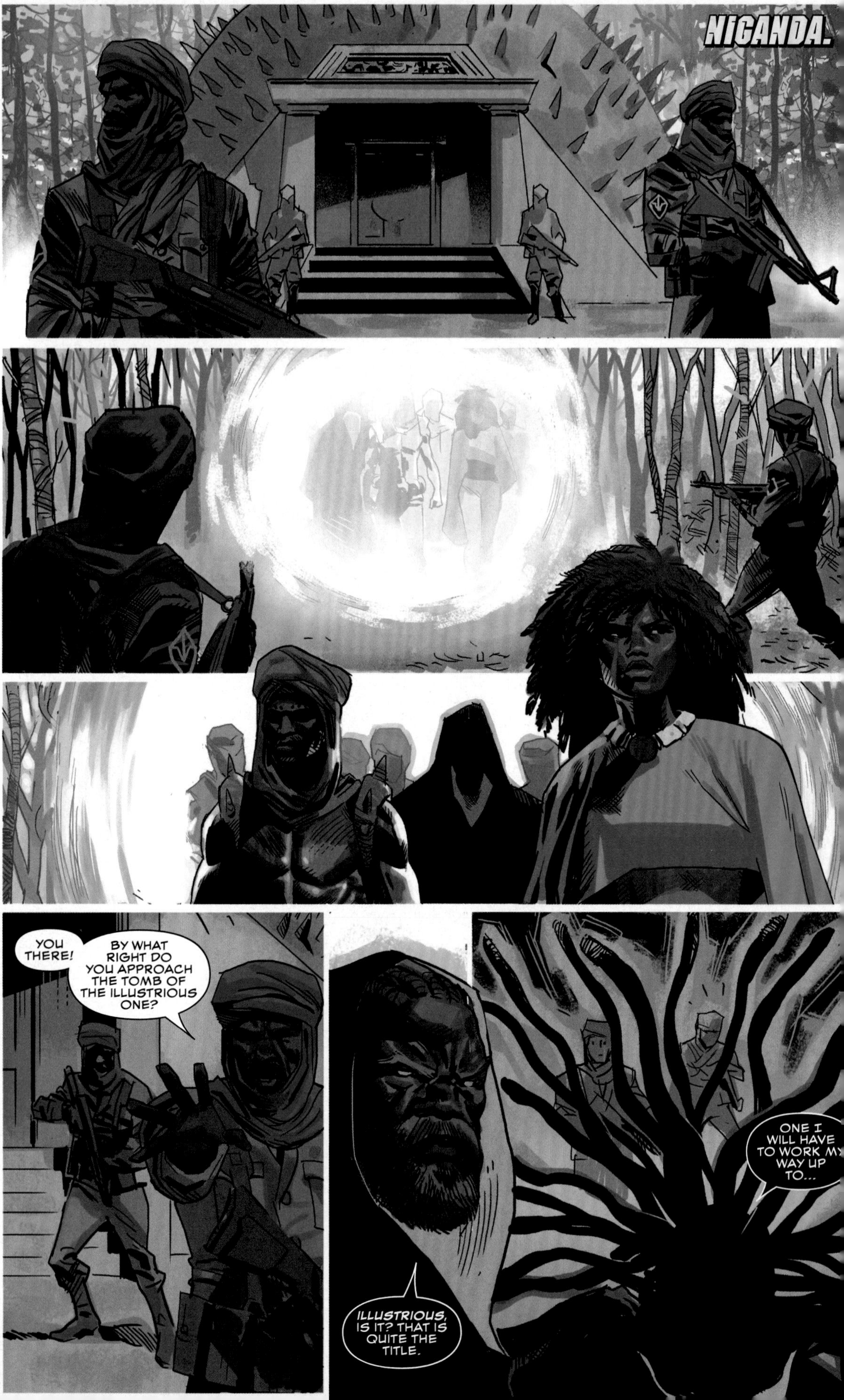
NIGANDA.
YOU THERE!
BY WHAT RIGHT DO YOU APPROACH THE TOMB OF THE ILLUSTRIOUS ONE?
ILLUSTRIOUS, IS IT? THAT IS QUITE THE TITLE.
ONE I WILL HAVE TO WORK MY WAY UP TO...

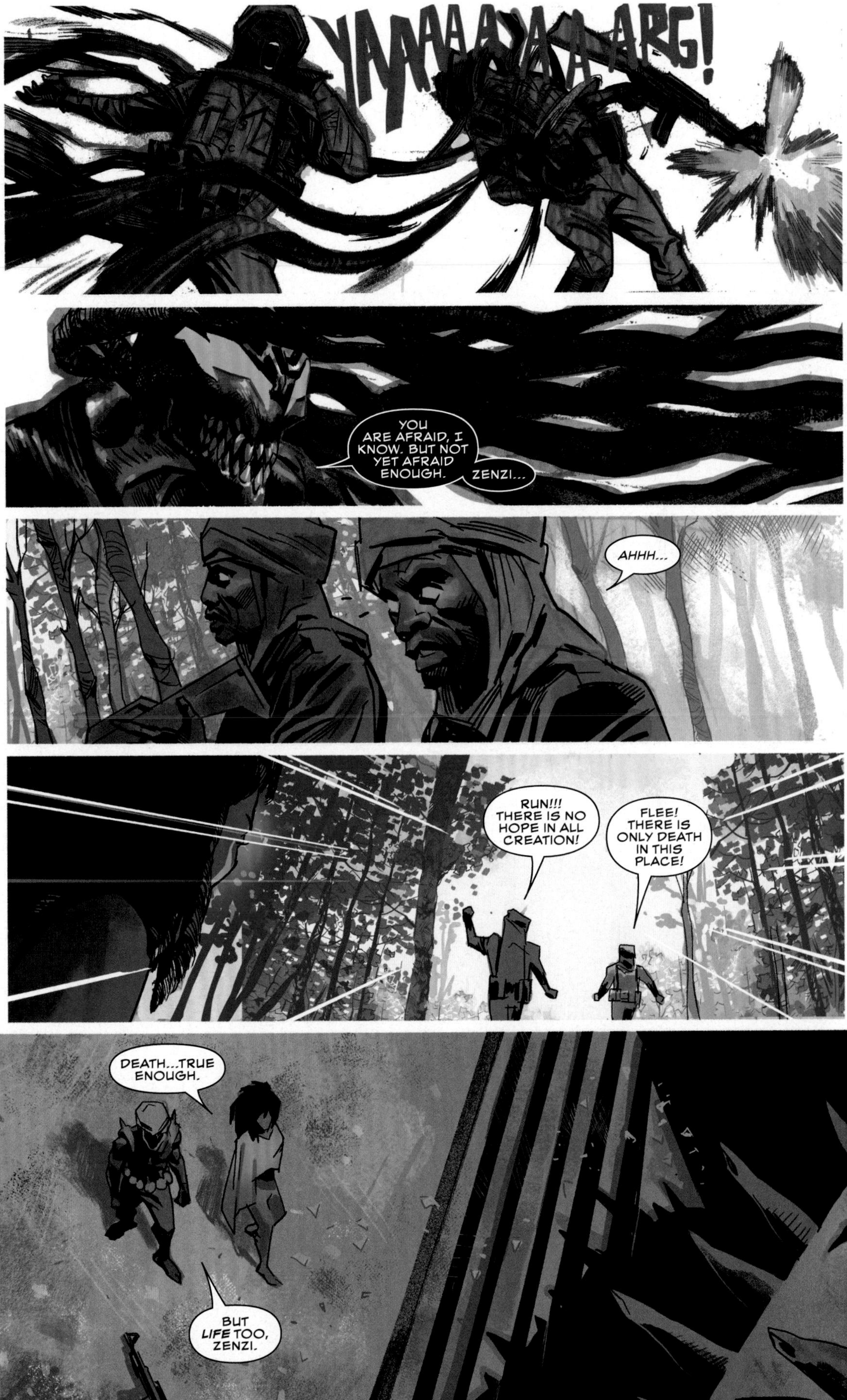
YAAAAAAA ARG!
YOU ARE AFRAID, I KNOW. BUT NOT YET AFRAID ENOUGH.
ZENZI...
AHHH...
RUN!!! THERE IS NO HOPE IN ALL CREATION!
FLEE! THERE IS ONLY DEATH IN THIS PLACE!
DEATH...TRUE ENOUGH.
BUT LIFE TOO, ZENZI.

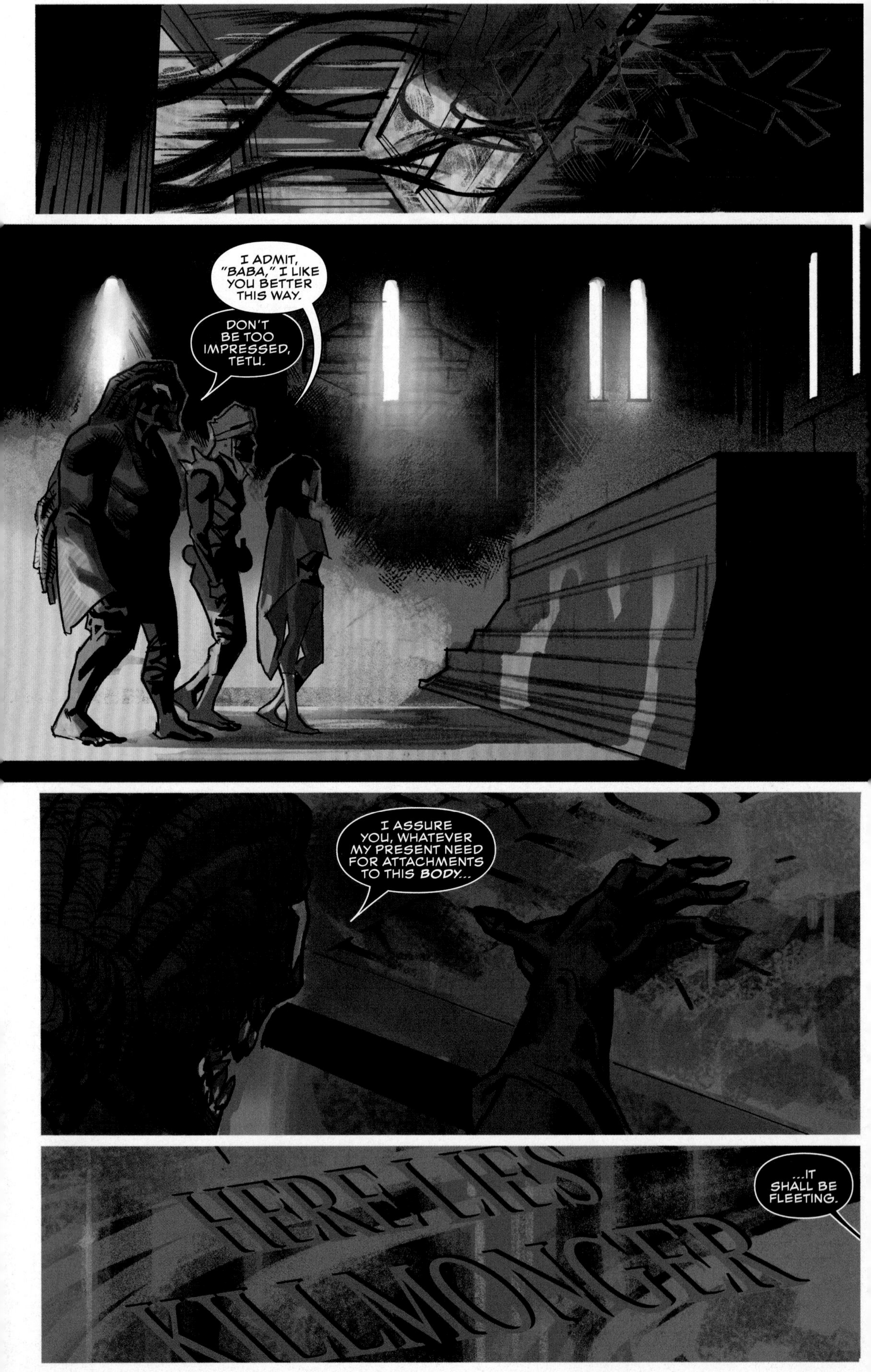
I ADMIT, "BABA," I LIKE YOU BETTER THIS WAY.
DON'T BE TOO IMPRESSED, TETU.
I ASSURE YOU, WHATEVER MY PRESENT NEED FOR ATTACHMENTS TO THIS *BODY*...
HERE LIES KILLMONGER
...IT SHALL BE FLEETING.

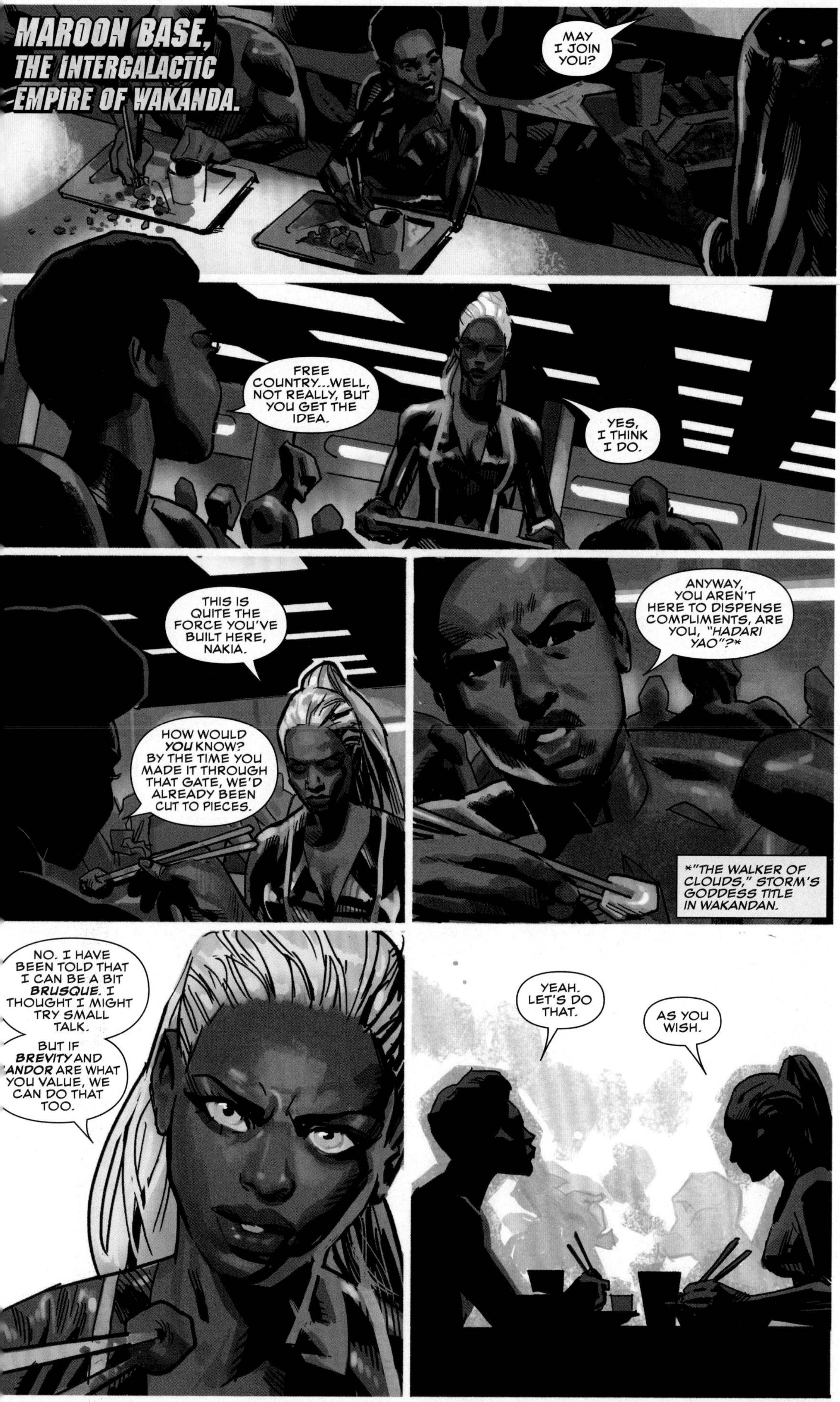

MAROON BASE, THE INTERGALACTIC EMPIRE OF WAKANDA.
MAY I JOIN YOU?
FREE COUNTRY...WELL, NOT REALLY, BUT YOU GET THE IDEA.
YES, I THINK I DO.
THIS IS QUITE THE FORCE YOU'VE BUILT HERE, NAKIA.
HOW WOULD YOU KNOW? BY THE TIME YOU MADE IT THROUGH THAT GATE, WE'D ALREADY BEEN CUT TO PIECES.
ANYWAY, YOU AREN'T HERE TO DISPENSE COMPLIMENTS, ARE YOU, "HADARI YAO"?*
*"THE WALKER OF CLOUDS," STORM'S GODDESS TITLE IN WAKANDAN.
NO. I HAVE BEEN TOLD THAT I CAN BE A BIT BRUSQUE. I THOUGHT I MIGHT TRY SMALL TALK.
BUT IF BREVITY AND ANDOR ARE WHAT YOU VALUE, WE CAN DO THAT TOO.
YEAH. LET'S DO THAT.
AS YOU WISH.

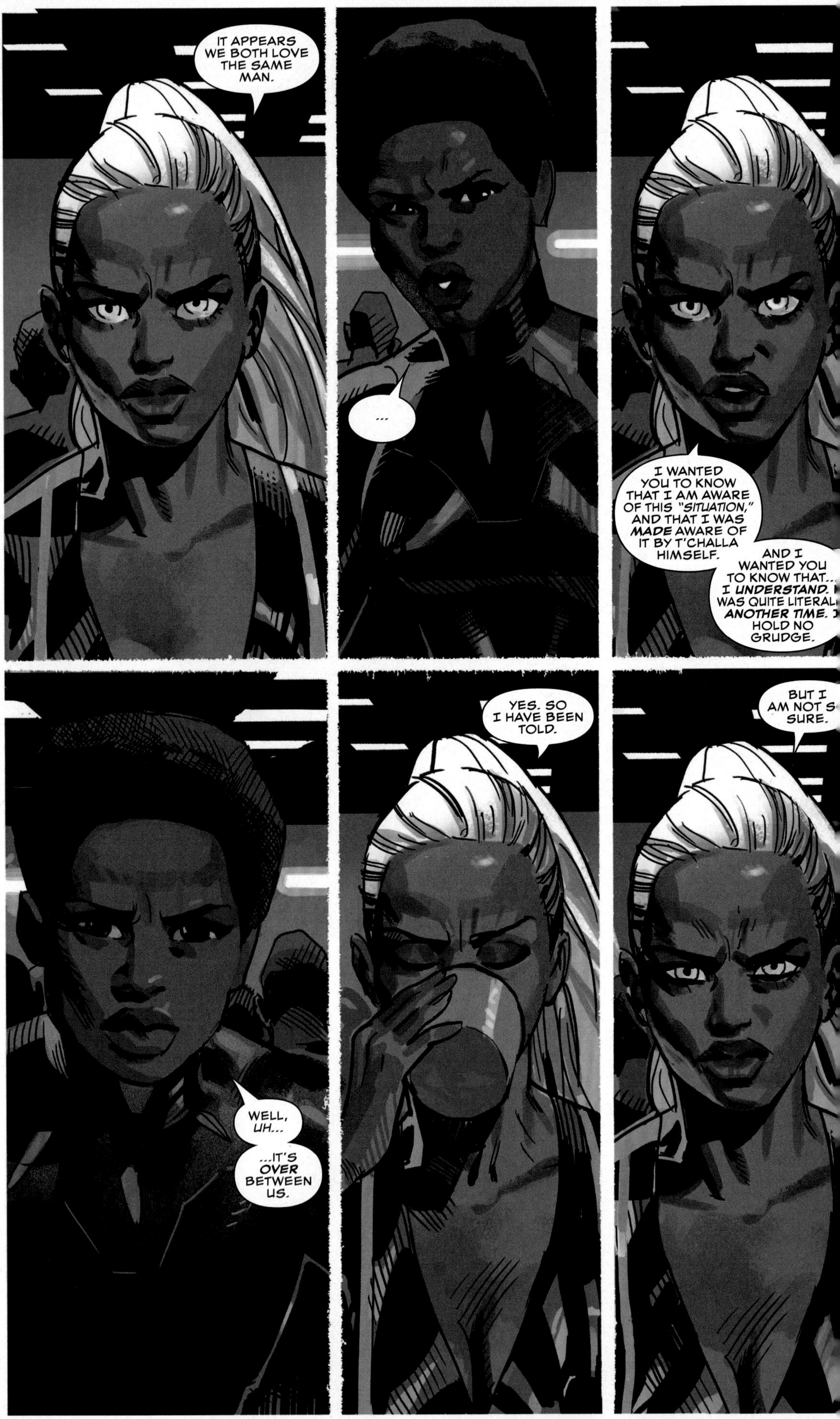
IT APPEARS WE BOTH LOVE THE SAME MAN.
...
I WANTED YOU TO KNOW THAT I AM AWARE OF THIS "SITUATION," AND THAT I WAS MADE AWARE OF IT BY T'CHALLA HIMSELF.
AND I WANTED YOU TO KNOW THAT... I UNDERSTAND. I WAS QUITE LITERAL ANOTHER TIME. I HOLD NO GRUDGE.
WELL, UH...
...IT'S OVER BETWEEN US.
YES. SO I HAVE BEEN TOLD.
BUT I AM NOT S SURE.

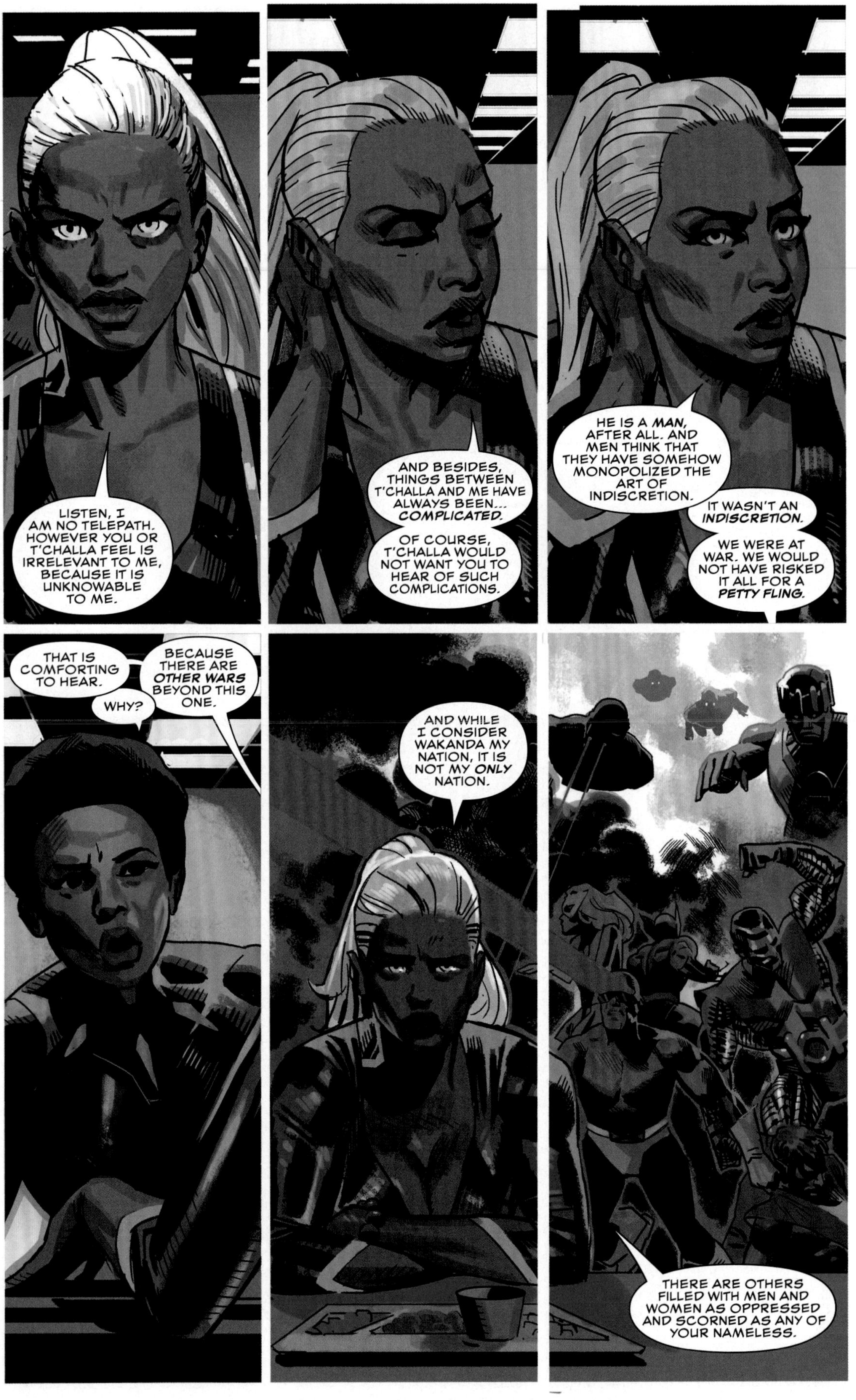
LISTEN, I AM NO TELEPATH. HOWEVER YOU OR T'CHALLA FEEL IS IRRELEVANT TO ME, BECAUSE IT IS UNKNOWABLE TO ME.
AND BESIDES, THINGS BETWEEN T'CHALLA AND ME HAVE ALWAYS BEEN... *COMPLICATED.*
OF COURSE, T'CHALLA WOULD NOT WANT YOU TO HEAR OF SUCH COMPLICATIONS.
HE IS A *MAN,* AFTER ALL. AND MEN THINK THAT THEY HAVE SOMEHOW MONOPOLIZED THE ART OF INDISCRETION.
IT WASN'T AN *INDISCRETION.*
WE WERE AT WAR. WE WOULD NOT HAVE RISKED IT ALL FOR A *PETTY FLING.*
THAT IS COMFORTING TO HEAR.
WHY?
BECAUSE THERE ARE *OTHER WARS* BEYOND THIS ONE.
AND WHILE I CONSIDER WAKANDA MY NATION, IT IS NOT MY *ONLY* NATION.
THERE ARE OTHERS FILLED WITH MEN AND WOMEN AS OPPRESSED AND SCORNED AS ANY OF YOUR NAMELESS.

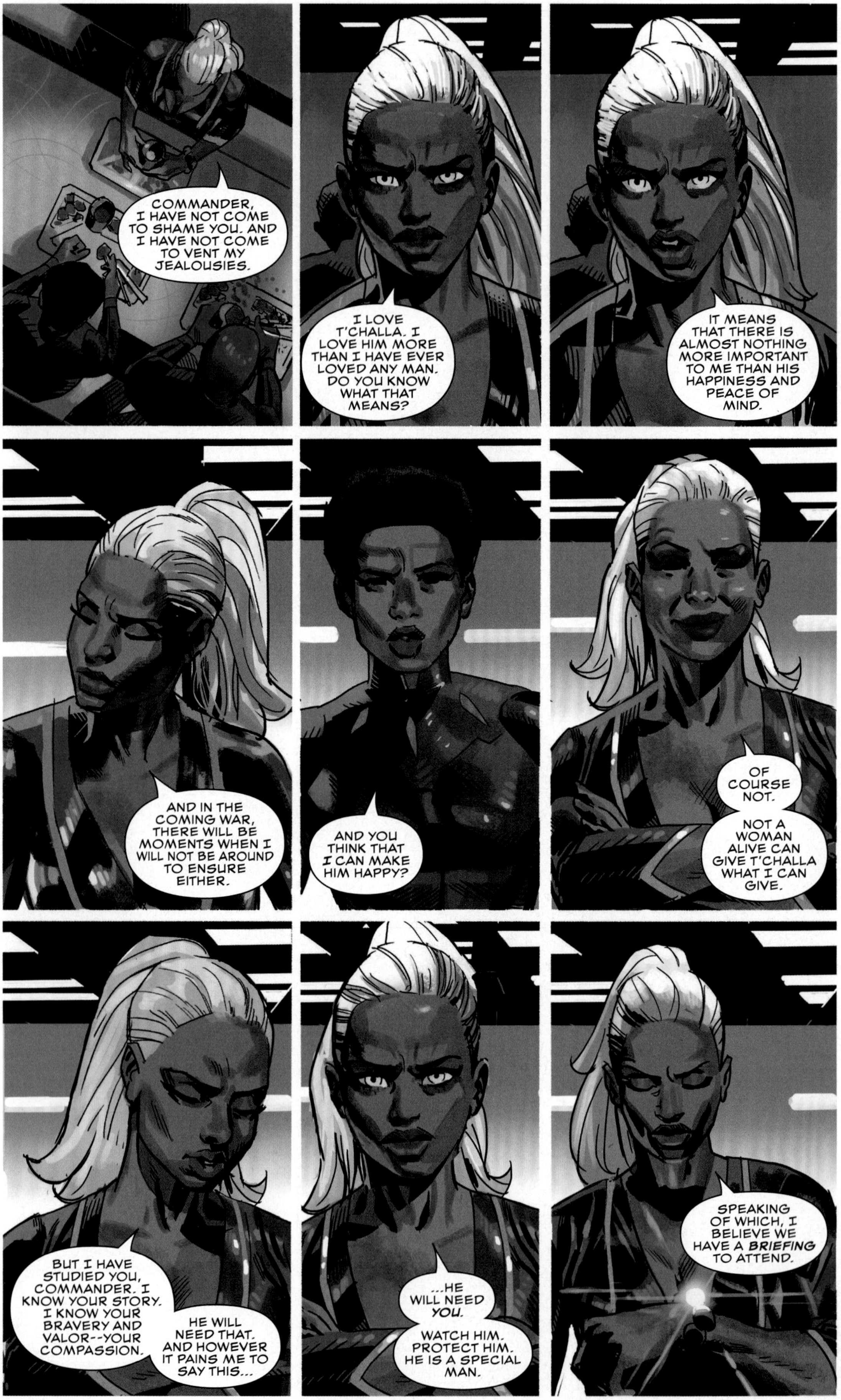
COMMANDER, I HAVE NOT COME TO SHAME YOU. AND I HAVE NOT COME TO VENT MY JEALOUSIES.
I LOVE T'CHALLA. I LOVE HIM MORE THAN I HAVE EVER LOVED ANY MAN. DO YOU KNOW WHAT THAT MEANS?
IT MEANS THAT THERE IS ALMOST NOTHING MORE IMPORTANT TO ME THAN HIS HAPPINESS AND PEACE OF MIND.
AND IN THE COMING WAR, THERE WILL BE MOMENTS WHEN I WILL NOT BE AROUND TO ENSURE EITHER.
AND YOU THINK THAT *I* CAN MAKE HIM HAPPY?
OF COURSE NOT.
NOT A WOMAN ALIVE CAN GIVE T'CHALLA WHAT I CAN GIVE.
BUT I HAVE STUDIED YOU, COMMANDER. I KNOW YOUR STORY. I KNOW YOUR BRAVERY AND VALOR--YOUR COMPASSION.
HE WILL NEED THAT. AND HOWEVER IT PAINS ME TO SAY THIS...
...HE WILL NEED *YOU*.
WATCH HIM. PROTECT HIM. HE IS A SPECIAL MAN.
SPEAKING OF WHICH, I BELIEVE WE HAVE A *BRIEFING* TO ATTEND.

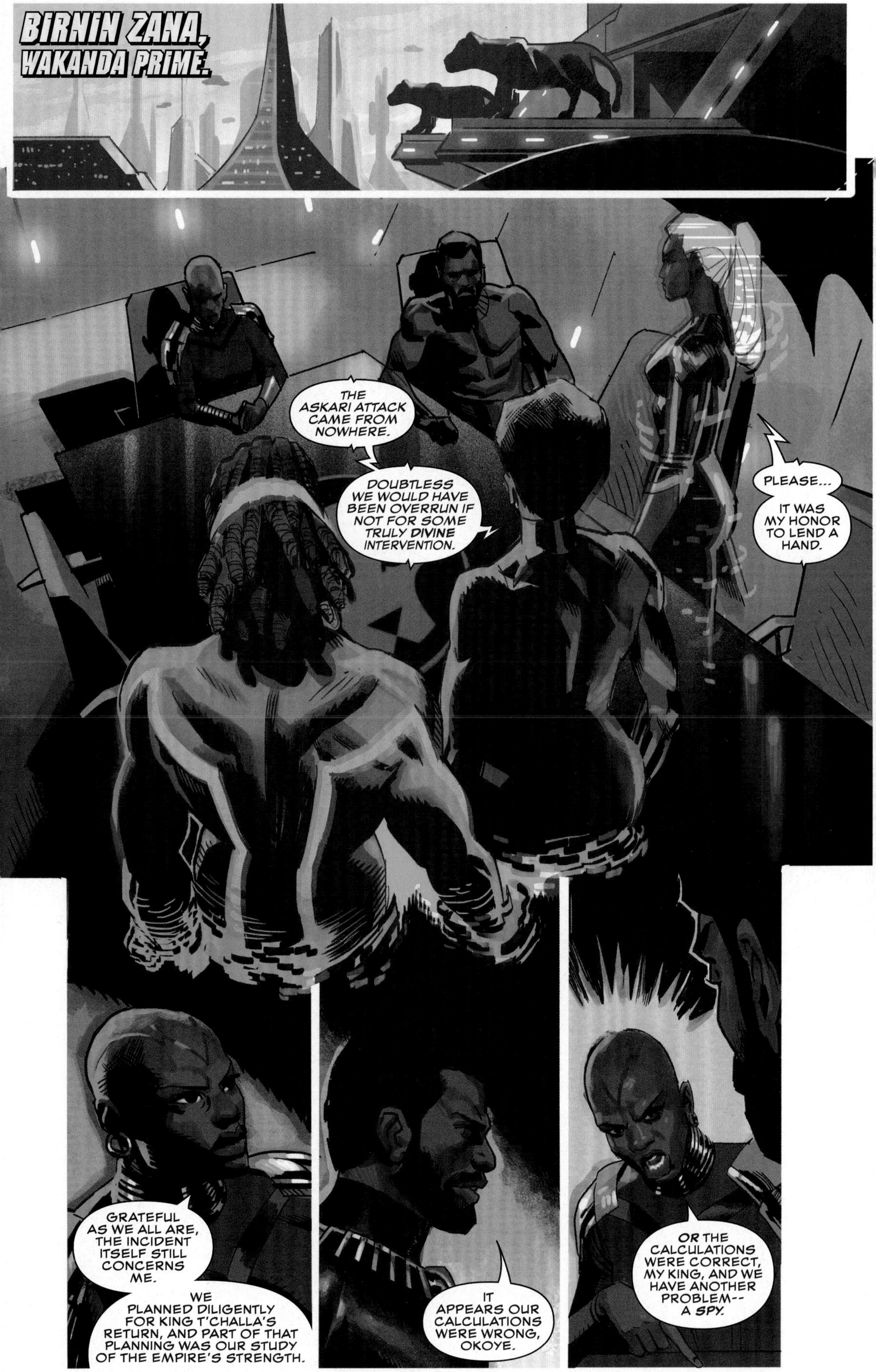
BIRNIN ZANA, WAKANDA PRIME.
THE ASKARI ATTACK CAME FROM NOWHERE.
DOUBTLESS WE WOULD HAVE BEEN OVERRUN IF NOT FOR SOME TRULY DIVINE INTERVENTION.
PLEASE...
IT WAS MY HONOR TO LEND A HAND.
GRATEFUL AS WE ALL ARE, THE INCIDENT ITSELF STILL CONCERNS ME.
WE PLANNED DILIGENTLY FOR KING T'CHALLA'S RETURN, AND PART OF THAT PLANNING WAS OUR STUDY OF THE EMPIRE'S STRENGTH.
IT APPEARS OUR CALCULATIONS WERE WRONG, OKOYE.
OR THE CALCULATIONS WERE CORRECT, MY KING, AND WE HAVE ANOTHER PROBLEM-- A SPY.

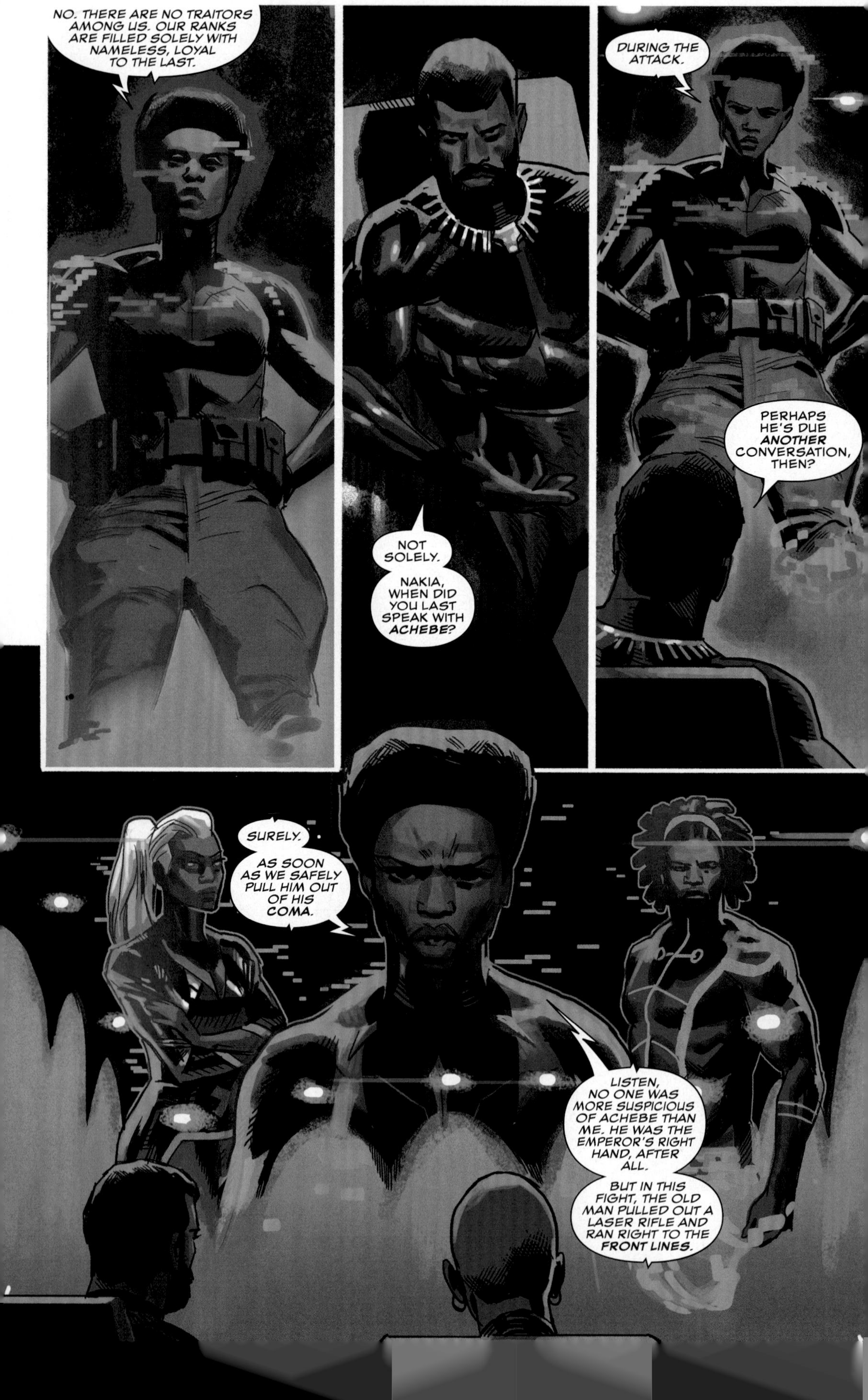
NO. THERE ARE NO TRAITORS AMONG US. OUR RANKS ARE FILLED SOLELY WITH NAMELESS, LOYAL TO THE LAST.
NOT SOLELY.
NAKIA, WHEN DID YOU LAST SPEAK WITH ACHEBE?
DURING THE ATTACK.
PERHAPS HE'S DUE ANOTHER CONVERSATION, THEN?
SURELY.
AS SOON AS WE SAFELY PULL HIM OUT OF HIS COMA.
LISTEN, NO ONE WAS MORE SUSPICIOUS OF ACHEBE THAN ME. HE WAS THE EMPEROR'S RIGHT HAND, AFTER ALL.
BUT IN THIS FIGHT, THE OLD MAN PULLED OUT A LASER RIFLE AND RAN RIGHT TO THE FRONT LINES.

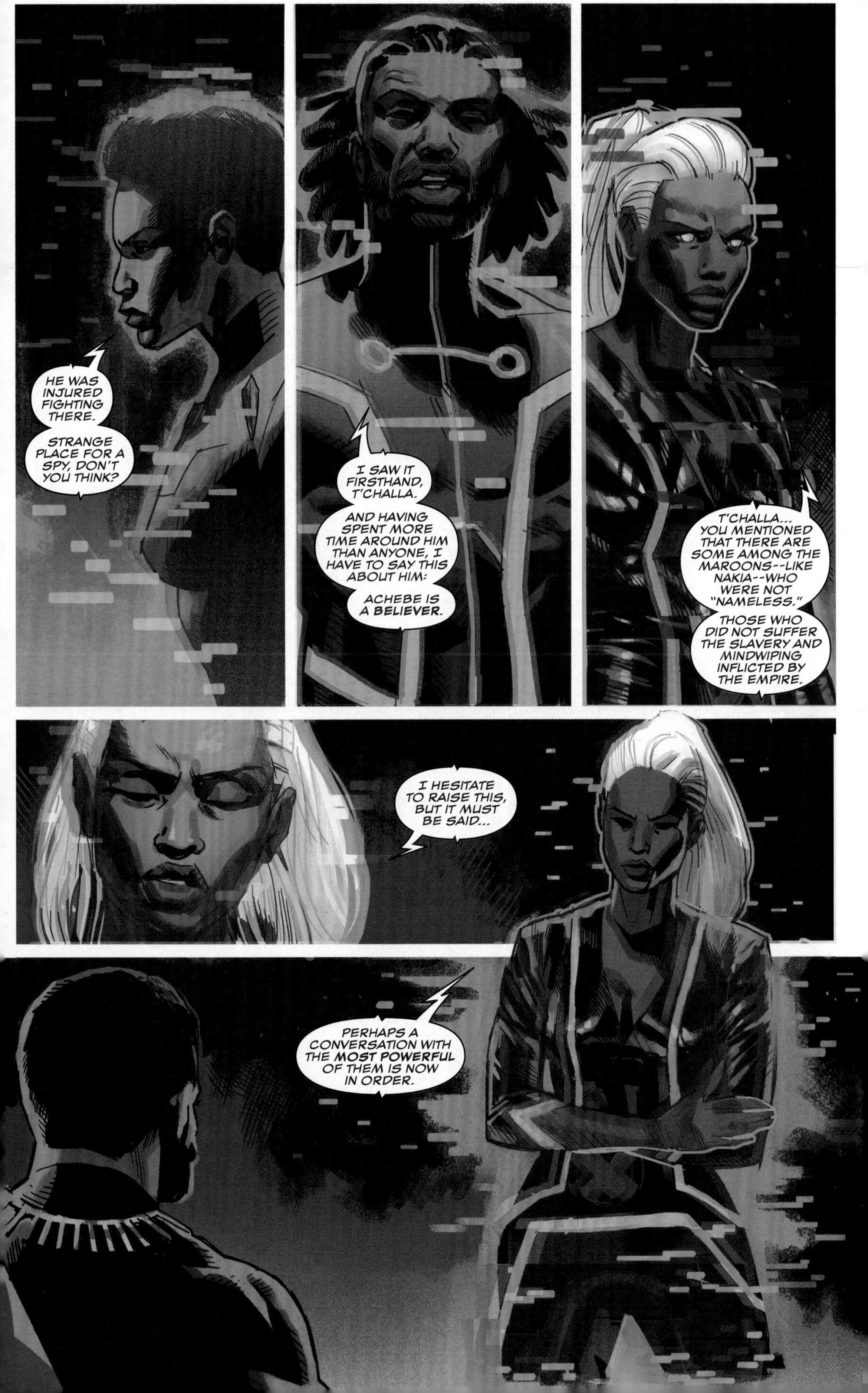

HE WAS INJURED FIGHTING THERE.
STRANGE PLACE FOR A SPY, DON'T YOU THINK?
I SAW IT FIRSTHAND, T'CHALLA.
AND HAVING SPENT MORE TIME AROUND HIM THAN ANYONE, I HAVE TO SAY THIS ABOUT HIM:
ACHEBE IS A BELIEVER.
T'CHALLA... YOU MENTIONED THAT THERE ARE SOME AMONG THE MAROONS--LIKE NAKIA--WHO WERE NOT "NAMELESS."
THOSE WHO DID NOT SUFFER THE SLAVERY AND MINDWIPING INFLICTED BY THE EMPIRE.
I HESITATE TO RAISE THIS, BUT IT MUST BE SAID...
PERHAPS A CONVERSATION WITH THE MOST POWERFUL OF THEM IS NOW IN ORDER.

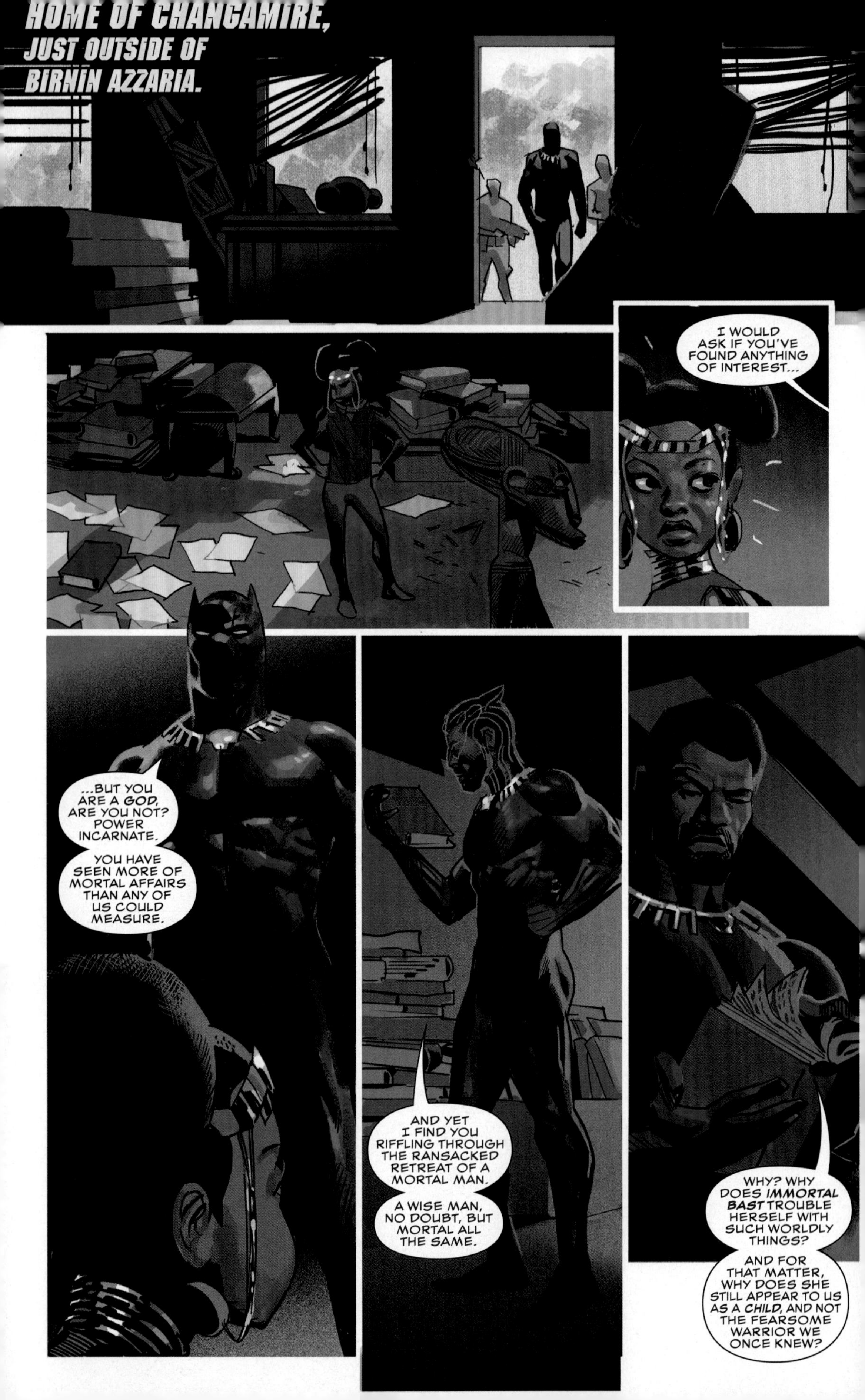
HOME OF CHANGAMIRE, JUST OUTSIDE OF BIRNIN AZZARIA.
I WOULD ASK IF YOU'VE FOUND ANYTHING OF INTEREST...
...BUT YOU ARE A GOD, ARE YOU NOT? POWER INCARNATE.
YOU HAVE SEEN MORE OF MORTAL AFFAIRS THAN ANY OF US COULD MEASURE.
AND YET I FIND YOU RIFFLING THROUGH THE RANSACKED RETREAT OF A MORTAL MAN.
A WISE MAN, NO DOUBT, BUT MORTAL ALL THE SAME.
WHY? WHY DOES IMMORTAL BAST TROUBLE HERSELF WITH SUCH WORLDLY THINGS?
AND FOR THAT MATTER, WHY DOES SHE STILL APPEAR TO US AS A CHILD, AND NOT THE FEARSOME WARRIOR WE ONCE KNEW?

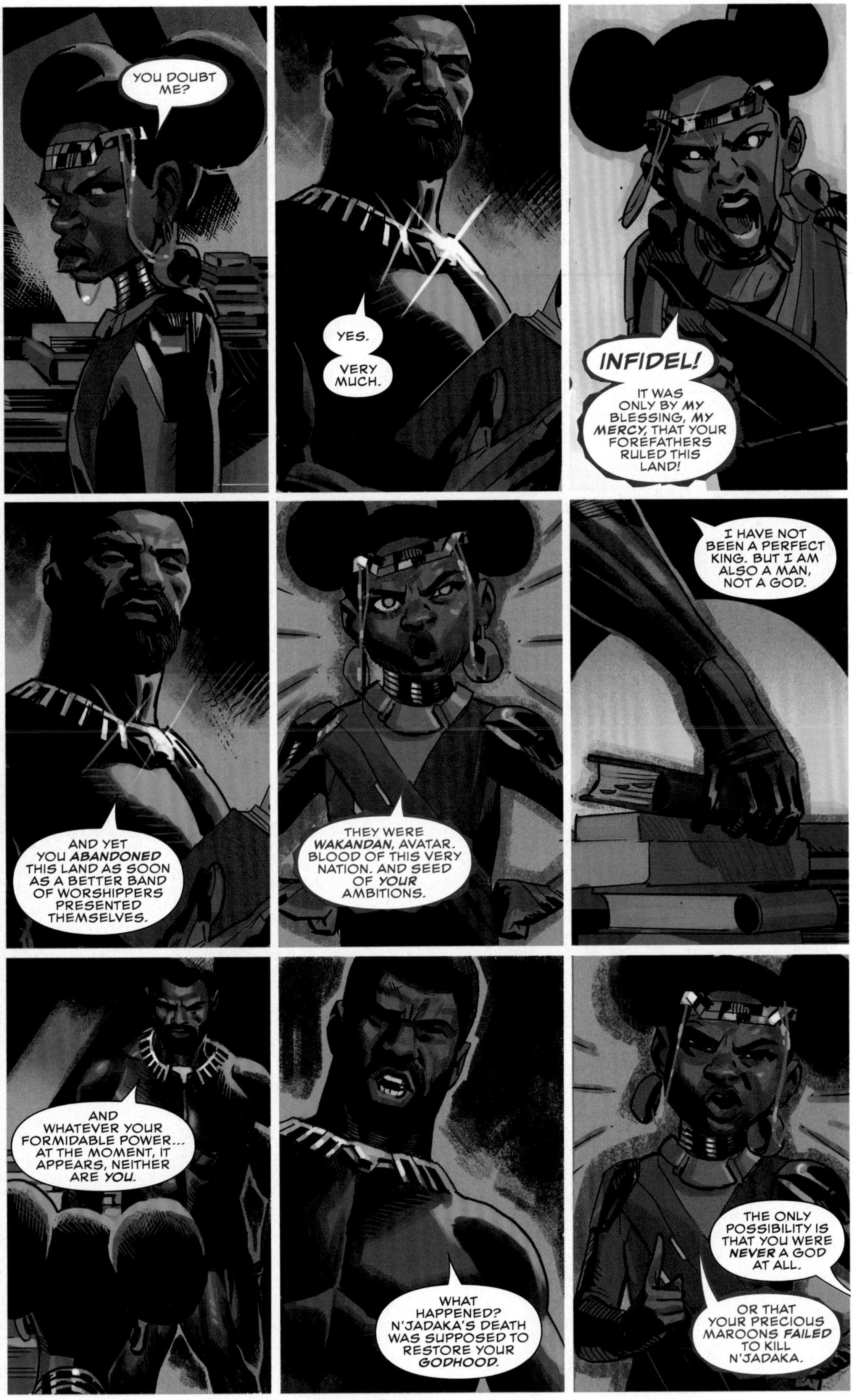
YOU DOUBT ME?
YES.
VERY MUCH.
INFIDEL!
IT WAS ONLY BY MY BLESSING, MY MERCY, THAT YOUR FOREFATHERS RULED THIS LAND!
AND YET YOU ABANDONED THIS LAND AS SOON AS A BETTER BAND OF WORSHIPPERS PRESENTED THEMSELVES.
THEY WERE WAKANDAN, AVATAR. BLOOD OF THIS VERY NATION. AND SEED OF YOUR AMBITIONS.
I HAVE NOT BEEN A PERFECT KING. BUT I AM ALSO A MAN, NOT A GOD.
AND WHATEVER YOUR FORMIDABLE POWER... AT THE MOMENT, IT APPEARS, NEITHER ARE YOU.
WHAT HAPPENED? N'JADAKA'S DEATH WAS SUPPOSED TO RESTORE YOUR GODHOOD.
THE ONLY POSSIBILITY IS THAT YOU WERE NEVER A GOD AT ALL.
OR THAT YOUR PRECIOUS MAROONS FAILED TO KILL N'JADAKA.

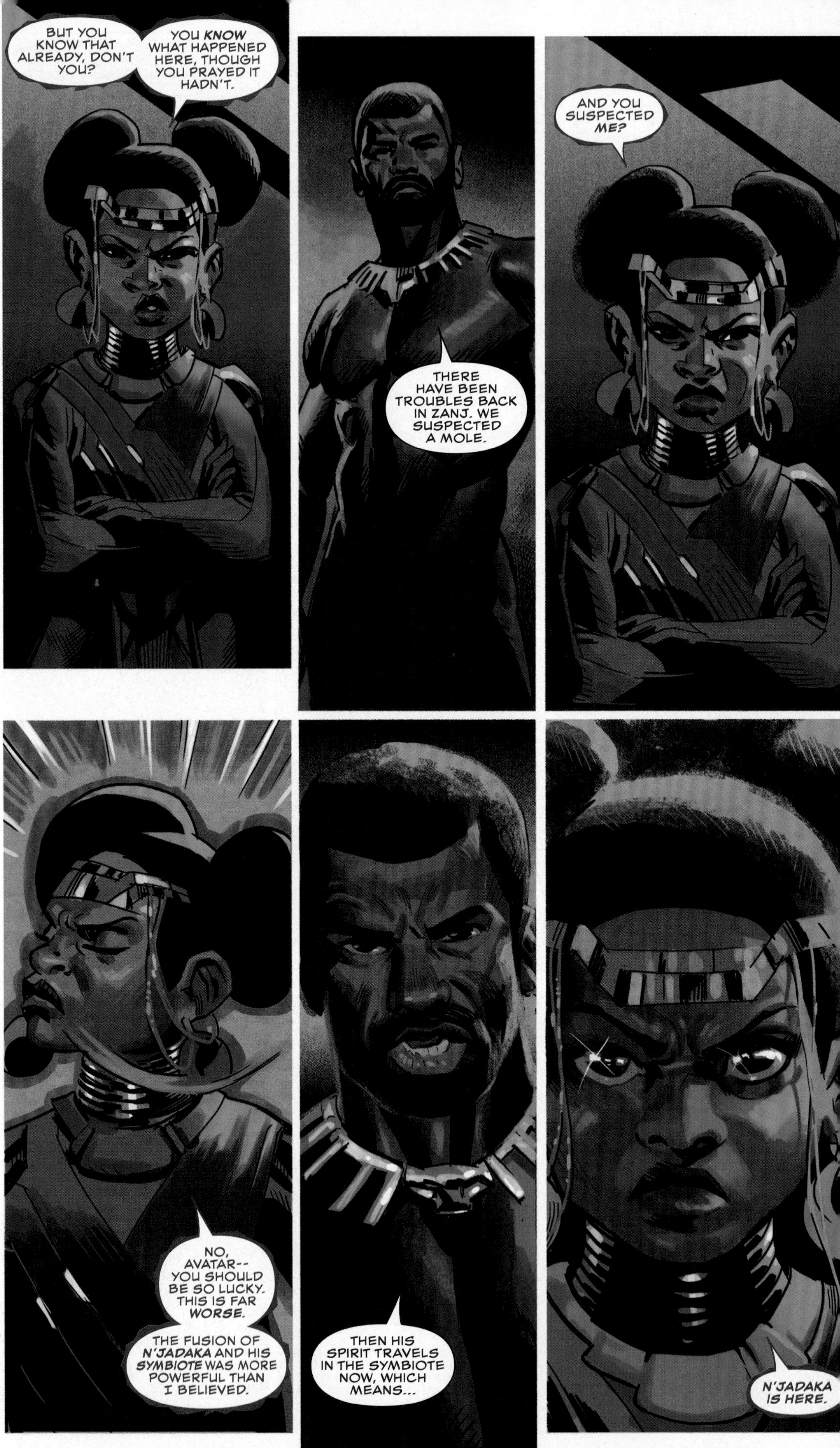
BUT YOU KNOW THAT ALREADY, DON'T YOU?
YOU KNOW WHAT HAPPENED HERE, THOUGH YOU PRAYED IT HADN'T.
THERE HAVE BEEN TROUBLES BACK IN ZANJ. WE SUSPECTED A MOLE.
AND YOU SUSPECTED ME?
NO, AVATAR-- YOU SHOULD BE SO LUCKY. THIS IS FAR WORSE.
THE FUSION OF N'JADAKA AND HIS SYMBIOTE WAS MORE POWERFUL THAN I BELIEVED.
THEN HIS SPIRIT TRAVELS IN THE SYMBIOTE NOW, WHICH MEANS...
N'JADAKA IS HERE.

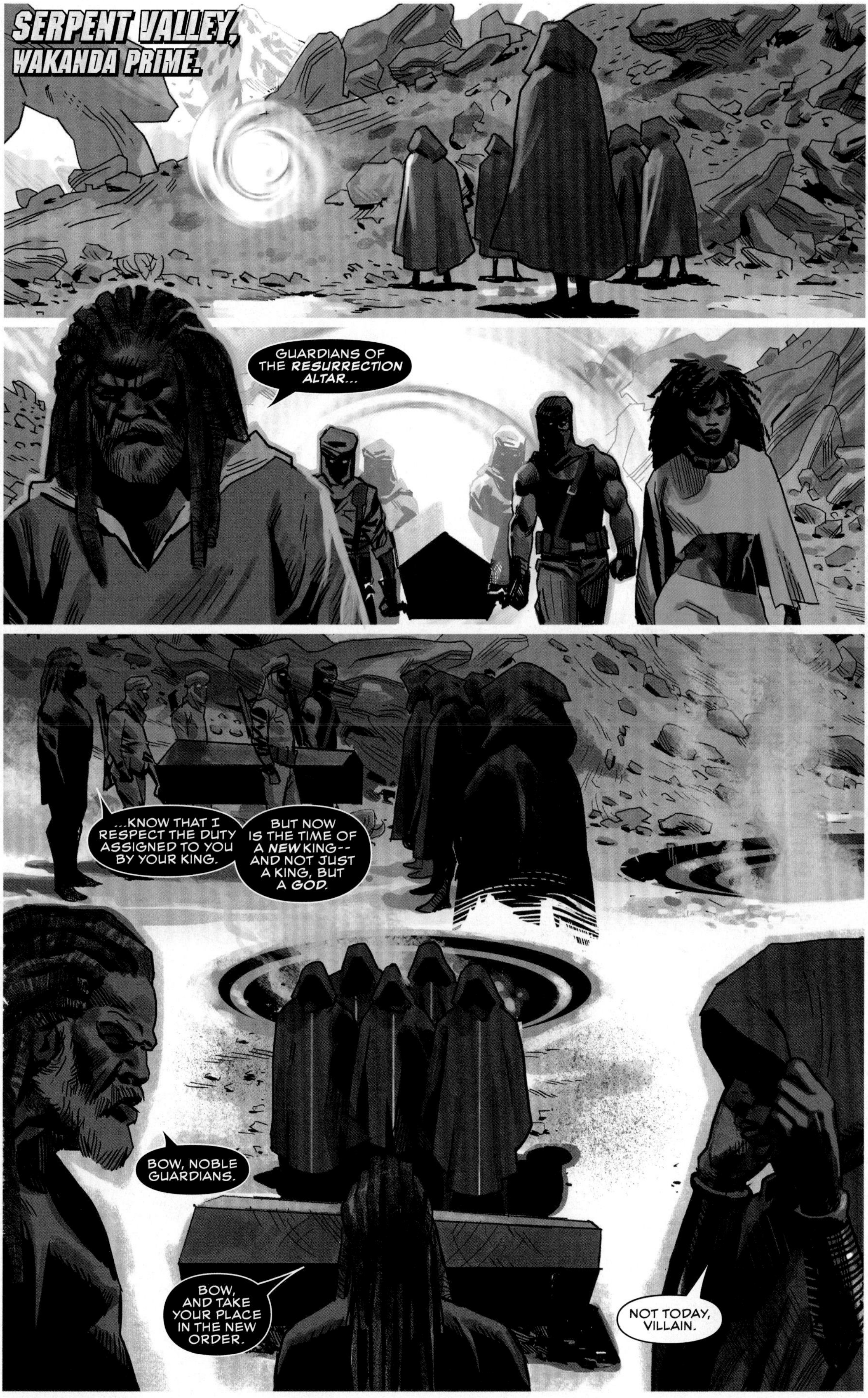
SERPENT VALLEY, WAKANDA PRIME.
GUARDIANS OF THE RESURRECTION ALTAR...
...KNOW THAT I RESPECT THE DUTY ASSIGNED TO YOU BY YOUR KING.
BUT NOW IS THE TIME OF A NEW KING--AND NOT JUST A KING, BUT A GOD.
BOW, NOBLE GUARDIANS.
BOW, AND TAKE YOUR PLACE IN THE NEW ORDER.
NOT TODAY, VILLAIN.

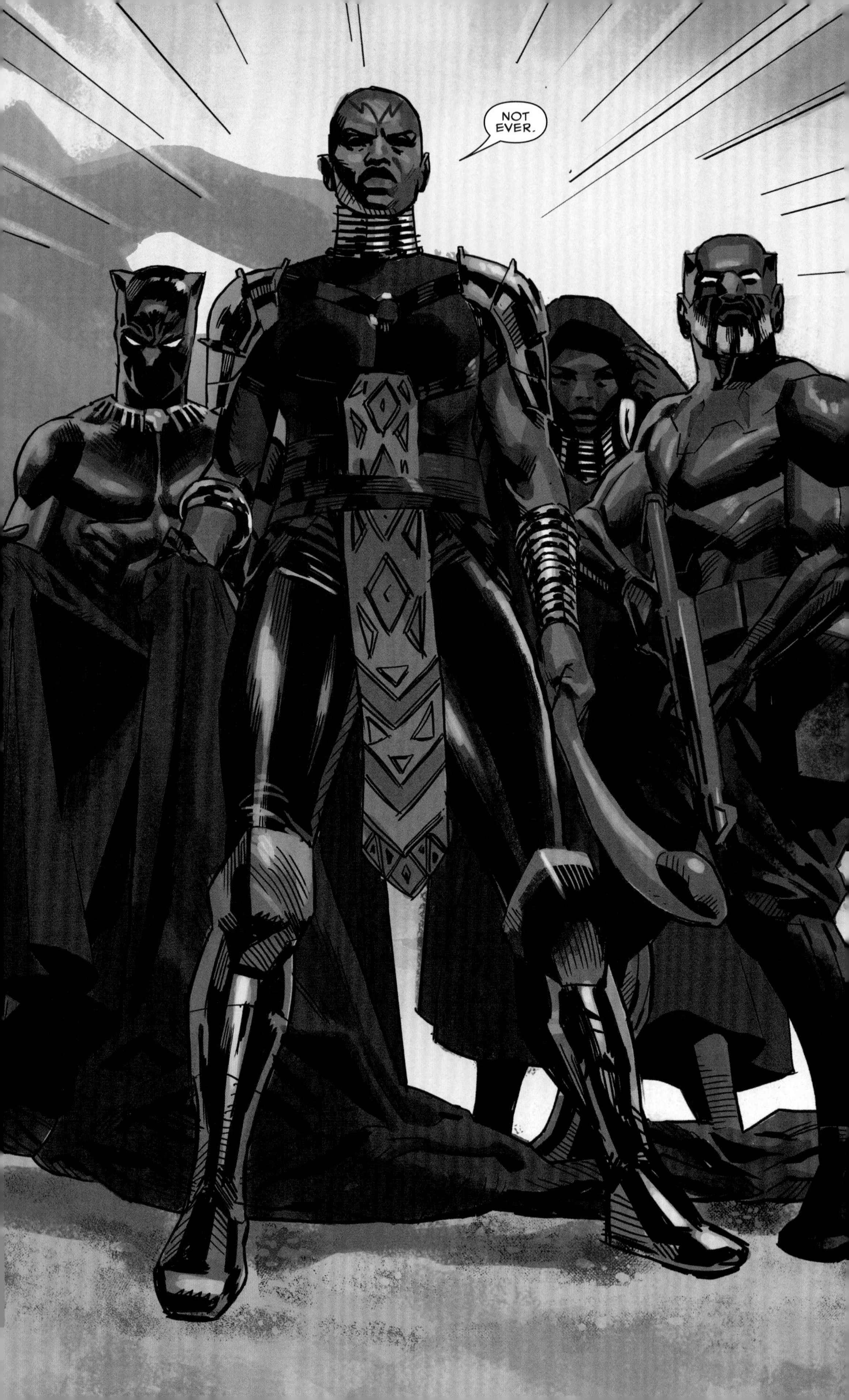
NOT EVER.

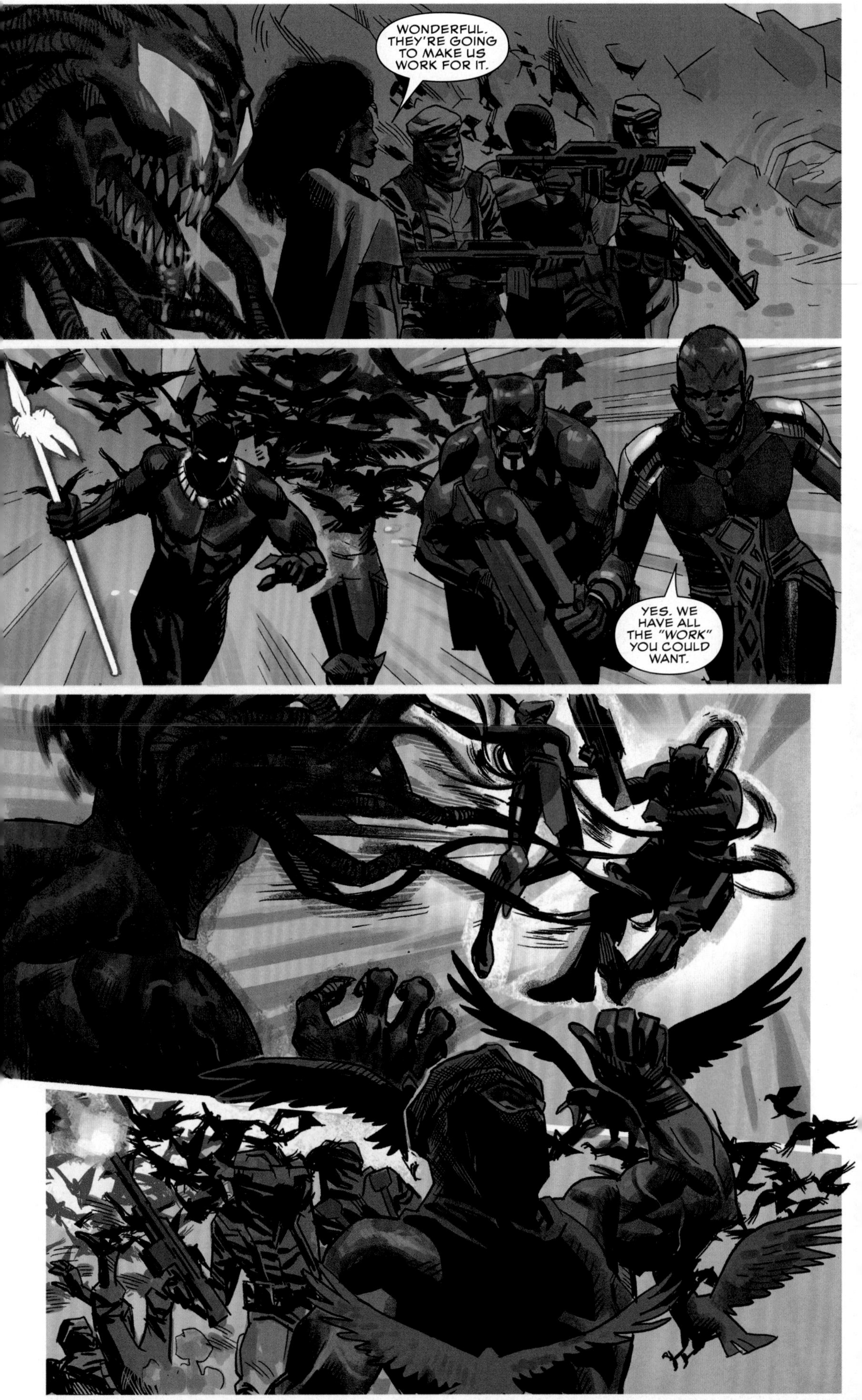
WONDERFUL. THEY'RE GOING TO MAKE US WORK FOR IT.
YES. WE HAVE ALL THE "WORK" YOU COULD WANT.

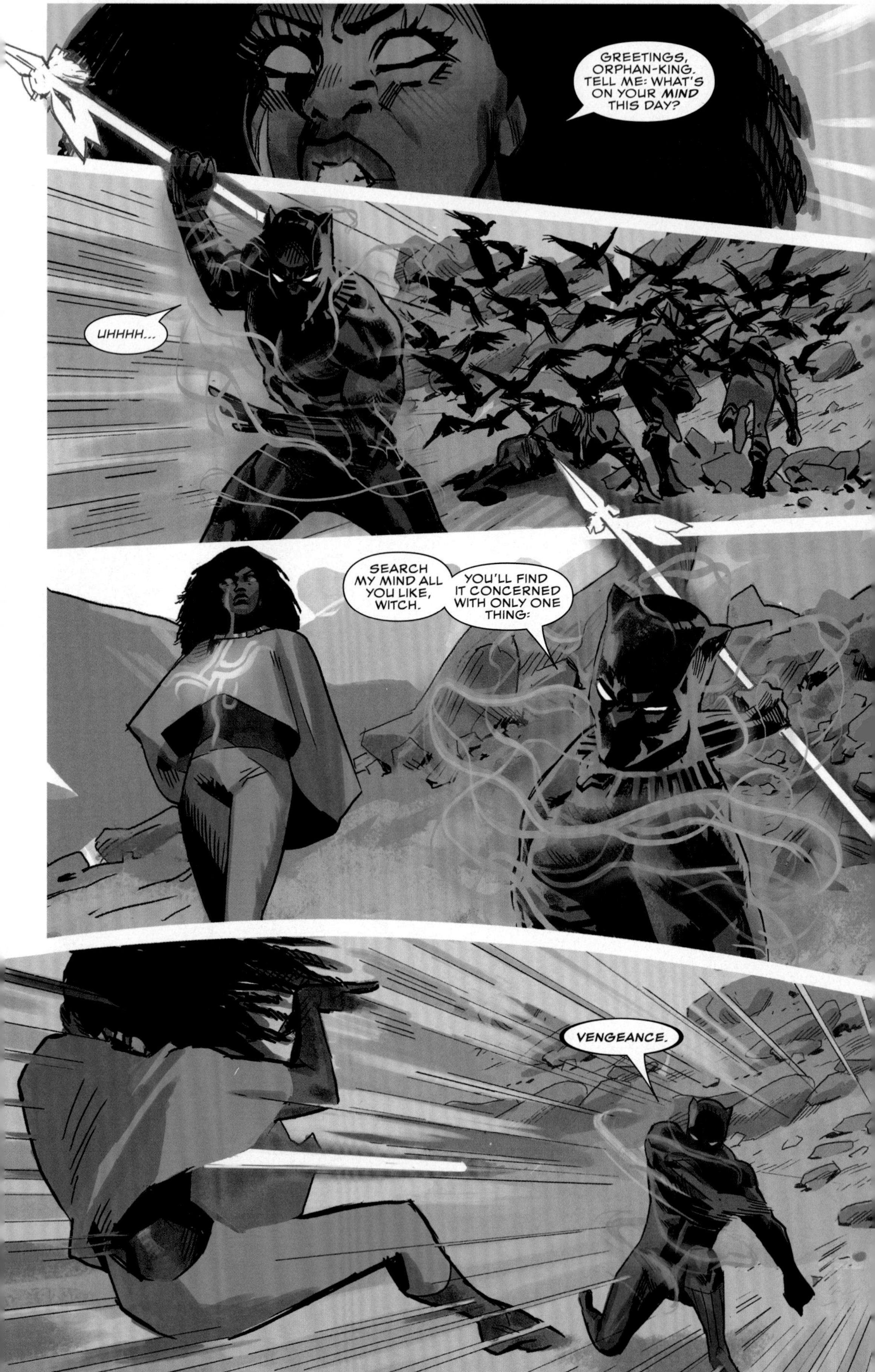
GREETINGS, ORPHAN-KING. TELL ME: WHAT'S ON YOUR MIND THIS DAY?
UHHHH...
SEARCH MY MIND ALL YOU LIKE, WITCH.
YOU'LL FIND IT CONCERNED WITH ONLY ONE THING:
VENGEANCE.

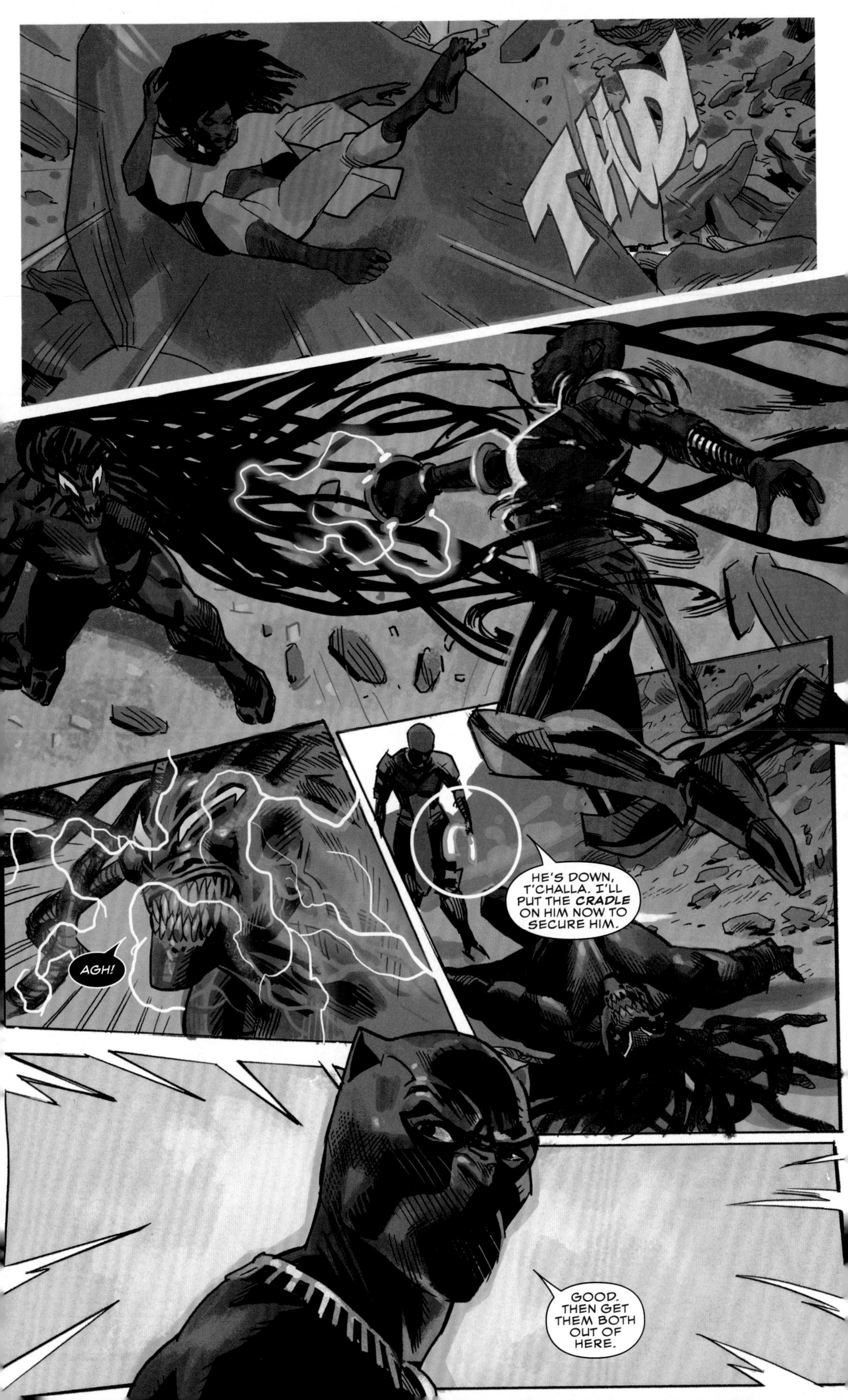
THUD!
AGH!
HE'S DOWN, T'CHALLA. I'LL PUT THE CRADLE ON HIM NOW TO SECURE HIM.
GOOD. THEN GET THEM BOTH OUT OF HERE.

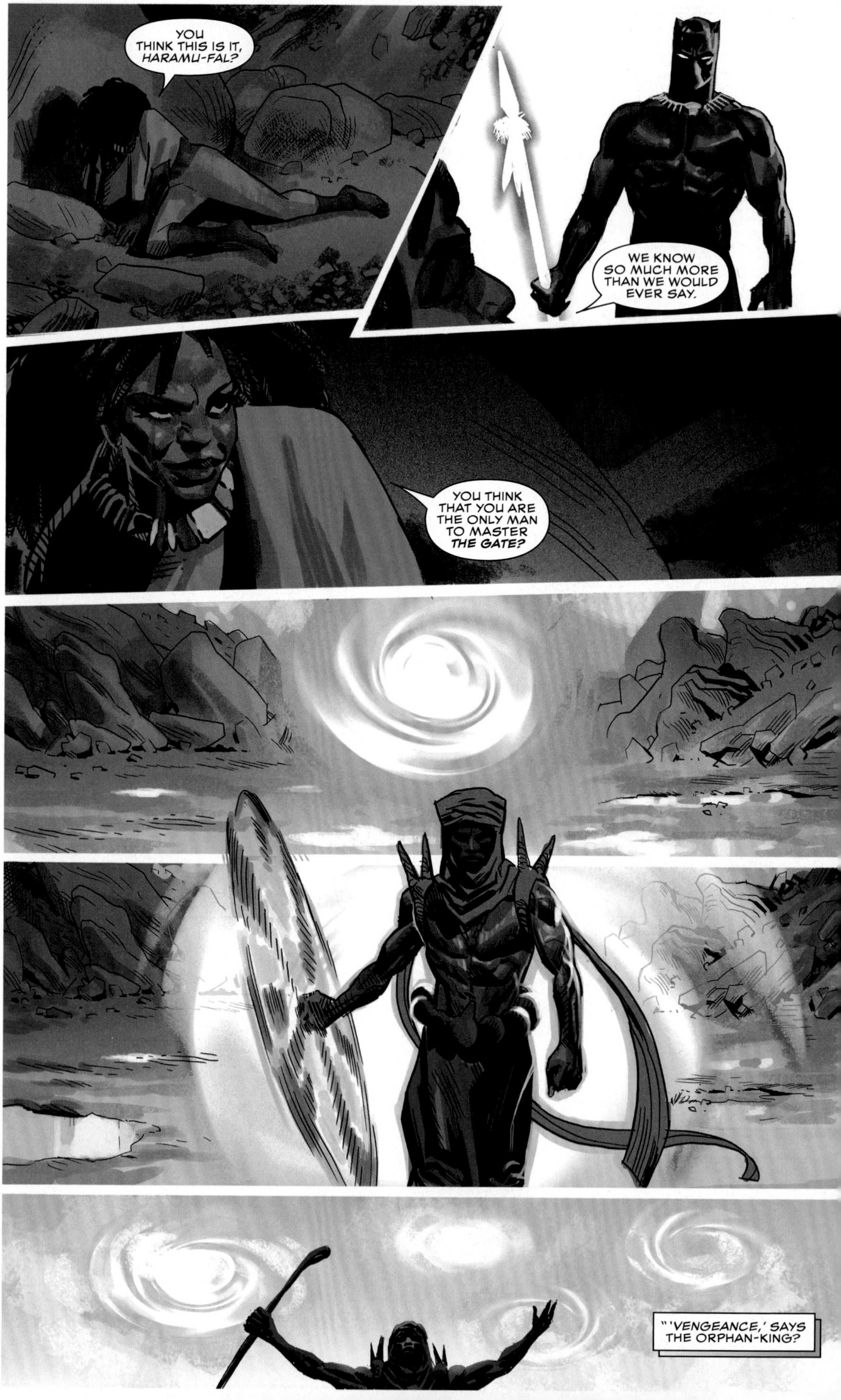
YOU THINK THIS IS IT, HARAMU-FAL?
WE KNOW SO MUCH MORE THAN WE WOULD EVER SAY.
YOU THINK THAT YOU ARE THE ONLY MAN TO MASTER THE GATE?
"'VENGEANCE,' SAYS THE ORPHAN-KING?

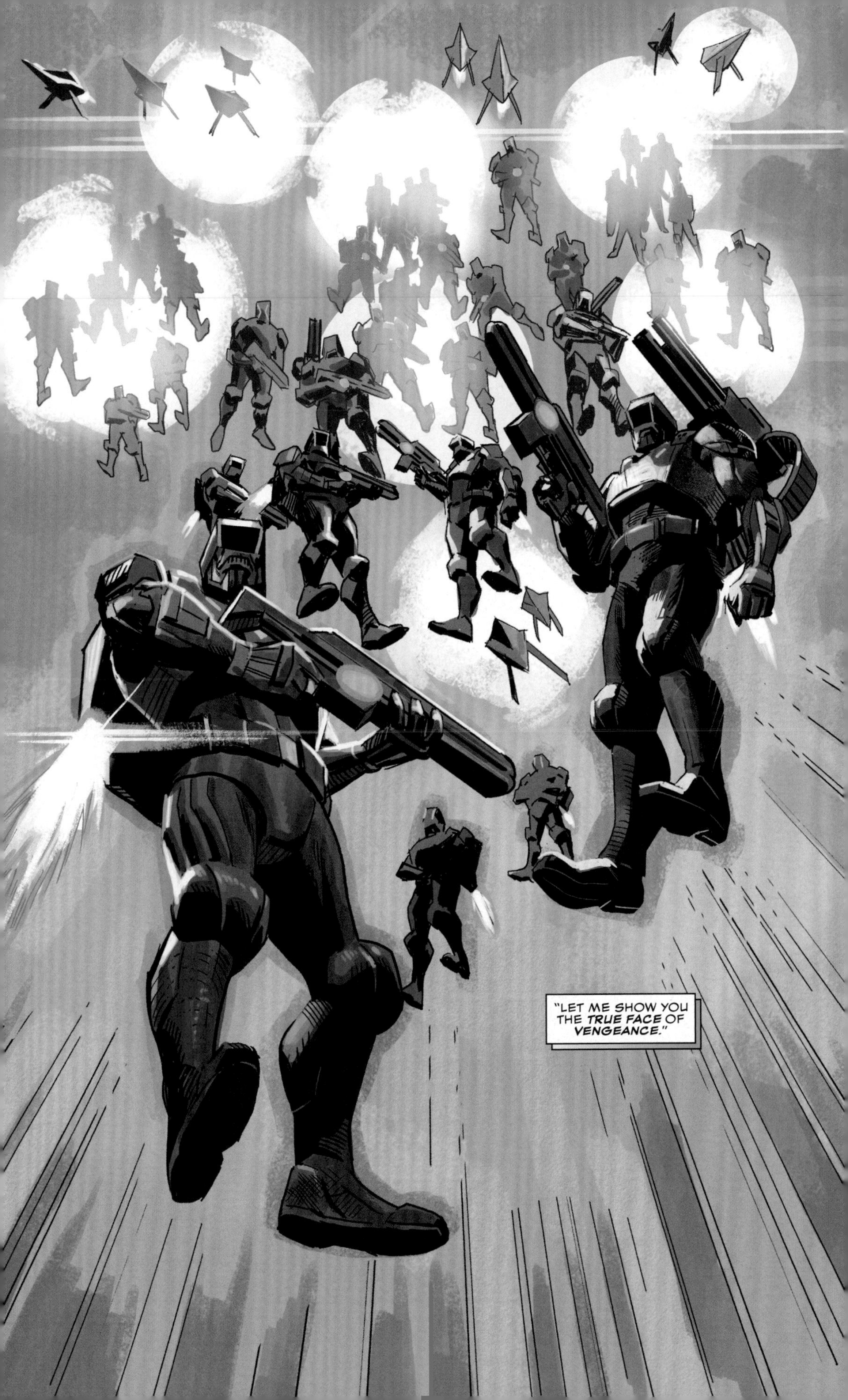
"LET ME SHOW YOU THE TRUE FACE OF VENGEANCE."

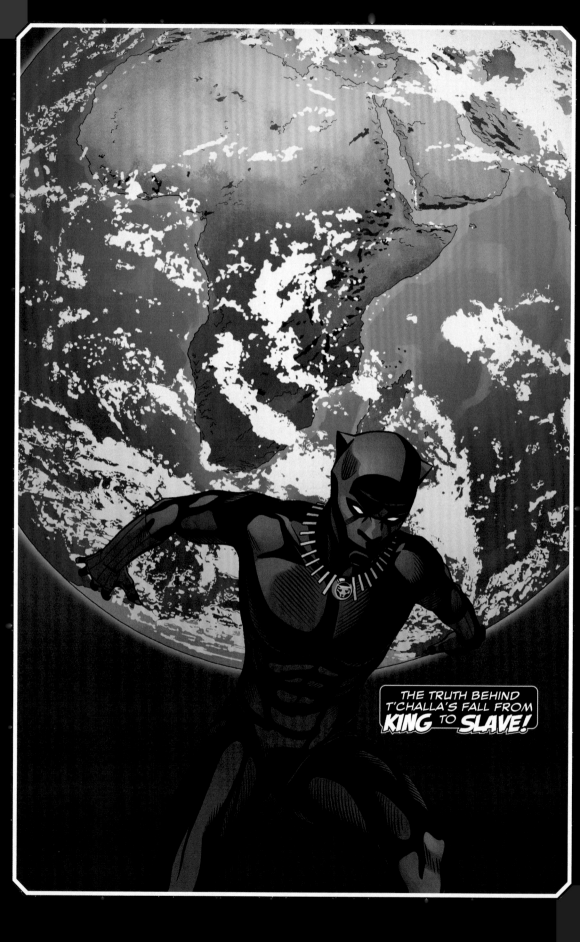

THE TRUTH BEHIND T'CHALLA'S FALL FROM **KING** TO **SLAVE!**

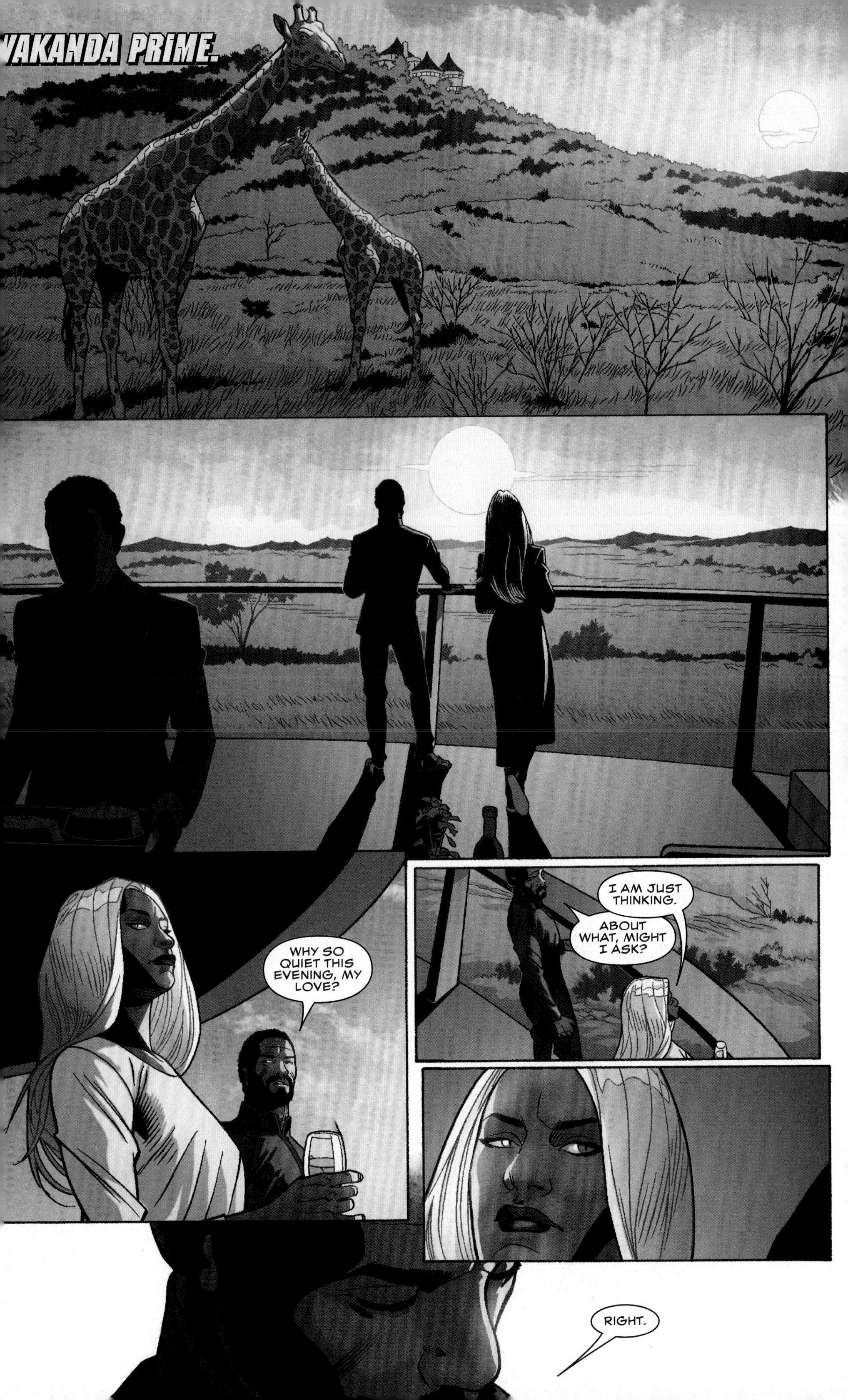
VAKANDA PRIME.
WHY SO QUIET THIS EVENING, MY LOVE?
I AM JUST THINKING.
ABOUT WHAT, MIGHT I ASK?
RIGHT.

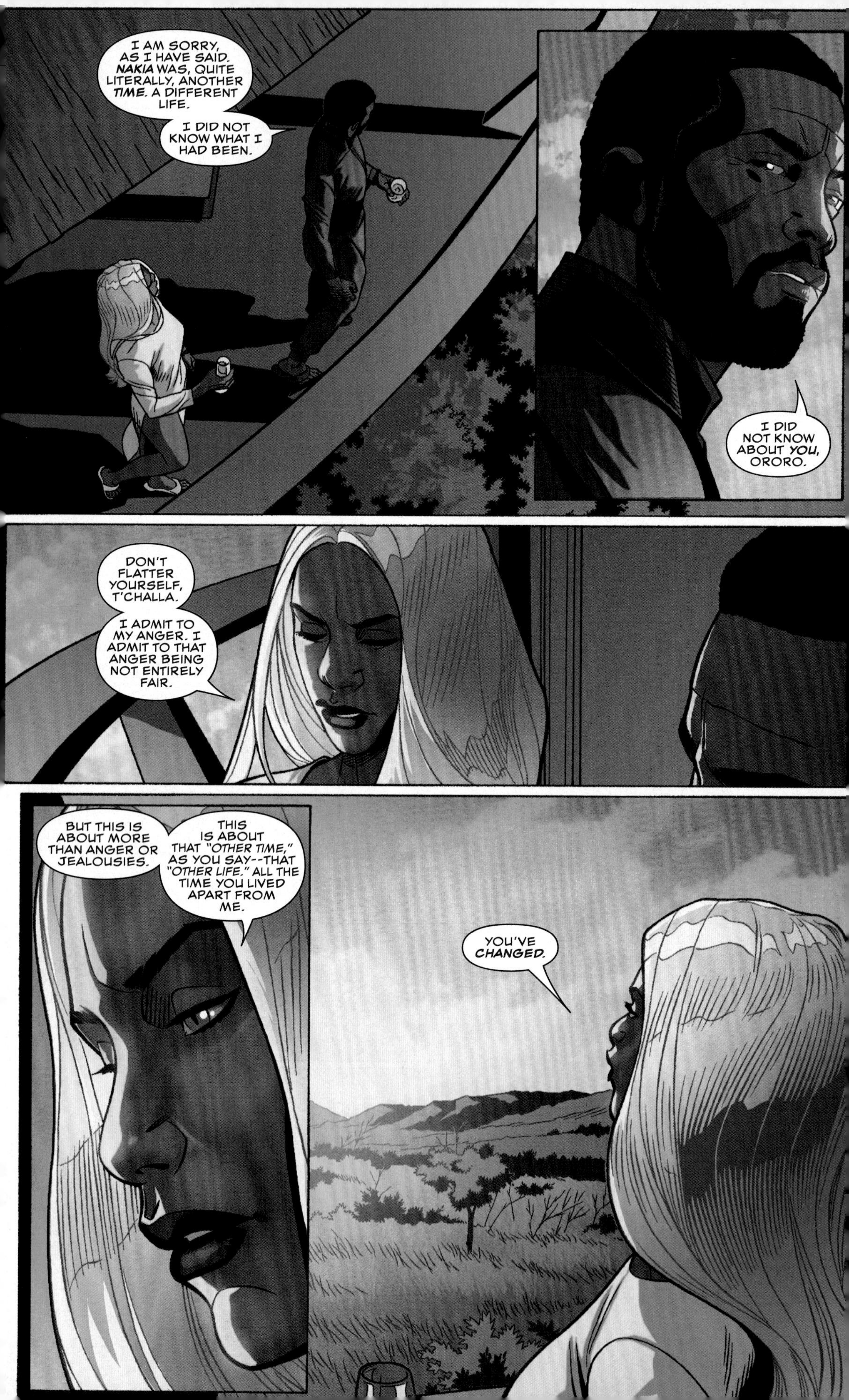
I AM SORRY, AS I HAVE SAID. NAKIA WAS, QUITE LITERALLY, ANOTHER TIME. A DIFFERENT LIFE.
I DID NOT KNOW WHAT I HAD BEEN.
I DID NOT KNOW ABOUT YOU, ORORO.
DON'T FLATTER YOURSELF, T'CHALLA.
I ADMIT TO MY ANGER. I ADMIT TO THAT ANGER BEING NOT ENTIRELY FAIR.
BUT THIS IS ABOUT MORE THAN ANGER OR JEALOUSIES.
THIS IS ABOUT THAT "OTHER TIME," AS YOU SAY--THAT "OTHER LIFE." ALL THE TIME YOU LIVED APART FROM ME.
YOU'VE CHANGED.

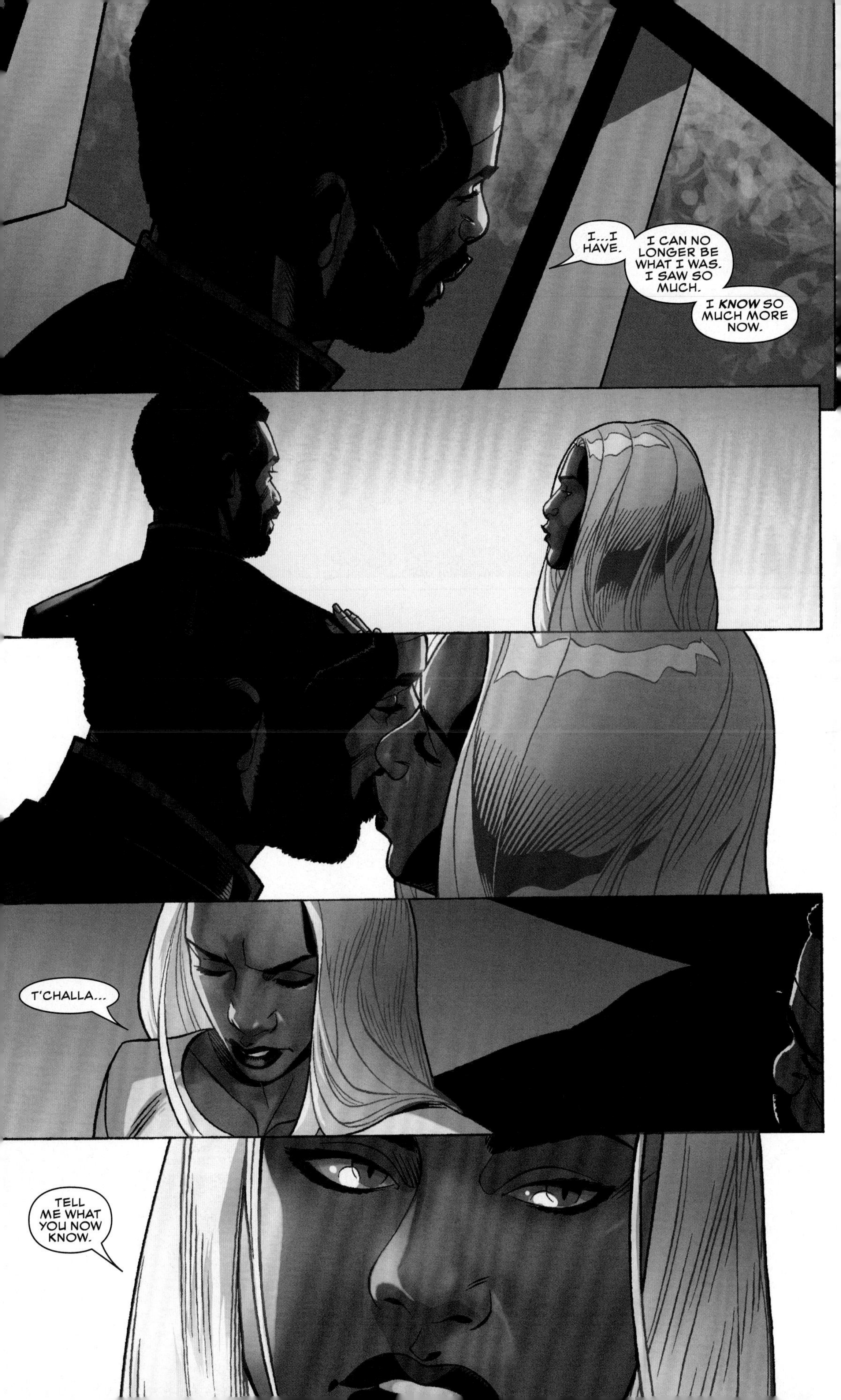

I...I HAVE.
I CAN NO LONGER BE WHAT I WAS. I SAW SO MUCH.
I KNOW SO MUCH MORE NOW.
T'CHALLA...
TELL ME WHAT YOU NOW KNOW.

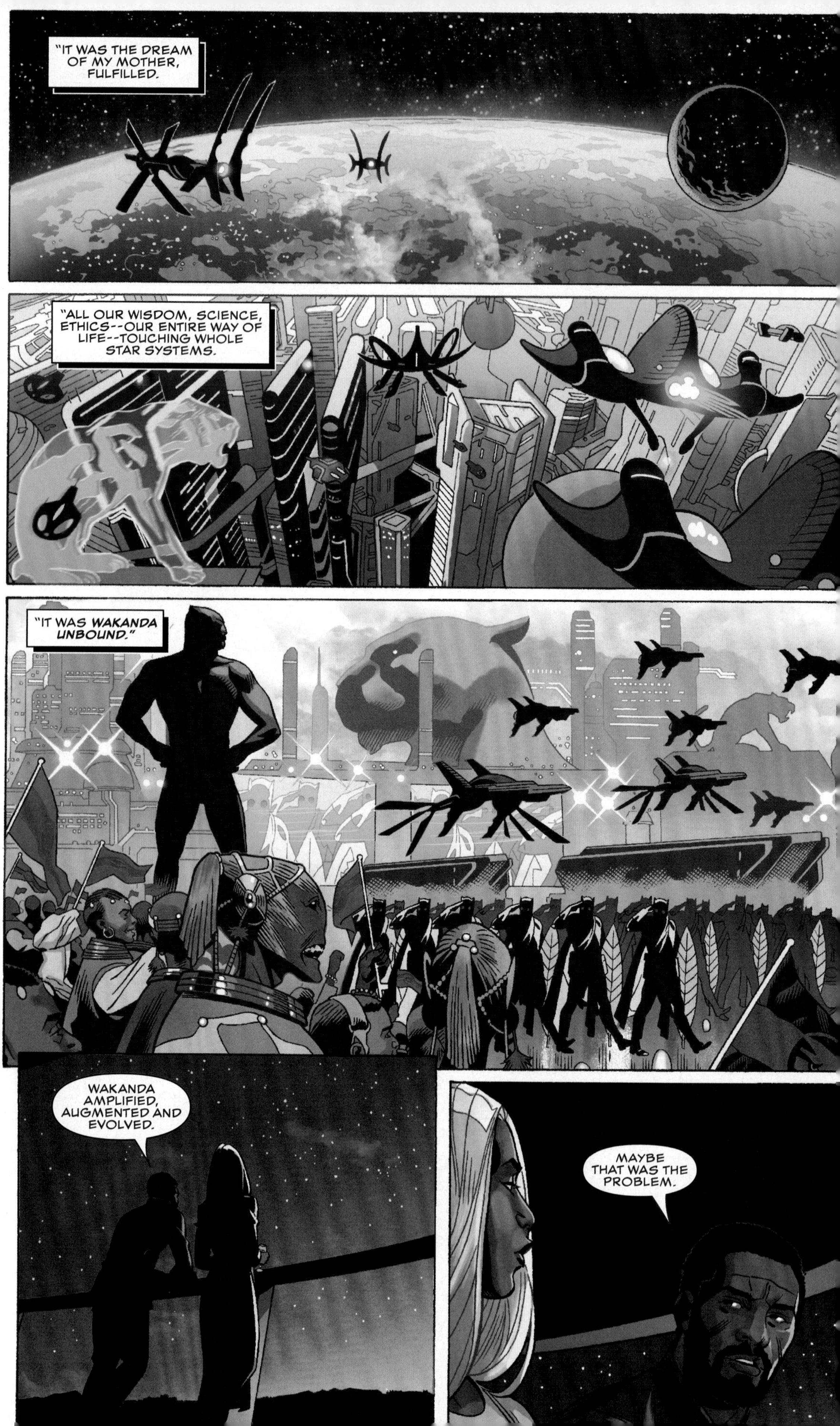
"IT WAS THE DREAM OF MY MOTHER, FULFILLED.
"ALL OUR WISDOM, SCIENCE, ETHICS--OUR ENTIRE WAY OF LIFE--TOUCHING WHOLE STAR SYSTEMS.
"IT WAS *WAKANDA UNBOUND.*"
WAKANDA AMPLIFIED, AUGMENTED AND EVOLVED.
MAYBE THAT WAS THE PROBLEM.

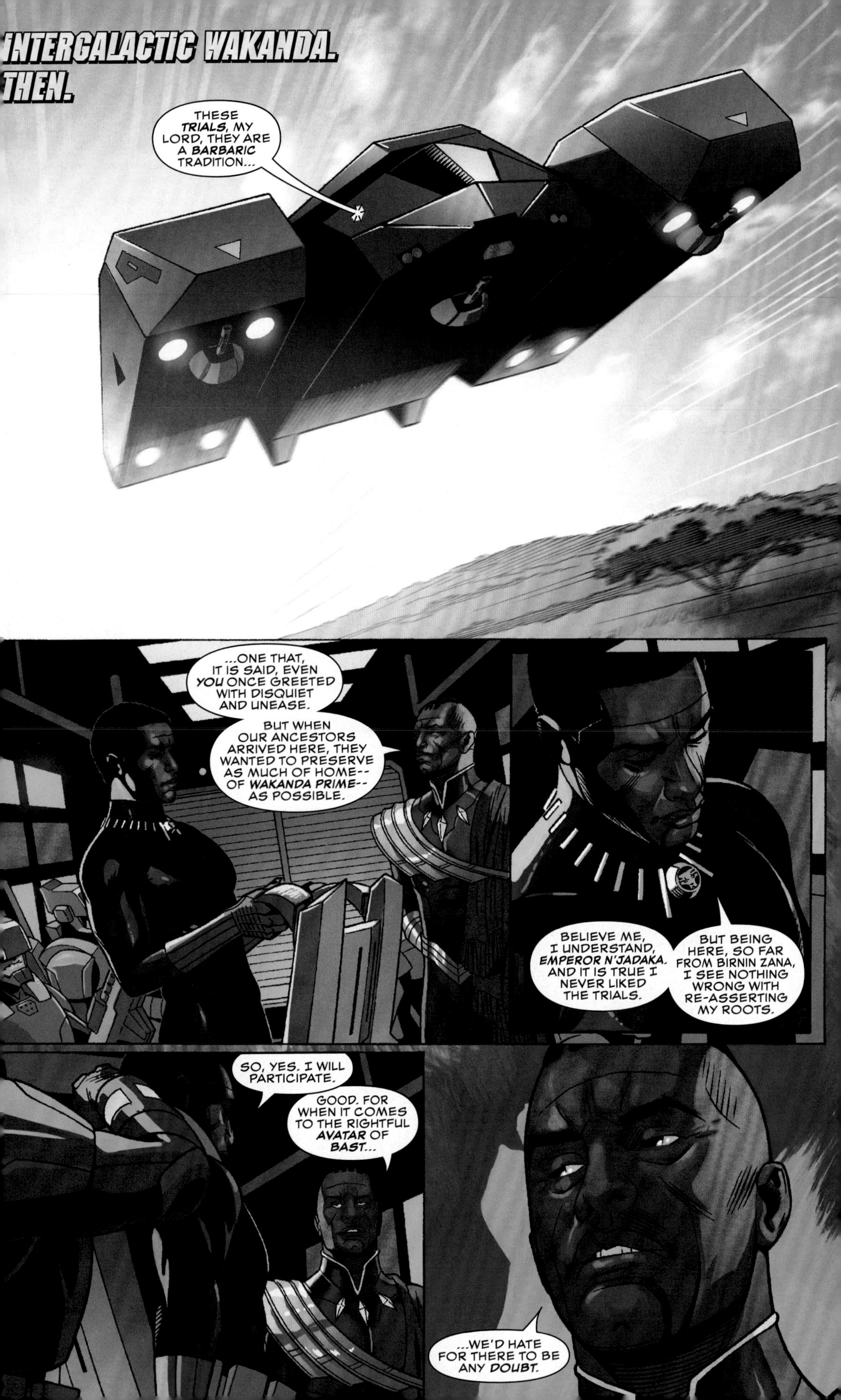

INTERGALACTIC WAKANDA. THEN.
THESE TRIALS, MY LORD, THEY ARE A BARBARIC TRADITION...
...ONE THAT, IT IS SAID, EVEN YOU ONCE GREETED WITH DISQUIET AND UNEASE.
BUT WHEN OUR ANCESTORS ARRIVED HERE, THEY WANTED TO PRESERVE AS MUCH OF HOME-- OF WAKANDA PRIME-- AS POSSIBLE.
BELIEVE ME, I UNDERSTAND, EMPEROR N'JADAKA. AND IT IS TRUE I NEVER LIKED THE TRIALS.
BUT BEING HERE, SO FAR FROM BIRNIN ZANA, I SEE NOTHING WRONG WITH RE-ASSERTING MY ROOTS.
SO, YES. I WILL PARTICIPATE.
GOOD. FOR WHEN IT COMES TO THE RIGHTFUL AVATAR OF BAST...
...WE'D HATE FOR THERE TO BE ANY DOUBT.

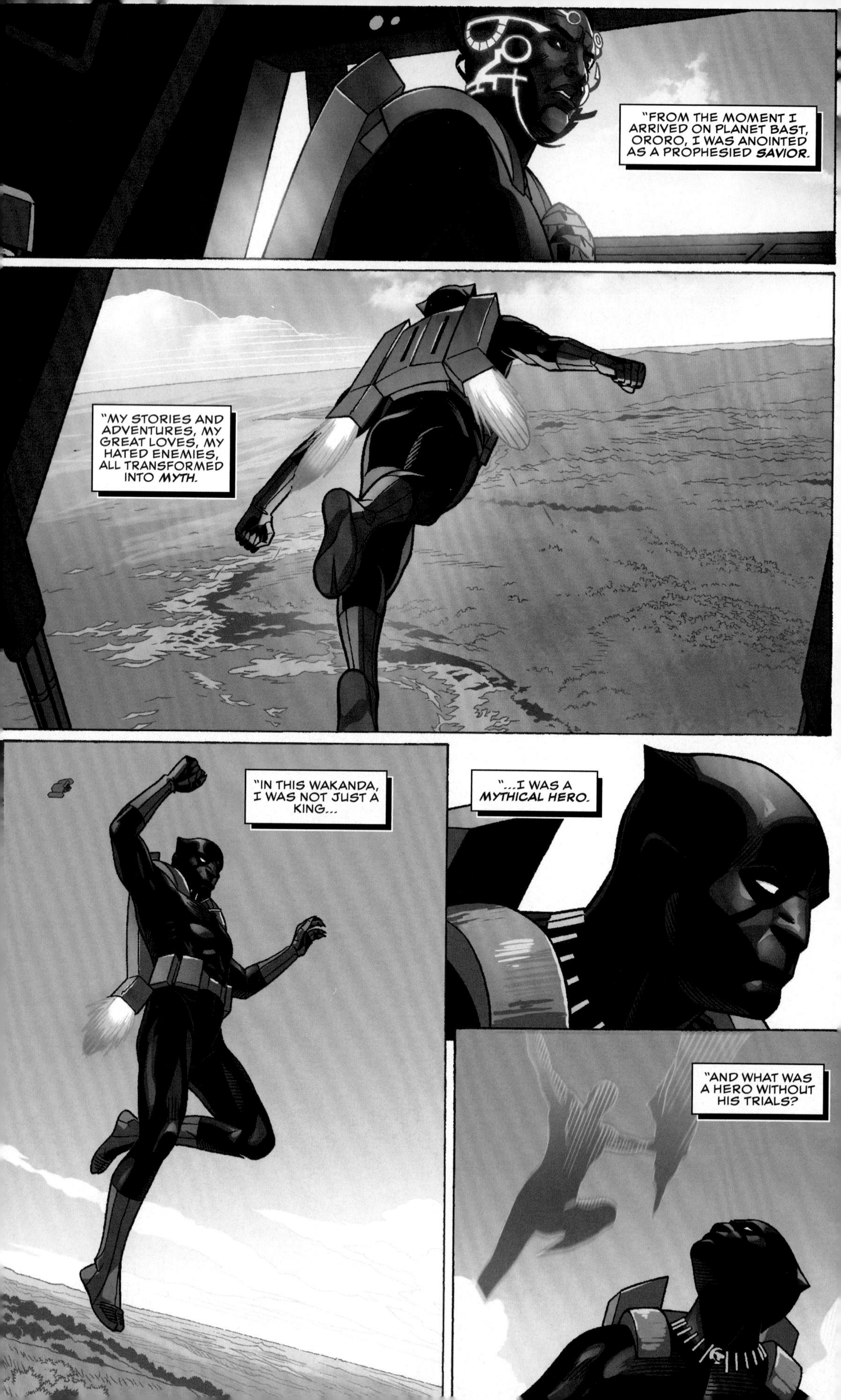
"FROM THE MOMENT I ARRIVED ON PLANET BAST, ORORO, I WAS ANOINTED AS A PROPHESIED *SAVIOR*.
"MY STORIES AND ADVENTURES, MY GREAT LOVES, MY HATED ENEMIES, ALL TRANSFORMED INTO *MYTH*.
"IN THIS WAKANDA, I WAS NOT JUST A KING...
"...I WAS A *MYTHICAL HERO*.
"AND WHAT WAS A HERO WITHOUT HIS TRIALS?

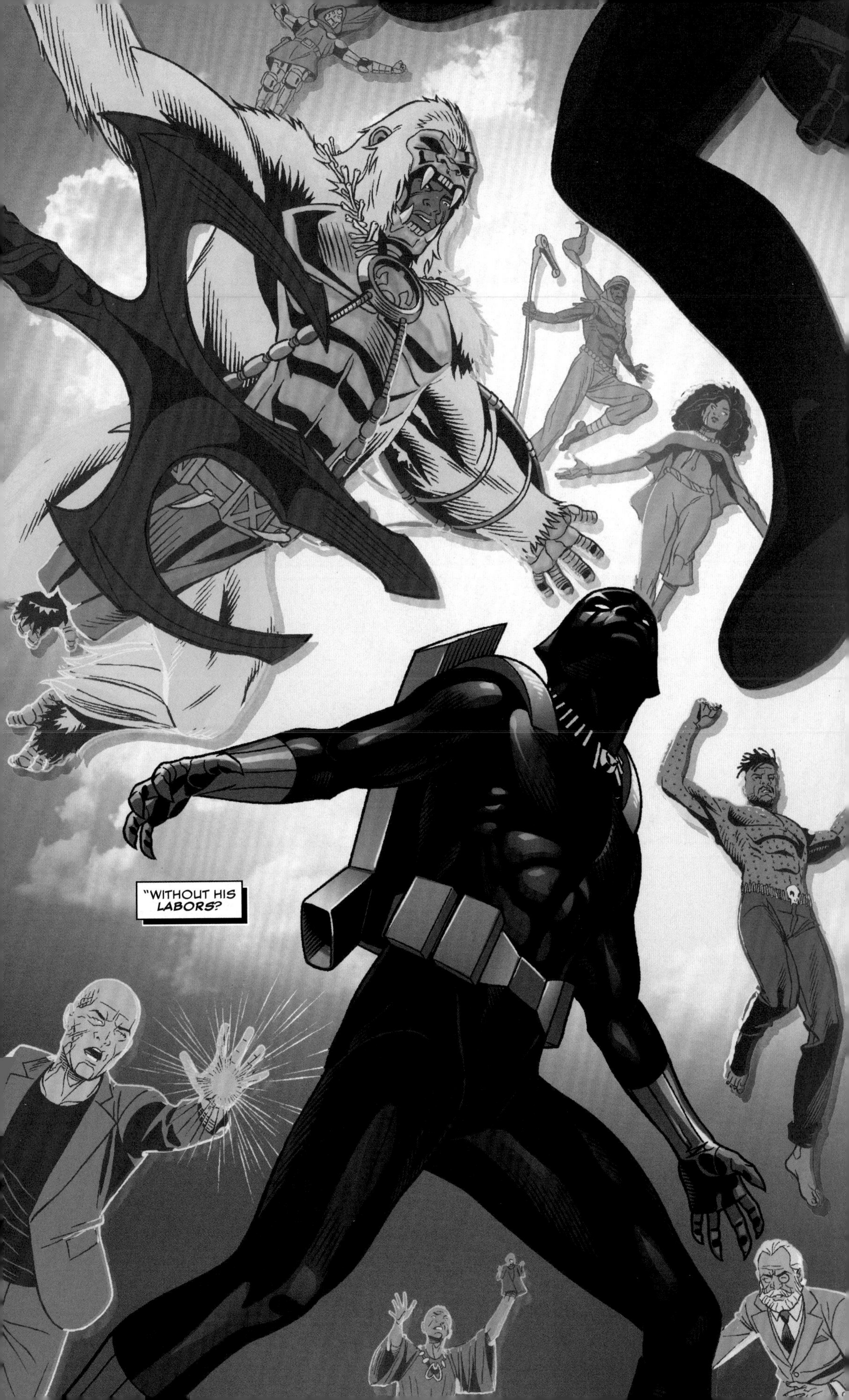
"WITHOUT HIS *LABORS*?

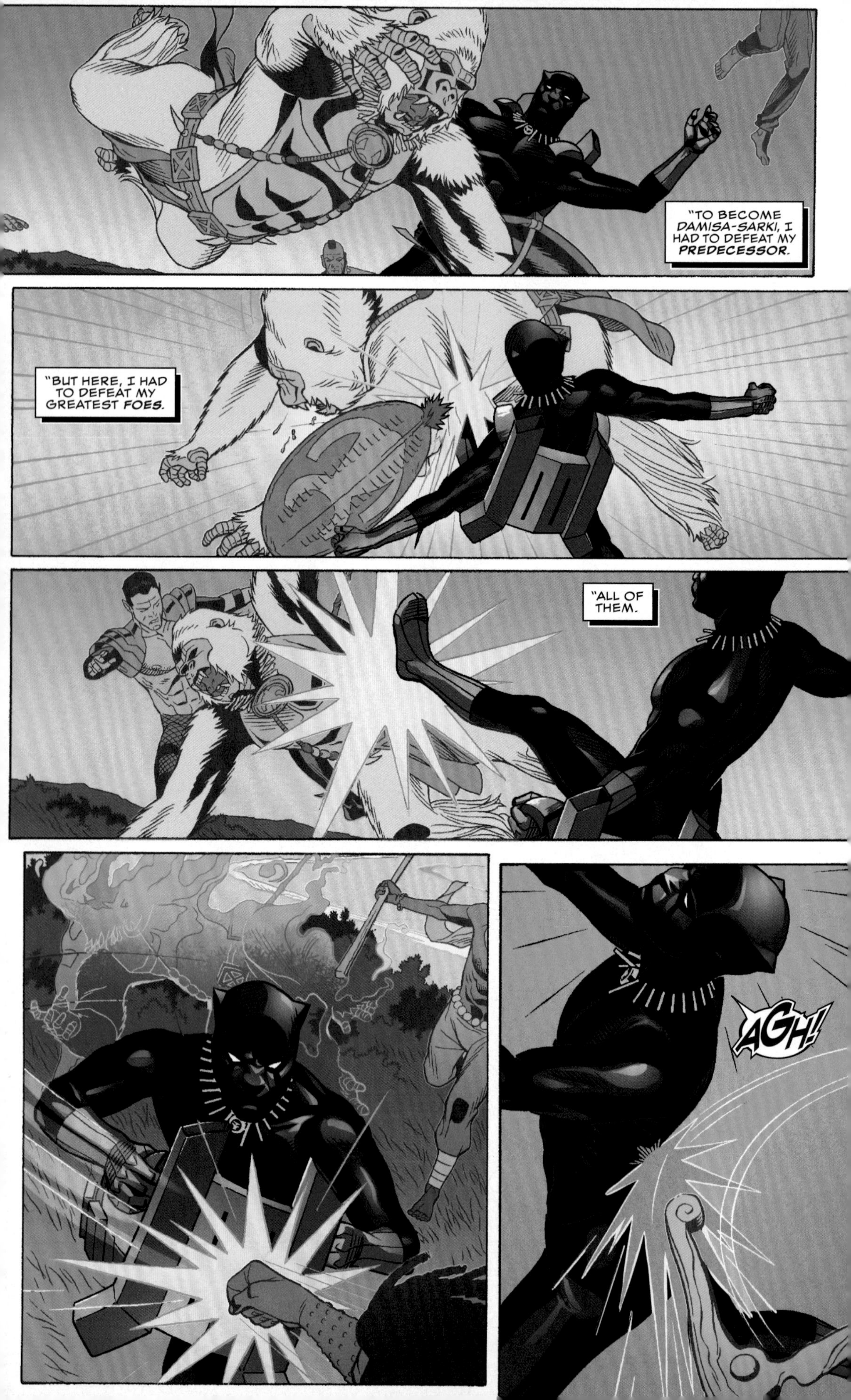
"TO BECOME DAMISA-SARKI, I HAD TO DEFEAT MY PREDECESSOR.
"BUT HERE, I HAD TO DEFEAT MY GREATEST FOES.
"ALL OF THEM.
AGH!!

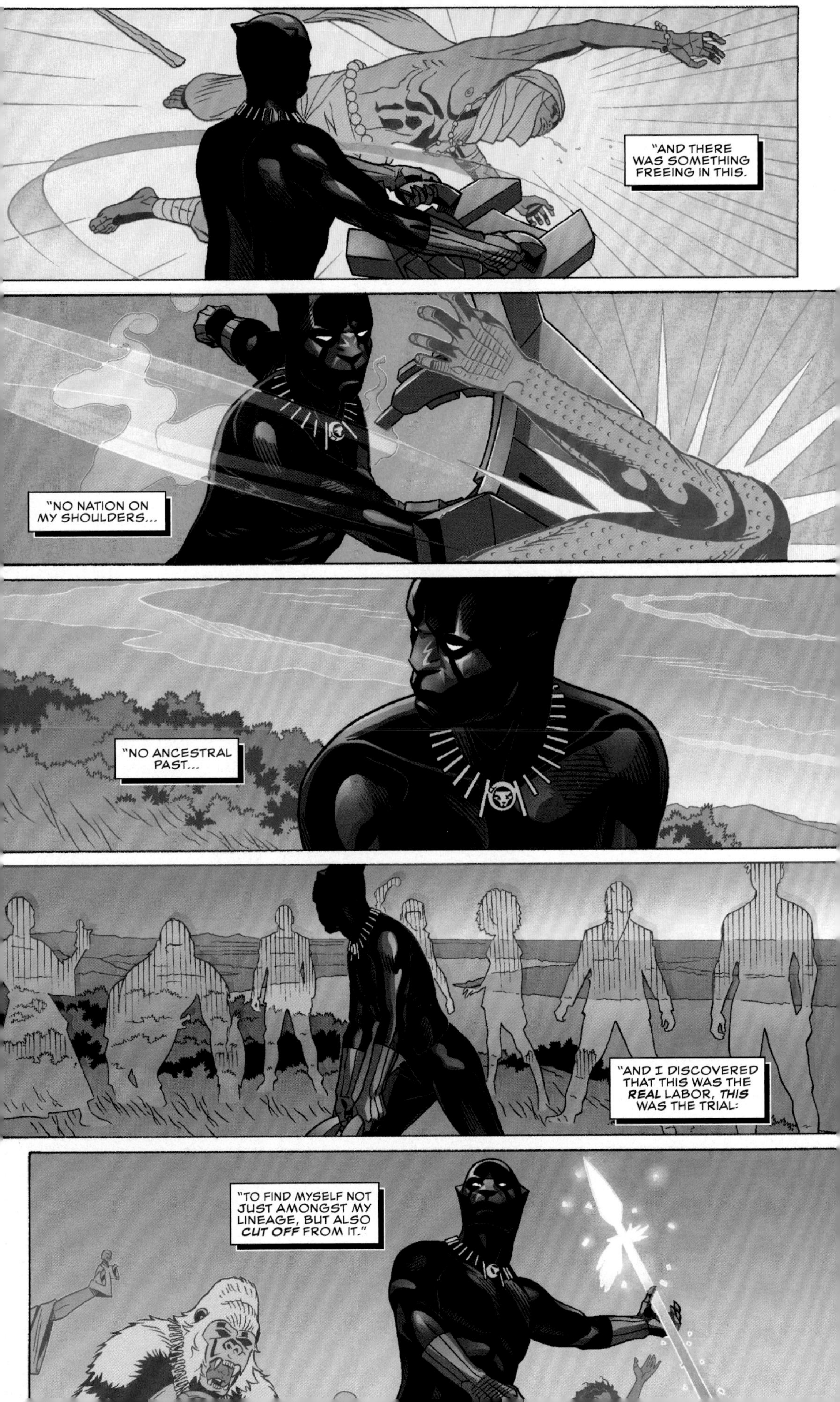
"AND THERE WAS SOMETHING FREEING IN THIS.
"NO NATION ON MY SHOULDERS...
"NO ANCESTRAL PAST...
"AND I DISCOVERED THAT THIS WAS THE REAL LABOR, THIS WAS THE TRIAL:
"TO FIND MYSELF NOT JUST AMONGST MY LINEAGE, BUT ALSO CUT OFF FROM IT."

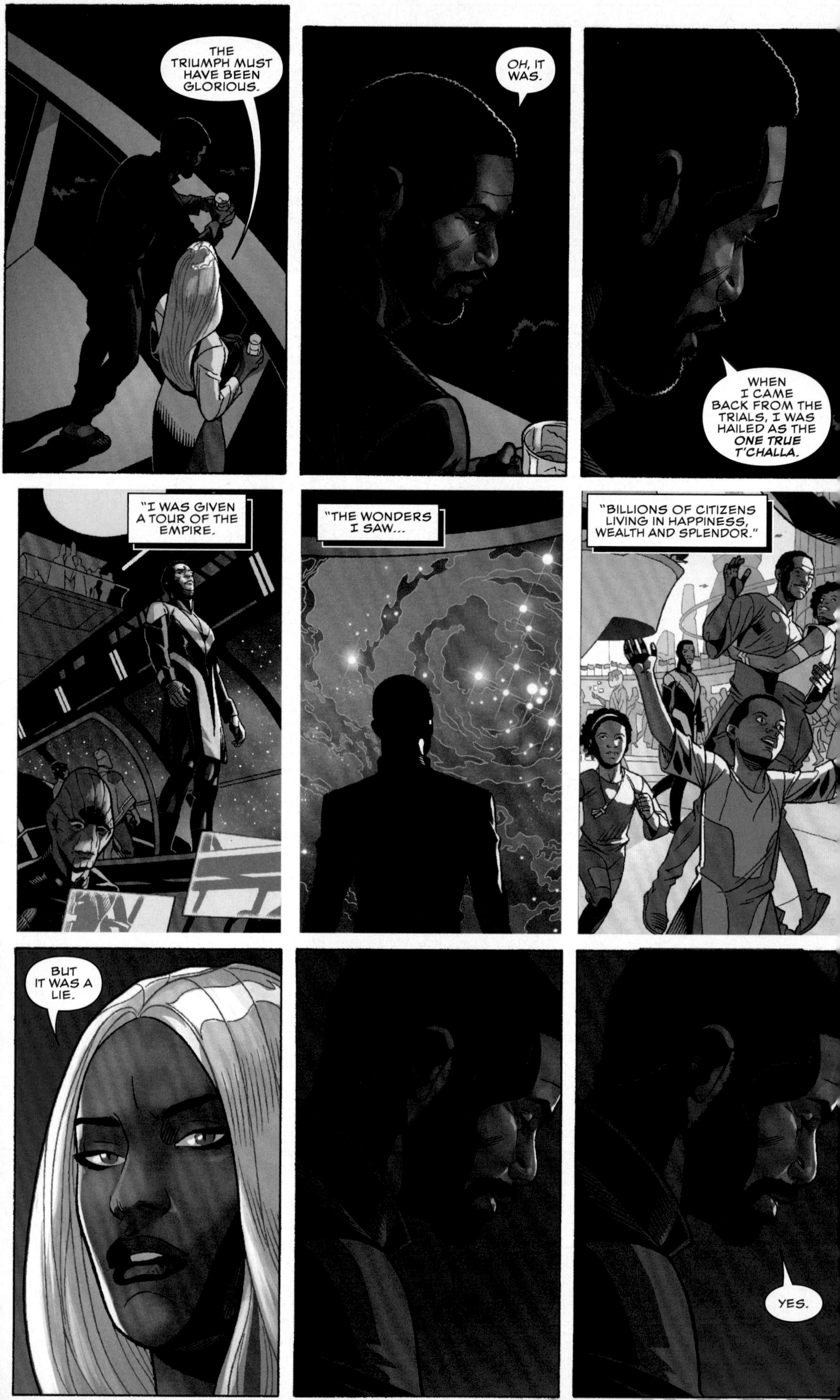
THE TRIUMPH MUST HAVE BEEN GLORIOUS.
OH, IT WAS.
WHEN I CAME BACK FROM THE TRIALS, I WAS HAILED AS THE *ONE TRUE T'CHALLA.*
"I WAS GIVEN A TOUR OF THE EMPIRE.
"THE WONDERS I SAW...
"BILLIONS OF CITIZENS LIVING IN HAPPINESS, WEALTH AND SPLENDOR."
BUT IT WAS A LIE.
YES.

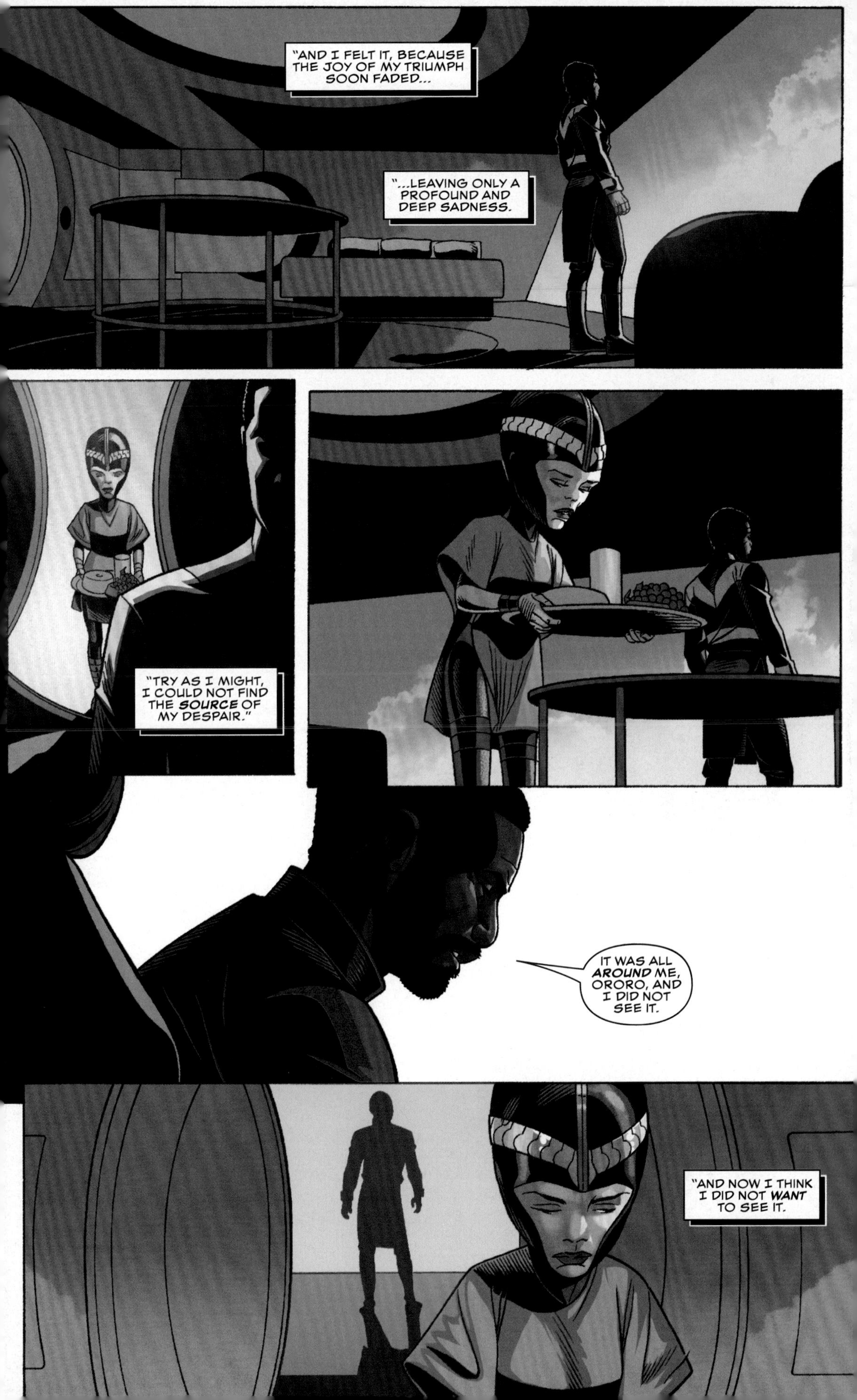
"AND I FELT IT, BECAUSE THE JOY OF MY TRIUMPH SOON FADED...
"...LEAVING ONLY A PROFOUND AND DEEP SADNESS.
"TRY AS I MIGHT, I COULD NOT FIND THE SOURCE OF MY DESPAIR."
IT WAS ALL AROUND ME, ORORO, AND I DID NOT SEE IT.
"AND NOW I THINK I DID NOT WANT TO SEE IT.

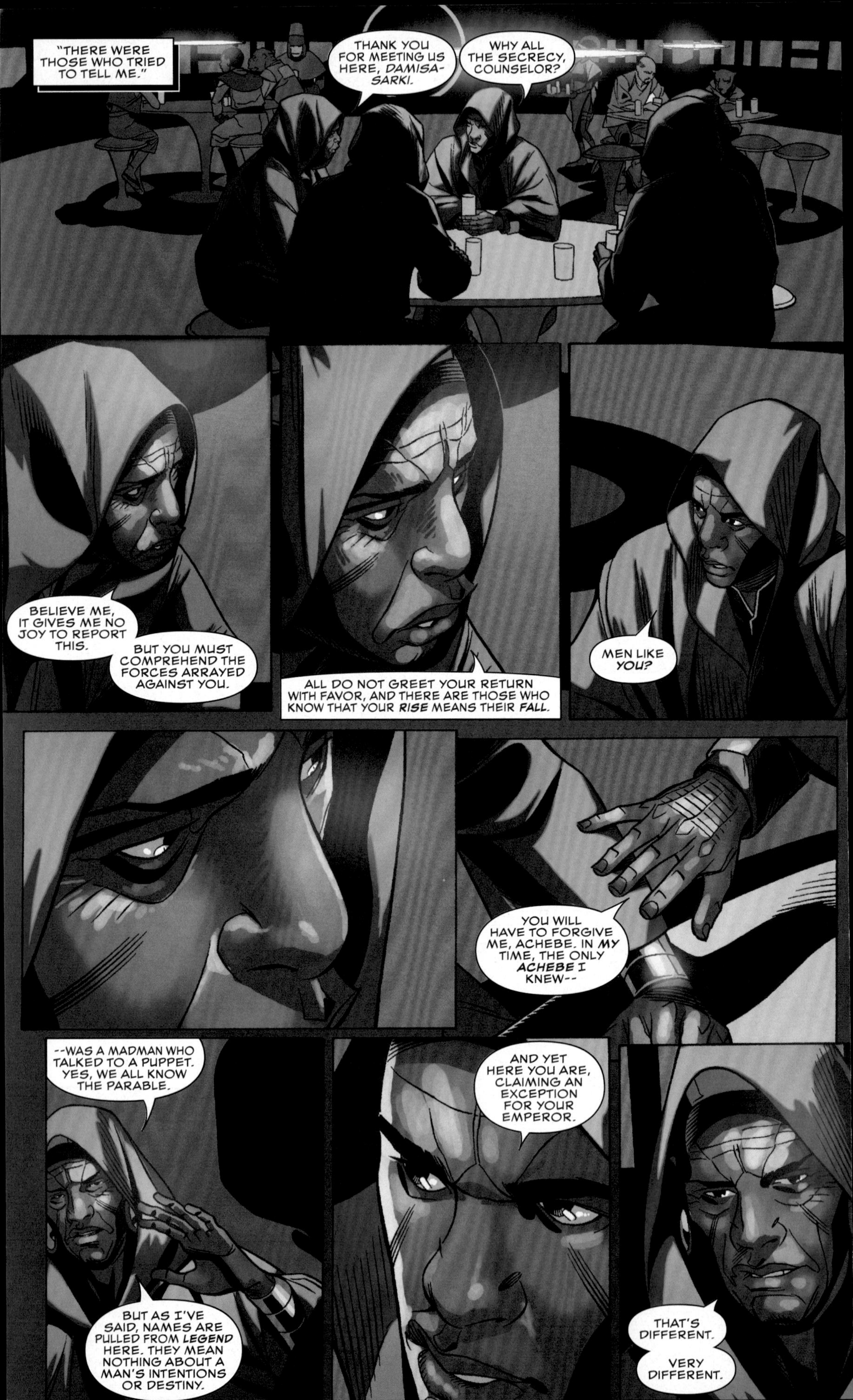
"THERE WERE THOSE WHO TRIED TO TELL ME."
THANK YOU FOR MEETING US HERE, DAMISA-SARKI.
WHY ALL THE SECRECY, COUNSELOR?
BELIEVE ME, IT GIVES ME NO JOY TO REPORT THIS.
BUT YOU MUST COMPREHEND THE FORCES ARRAYED AGAINST YOU.
ALL DO NOT GREET YOUR RETURN WITH FAVOR, AND THERE ARE THOSE WHO KNOW THAT YOUR RISE MEANS THEIR FALL.
MEN LIKE YOU?
YOU WILL HAVE TO FORGIVE ME, ACHEBE. IN MY TIME, THE ONLY ACHEBE I KNEW--
--WAS A MADMAN WHO TALKED TO A PUPPET. YES, WE ALL KNOW THE PARABLE.
BUT AS I'VE SAID, NAMES ARE PULLED FROM LEGEND HERE. THEY MEAN NOTHING ABOUT A MAN'S INTENTIONS OR DESTINY.
AND YET HERE YOU ARE, CLAIMING AN EXCEPTION FOR YOUR EMPEROR.
THAT'S DIFFERENT.
VERY DIFFERENT.

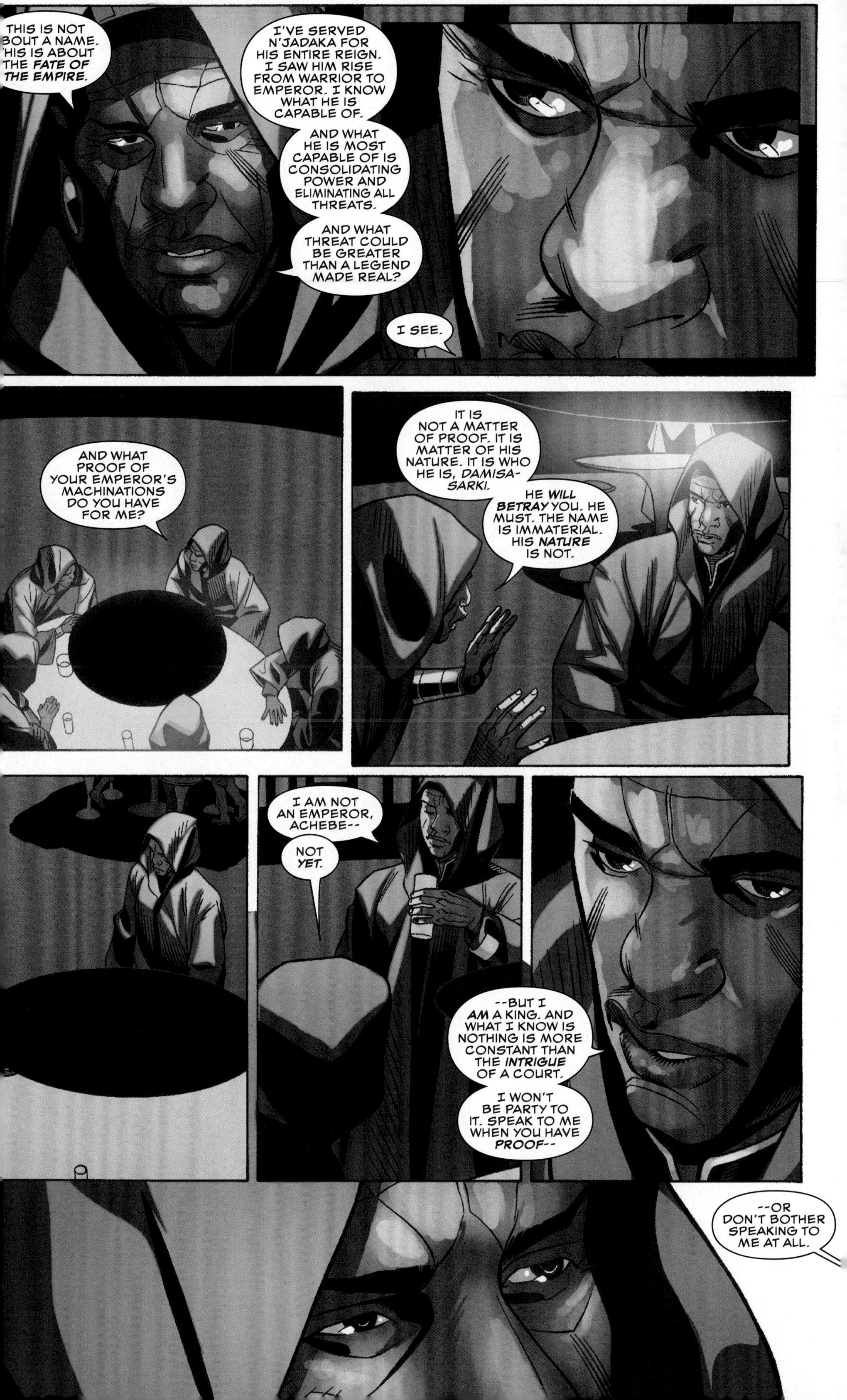

THIS IS NOT BOUT A NAME. HIS IS ABOUT THE FATE OF THE EMPIRE.
I'VE SERVED N'JADAKA FOR HIS ENTIRE REIGN. I SAW HIM RISE FROM WARRIOR TO EMPEROR. I KNOW WHAT HE IS CAPABLE OF.
AND WHAT HE IS MOST CAPABLE OF IS CONSOLIDATING POWER AND ELIMINATING ALL THREATS.
AND WHAT THREAT COULD BE GREATER THAN A LEGEND MADE REAL?
I SEE.
AND WHAT PROOF OF YOUR EMPEROR'S MACHINATIONS DO YOU HAVE FOR ME?
IT IS NOT A MATTER OF PROOF. IT IS MATTER OF HIS NATURE. IT IS WHO HE IS, DAMISA-SARKI.
HE WILL BETRAY YOU. HE MUST. THE NAME IS IMMATERIAL. HIS NATURE IS NOT.
I AM NOT AN EMPEROR, ACHEBE--
NOT YET.
--BUT I AM A KING. AND WHAT I KNOW IS NOTHING IS MORE CONSTANT THAN THE INTRIGUE OF A COURT.
I WON'T BE PARTY TO IT. SPEAK TO ME WHEN YOU HAVE PROOF--
--OR DON'T BOTHER SPEAKING TO ME AT ALL.

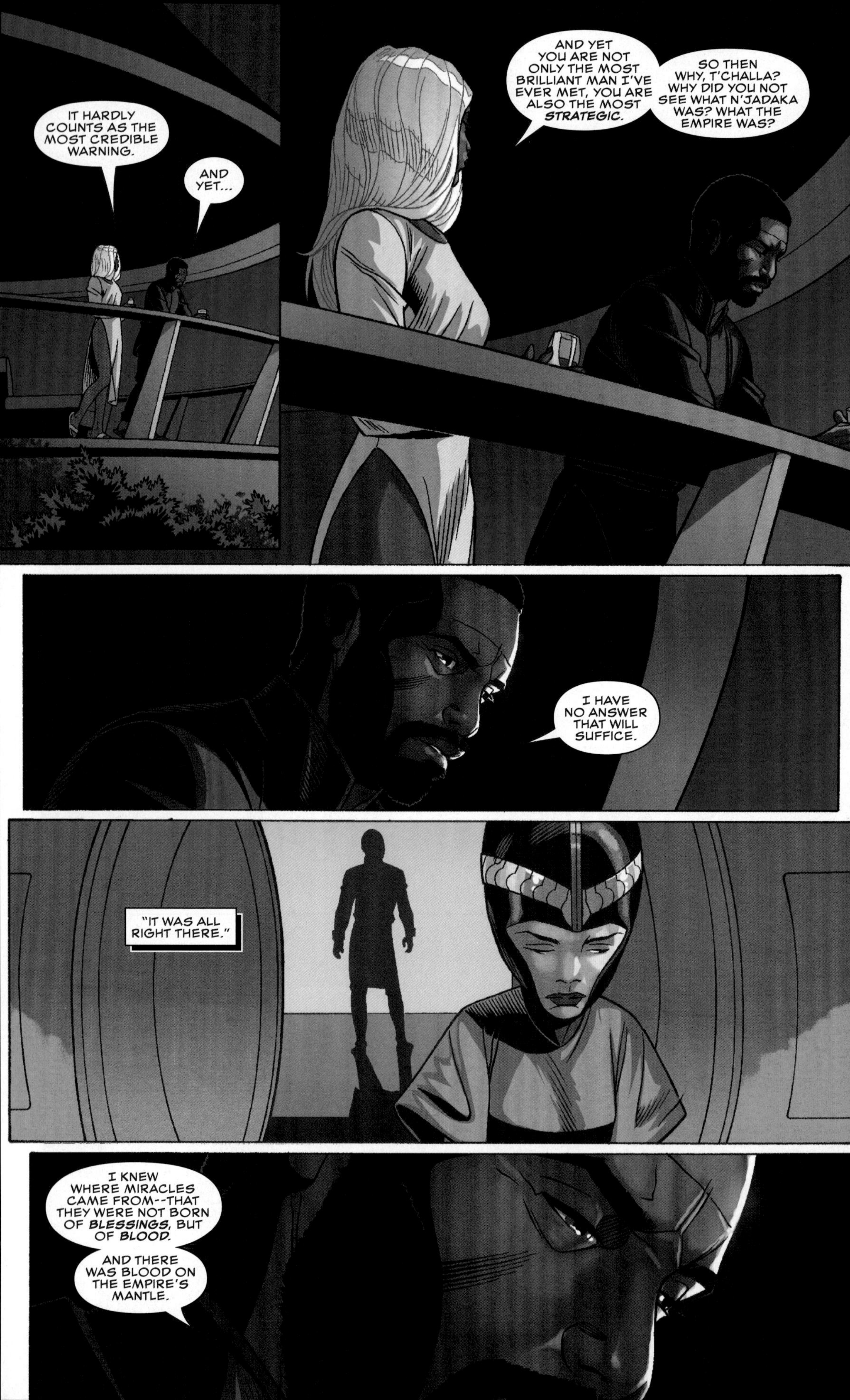
IT HARDLY COUNTS AS THE MOST CREDIBLE WARNING.
AND YET...
AND YET YOU ARE NOT ONLY THE MOST BRILLIANT MAN I'VE EVER MET, YOU ARE ALSO THE MOST STRATEGIC.
SO THEN WHY, T'CHALLA? WHY DID YOU NOT SEE WHAT N'JADAKA WAS? WHAT THE EMPIRE WAS?
I HAVE NO ANSWER THAT WILL SUFFICE.
"IT WAS ALL RIGHT THERE."
I KNEW WHERE MIRACLES CAME FROM--THAT THEY WERE NOT BORN OF BLESSINGS, BUT OF BLOOD.
AND THERE WAS BLOOD ON THE EMPIRE'S MANTLE.

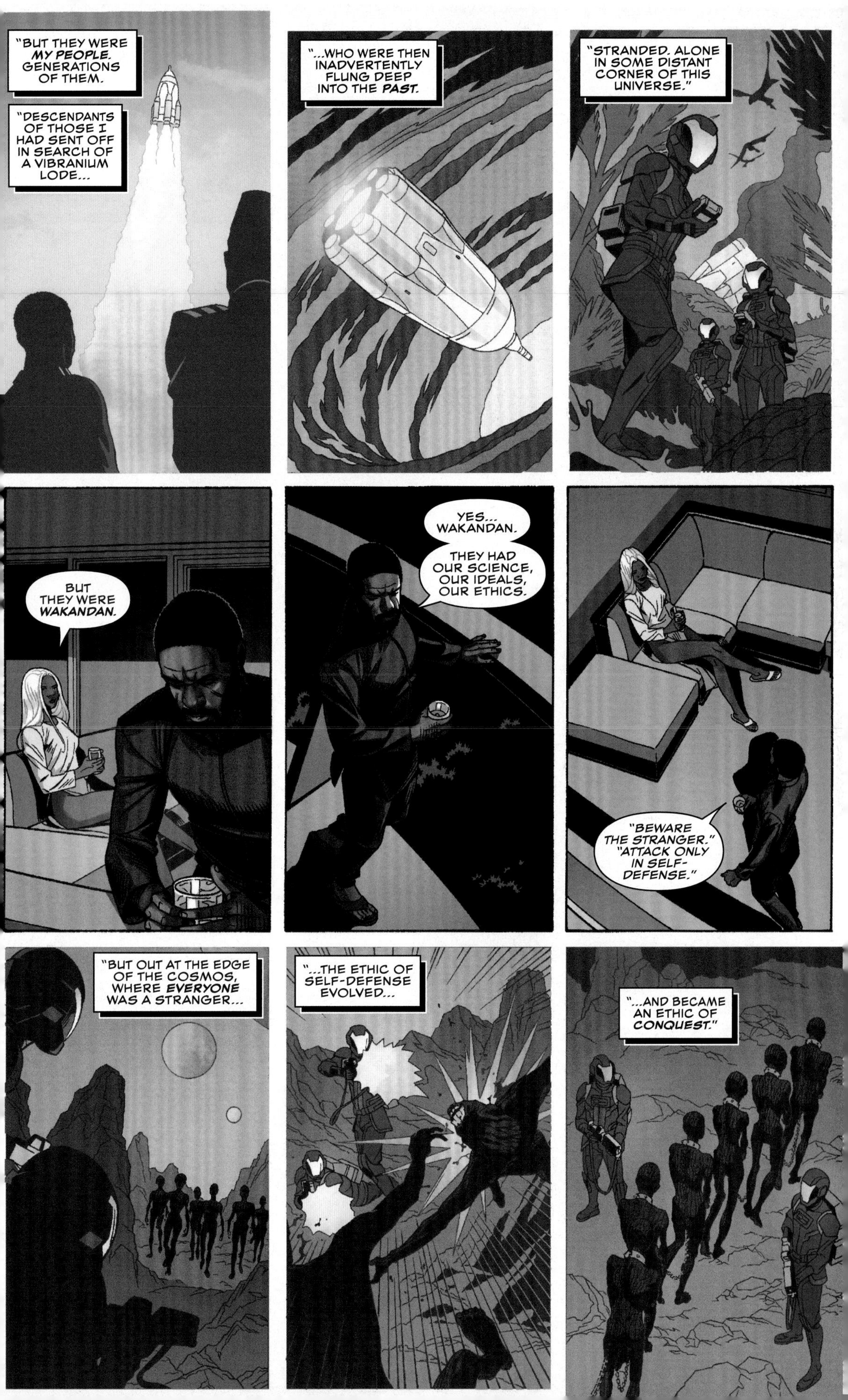
"BUT THEY WERE MY PEOPLE. GENERATIONS OF THEM.
"DESCENDANTS OF THOSE I HAD SENT OFF IN SEARCH OF A VIBRANIUM LODE...
"...WHO WERE THEN INADVERTENTLY FLUNG DEEP INTO THE PAST.
"STRANDED. ALONE IN SOME DISTANT CORNER OF THIS UNIVERSE."
BUT THEY WERE WAKANDAN.
YES... WAKANDAN.
THEY HAD OUR SCIENCE, OUR IDEALS, OUR ETHICS.
"BEWARE THE STRANGER." "ATTACK ONLY IN SELF-DEFENSE."
"BUT OUT AT THE EDGE OF THE COSMOS, WHERE EVERYONE WAS A STRANGER...
"...THE ETHIC OF SELF-DEFENSE EVOLVED...
"...AND BECAME AN ETHIC OF CONQUEST."

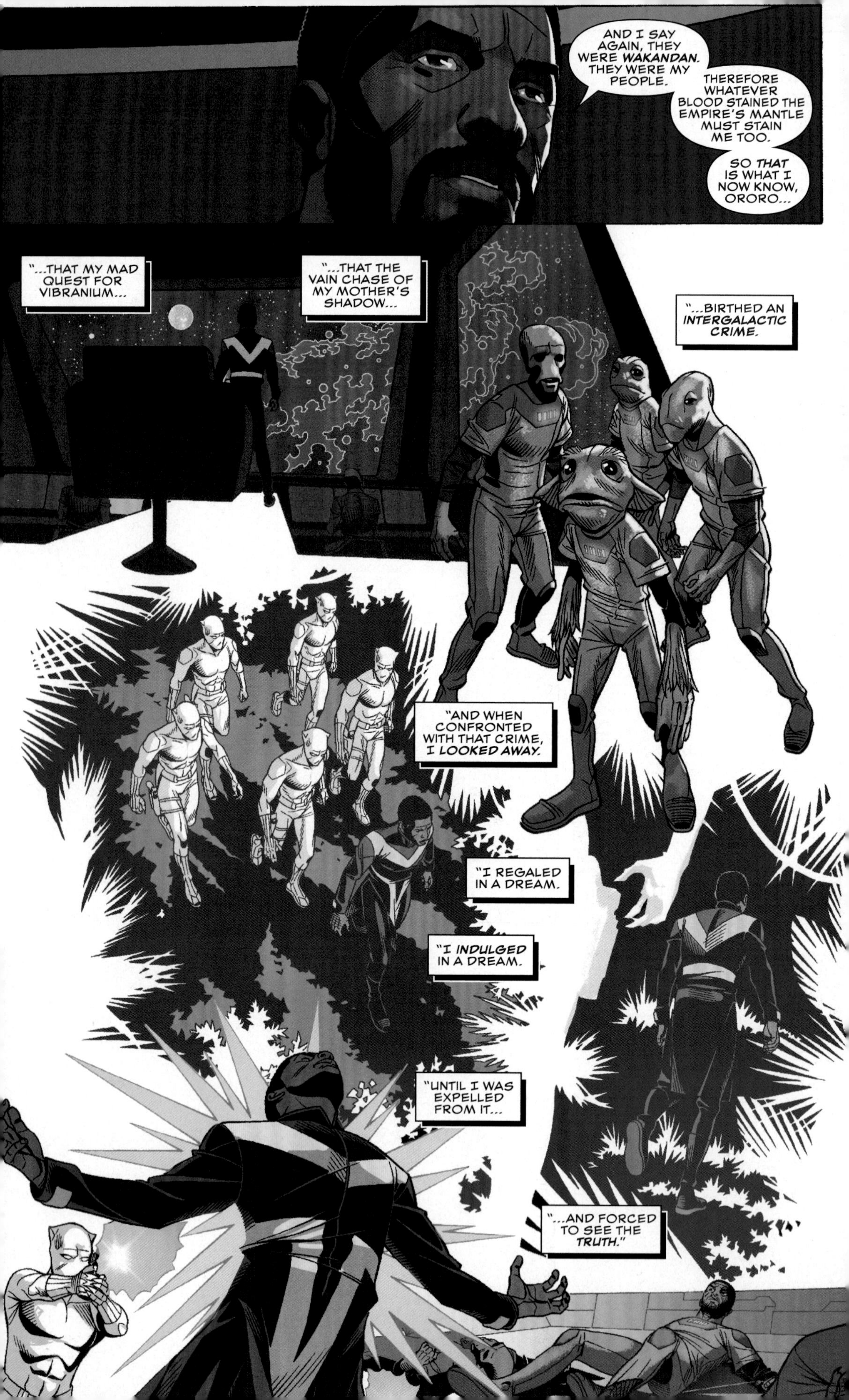
AND I SAY AGAIN, THEY WERE WAKANDAN. THEY WERE MY PEOPLE.
THEREFORE WHATEVER BLOOD STAINED THE EMPIRE'S MANTLE MUST STAIN ME TOO.
SO THAT IS WHAT I NOW KNOW, ORORO...
"...THAT MY MAD QUEST FOR VIBRANIUM...
"...THAT THE VAIN CHASE OF MY MOTHER'S SHADOW...
"...BIRTHED AN INTERGALACTIC CRIME.
"AND WHEN CONFRONTED WITH THAT CRIME, I LOOKED AWAY.
"I REGALED IN A DREAM.
"I INDULGED IN A DREAM.
"UNTIL I WAS EXPELLED FROM IT...
"...AND FORCED TO SEE THE TRUTH."

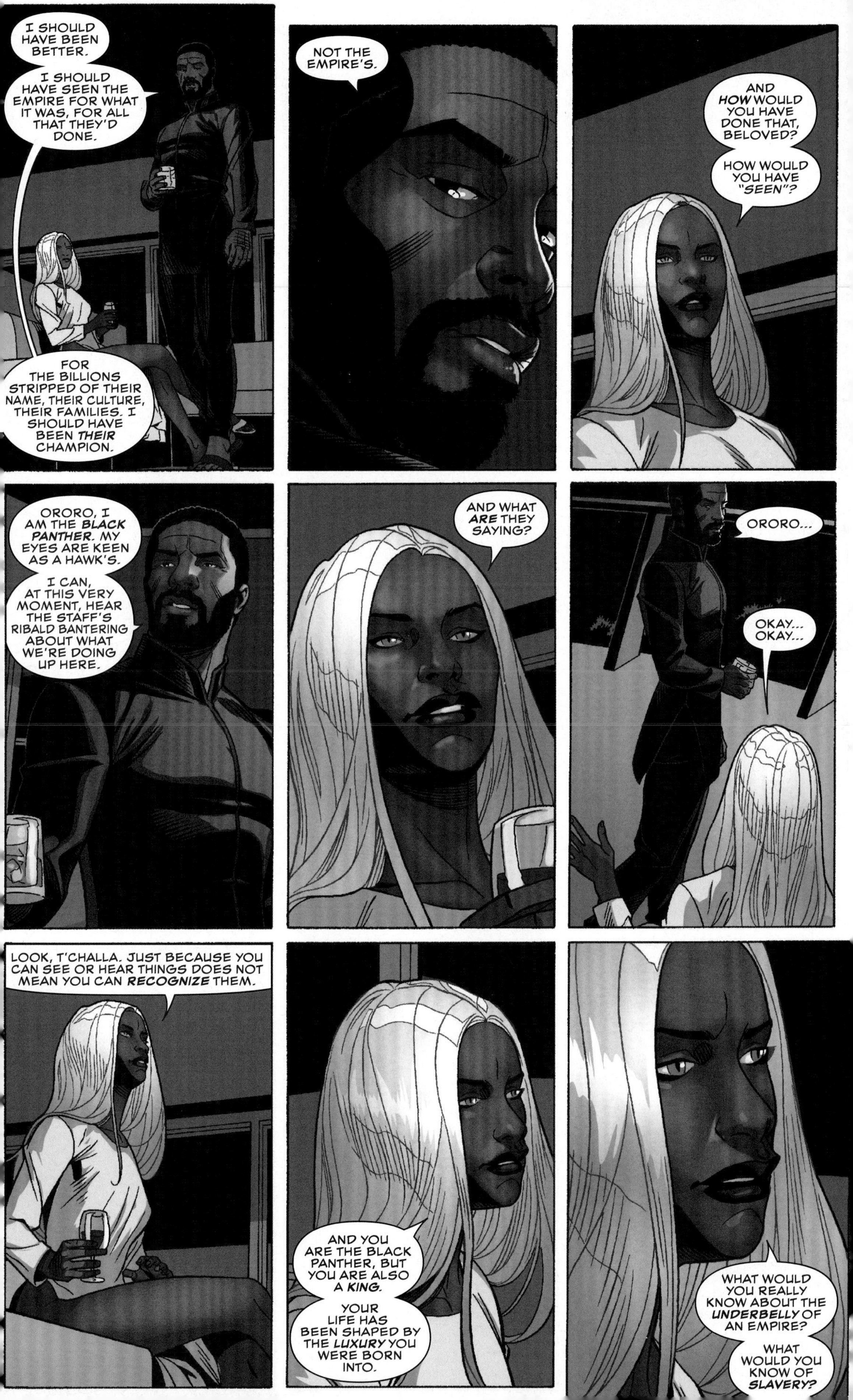
I SHOULD HAVE BEEN BETTER.
I SHOULD HAVE SEEN THE EMPIRE FOR WHAT IT WAS, FOR ALL THAT THEY'D DONE.
FOR THE BILLIONS STRIPPED OF THEIR NAME, THEIR CULTURE, THEIR FAMILIES. I SHOULD HAVE BEEN THEIR CHAMPION.
NOT THE EMPIRE'S.
AND HOW WOULD YOU HAVE DONE THAT, BELOVED?
HOW WOULD YOU HAVE "SEEN"?
ORORO, I AM THE BLACK PANTHER. MY EYES ARE KEEN AS A HAWK'S.
I CAN, AT THIS VERY MOMENT, HEAR THE STAFF'S RIBALD BANTERING ABOUT WHAT WE'RE DOING UP HERE.
AND WHAT ARE THEY SAYING?
ORORO...
OKAY... OKAY...
LOOK, T'CHALLA. JUST BECAUSE YOU CAN SEE OR HEAR THINGS DOES NOT MEAN YOU CAN RECOGNIZE THEM.
AND YOU ARE THE BLACK PANTHER, BUT YOU ARE ALSO A KING.
YOUR LIFE HAS BEEN SHAPED BY THE LUXURY YOU WERE BORN INTO.
WHAT WOULD YOU REALLY KNOW ABOUT THE UNDERBELLY OF AN EMPIRE?
WHAT WOULD YOU KNOW OF SLAVERY?

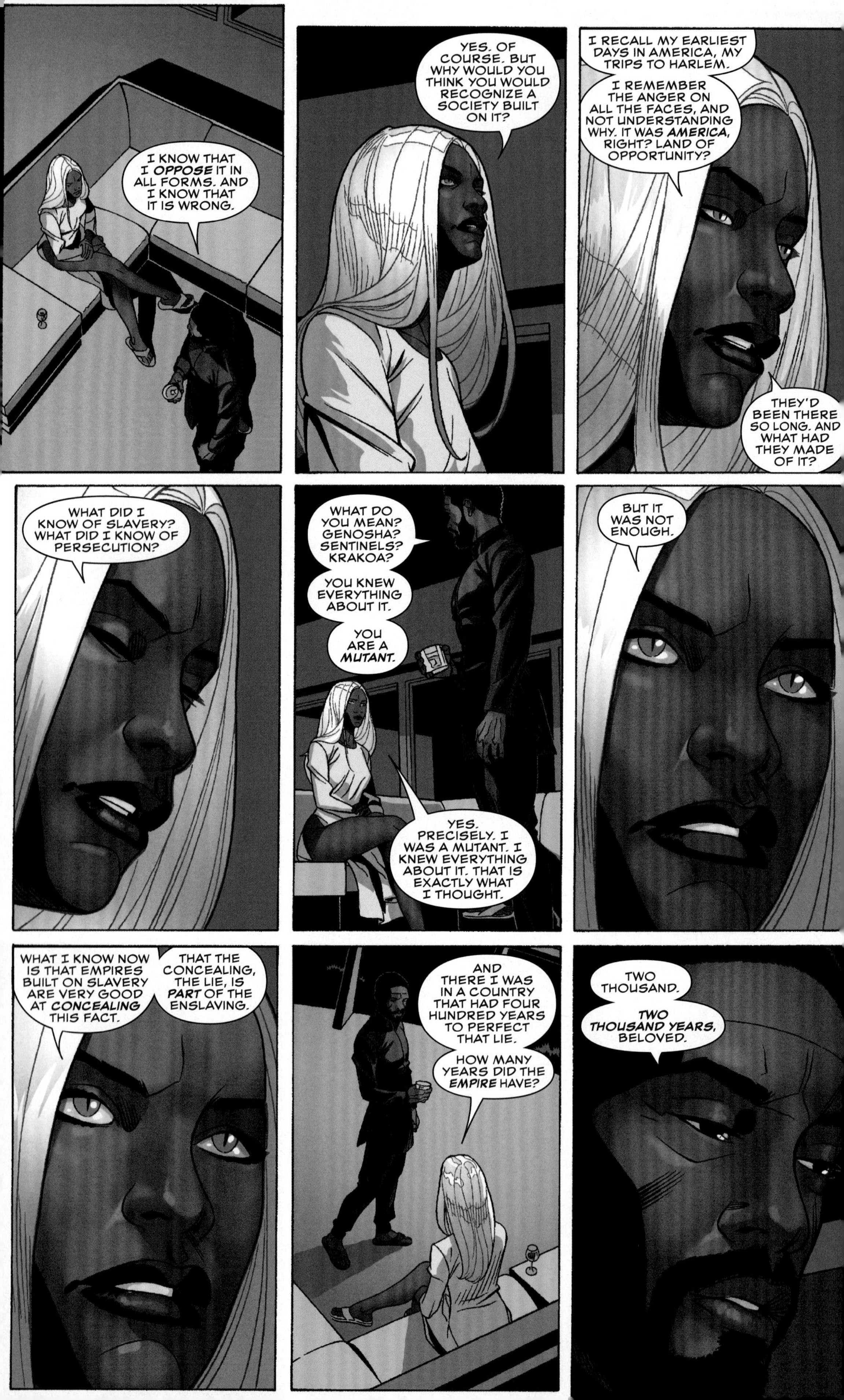
I KNOW THAT I OPPOSE IT IN ALL FORMS. AND I KNOW THAT IT IS WRONG.
YES. OF COURSE. BUT WHY WOULD YOU THINK YOU WOULD RECOGNIZE A SOCIETY BUILT ON IT?
I RECALL MY EARLIEST DAYS IN AMERICA, MY TRIPS TO HARLEM.
I REMEMBER THE ANGER ON ALL THE FACES, AND NOT UNDERSTANDING WHY. IT WAS AMERICA, RIGHT? LAND OF OPPORTUNITY?
THEY'D BEEN THERE SO LONG. AND WHAT HAD THEY MADE OF IT?
WHAT DID I KNOW OF SLAVERY? WHAT DID I KNOW OF PERSECUTION?
WHAT DO YOU MEAN? GENOSHA? SENTINELS? KRAKOA?
YOU KNEW EVERYTHING ABOUT IT.
YOU ARE A MUTANT.
YES. PRECISELY. I WAS A MUTANT. I KNEW EVERYTHING ABOUT IT. THAT IS EXACTLY WHAT I THOUGHT.
BUT IT WAS NOT ENOUGH.
WHAT I KNOW NOW IS THAT EMPIRES BUILT ON SLAVERY ARE VERY GOOD AT CONCEALING THIS FACT.
THAT THE CONCEALING, THE LIE, IS PART OF THE ENSLAVING.
AND THERE I WAS IN A COUNTRY THAT HAD FOUR HUNDRED YEARS TO PERFECT THAT LIE.
HOW MANY YEARS DID THE EMPIRE HAVE?
TWO THOUSAND.
TWO THOUSAND YEARS, BELOVED.

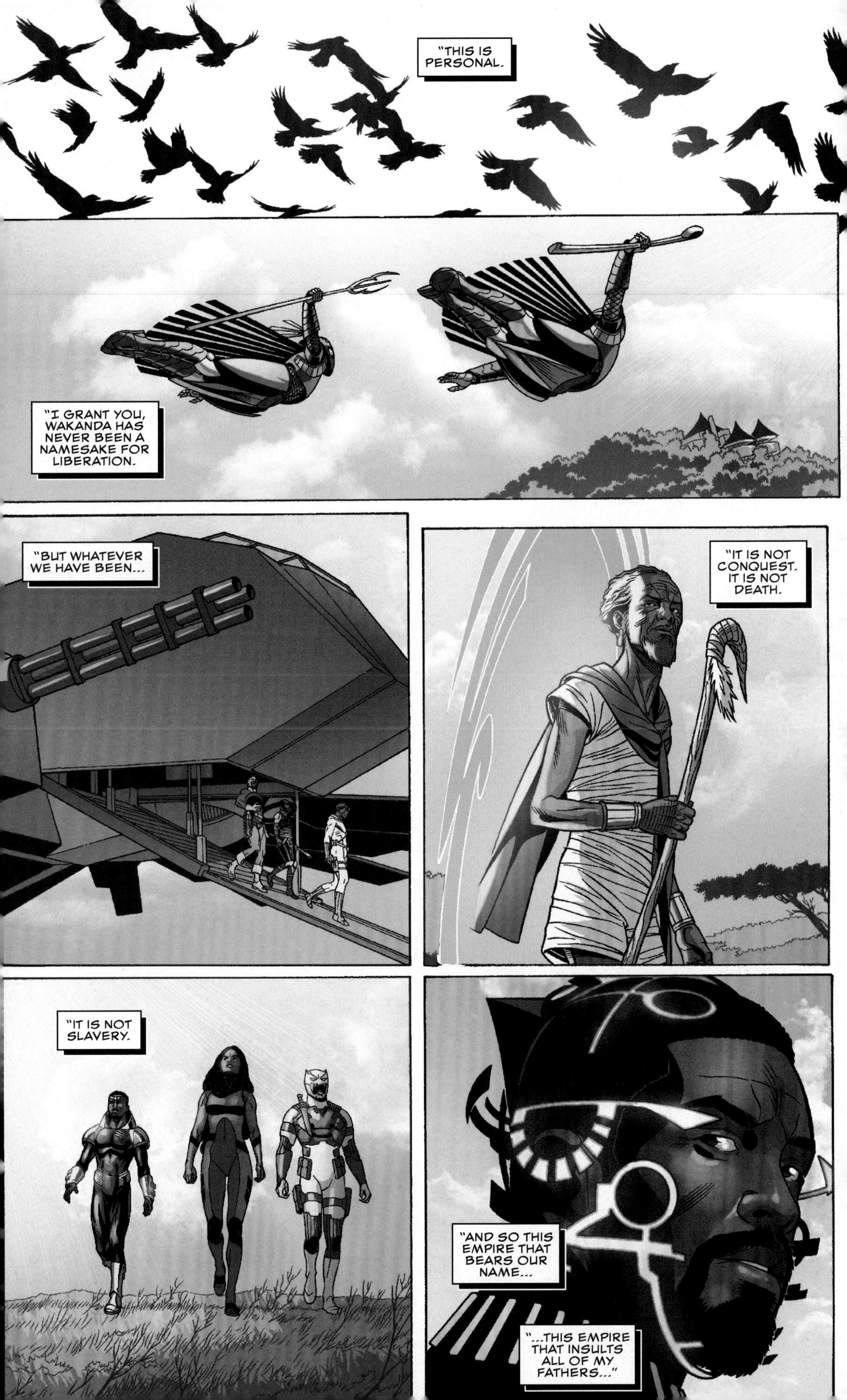
"THIS IS PERSONAL.
"I GRANT YOU, WAKANDA HAS NEVER BEEN A NAMESAKE FOR LIBERATION.
"BUT WHATEVER WE HAVE BEEN...
"IT IS NOT CONQUEST. IT IS NOT DEATH.
"IT IS NOT SLAVERY.
"AND SO THIS EMPIRE THAT BEARS OUR NAME...
"...THIS EMPIRE THAT INSULTS ALL OF MY FATHERS..."

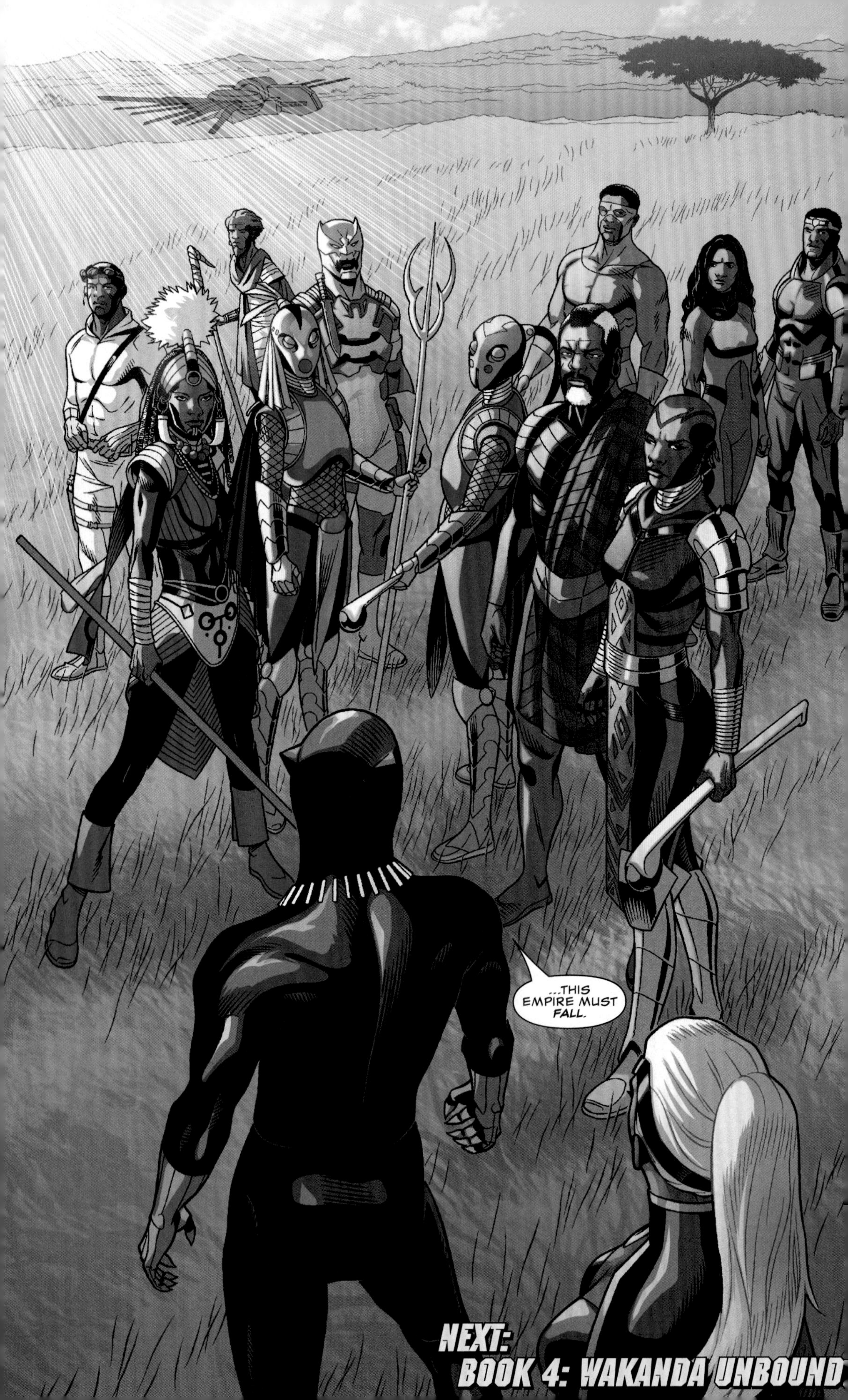
...THIS EMPIRE MUST FALL.
NEXT:
BOOK 4: WAKANDA UNBOUND

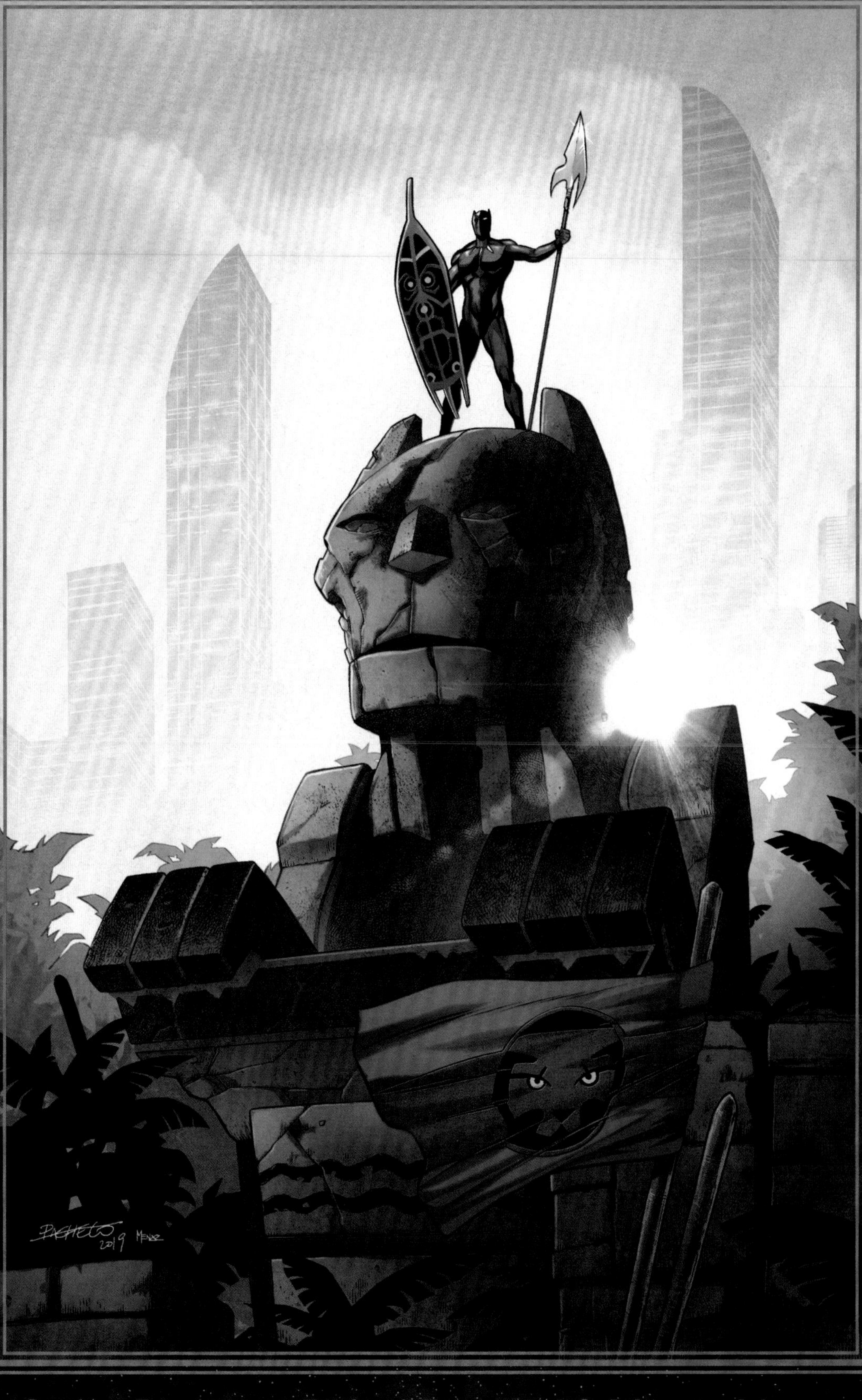

Carlos Pacheco, Rafael Fonteriz & Marcio Menyz

13 VARIANT

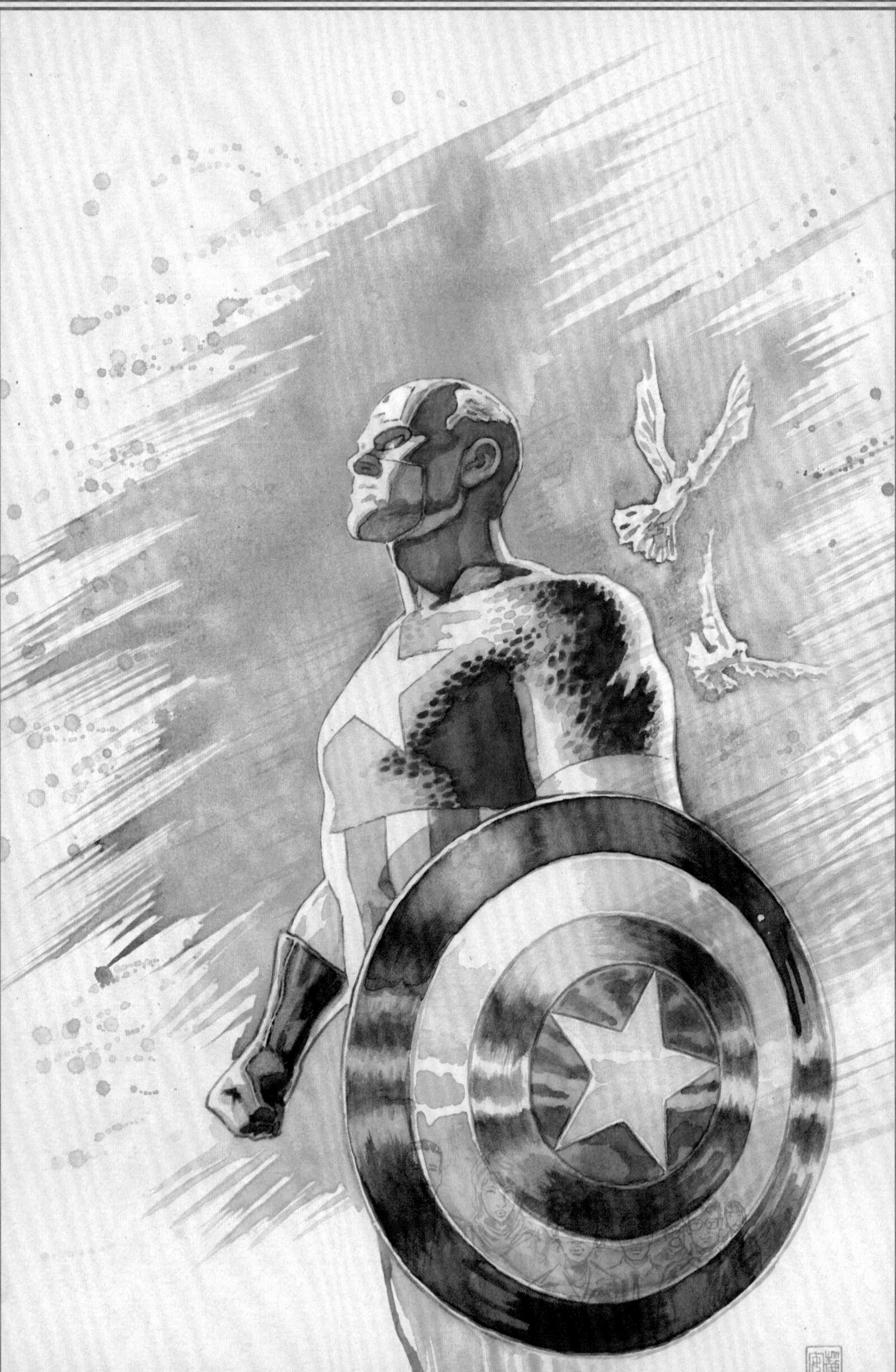
MACK

David Mack

13 MARVELS 25TH TRIBUTE VARIANT

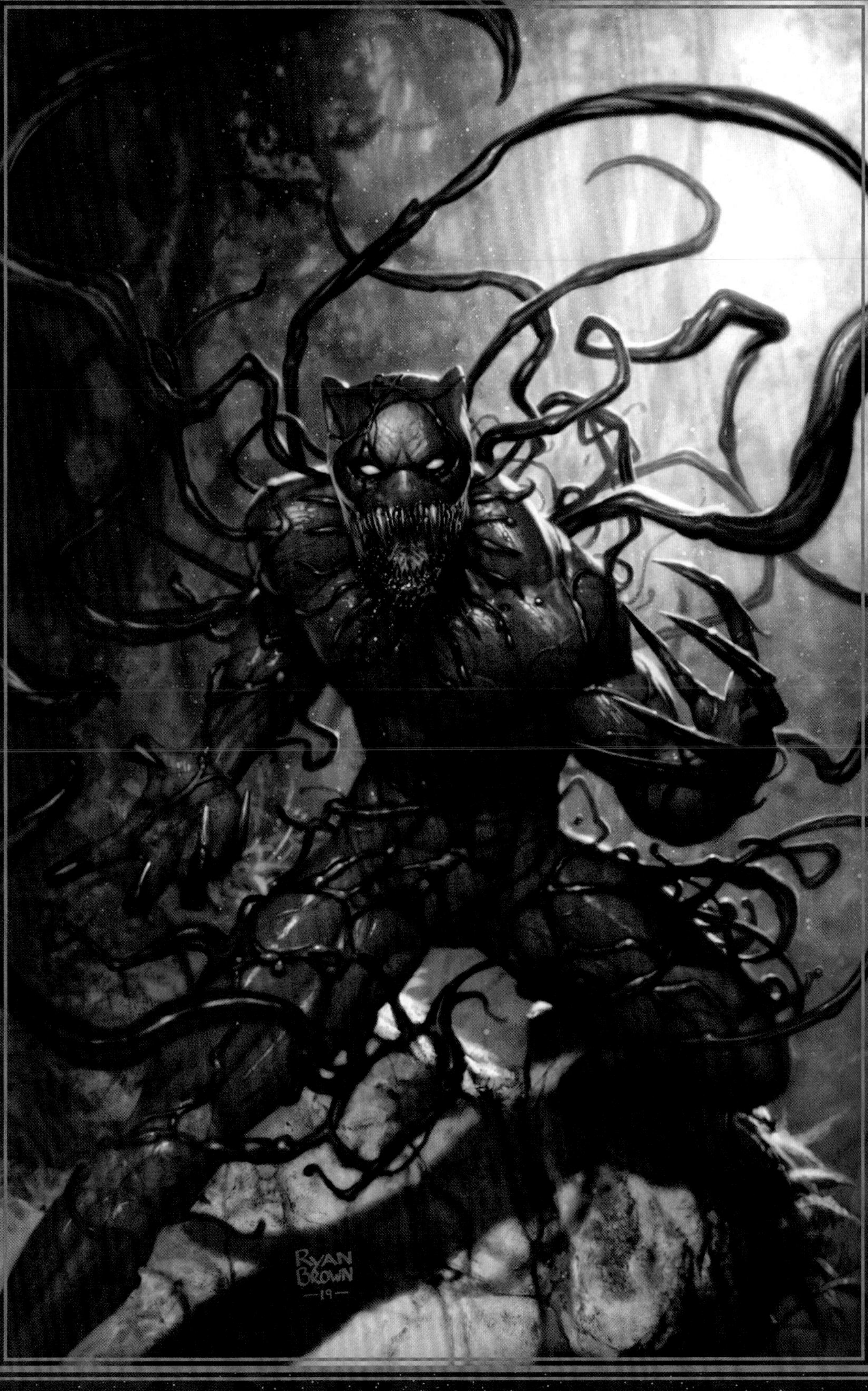
RYAN
BROWN
-19-

Ryan Brown

14 CARNAGE-IZED VARIANT

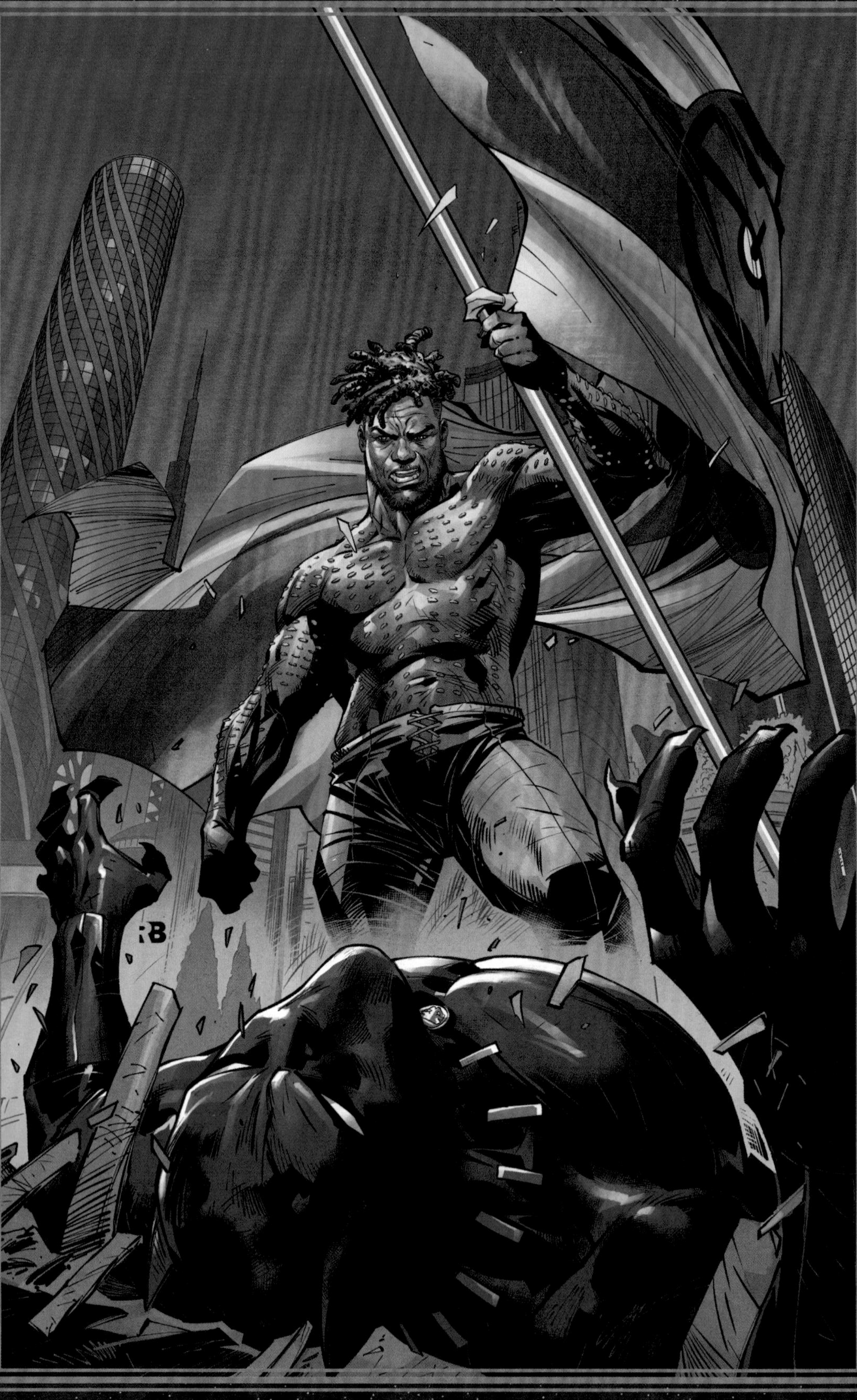
RB

Ryan Benjamin & Rain Beredo

15 BRING ON THE BAD GUYS VARIANT

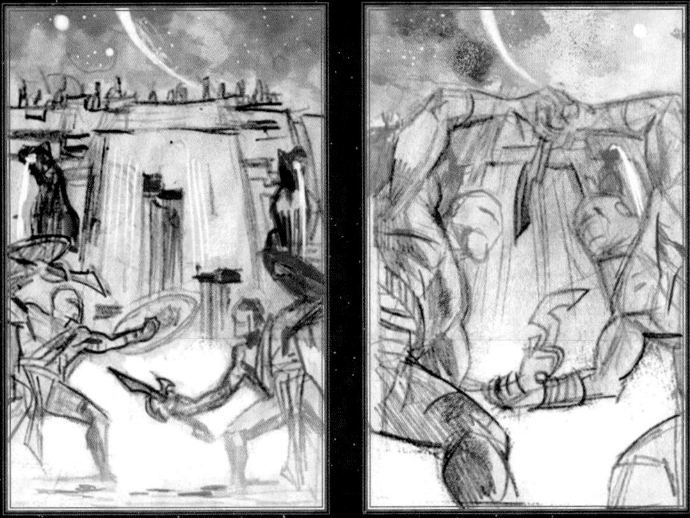

Daniel Acuña
13 COVER SKETCHES

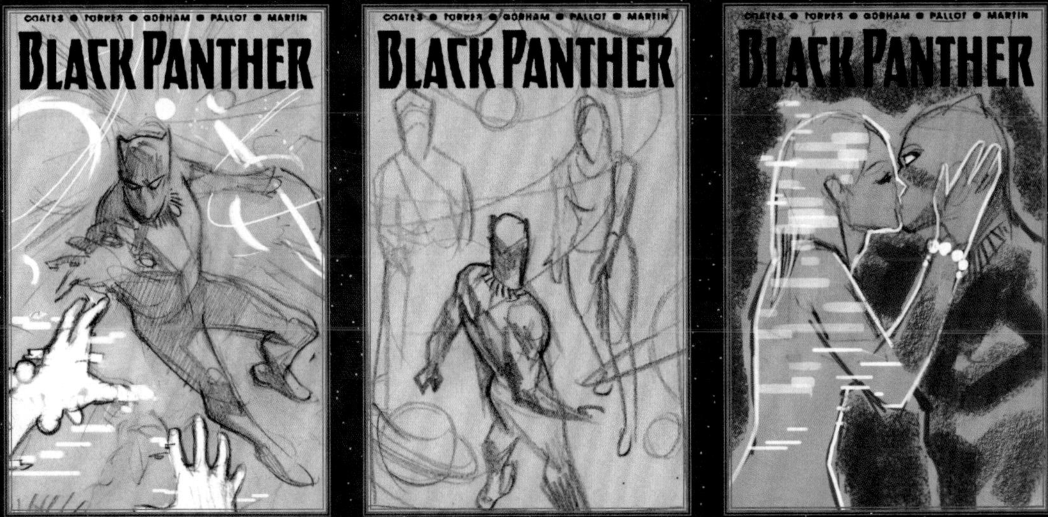

COATES • TORRES • GORHAM • PALLOT • MARTIN
BLACK PANTHER
COATES • TORRES • GORHAM • PALLOT • MARTIN
BLACK PANTHER
COATES • TORRES • GORHAM • PALLOT • MARTIN
BLACK PANTHER

Daniel Acuña
14 COVER SKETCHES

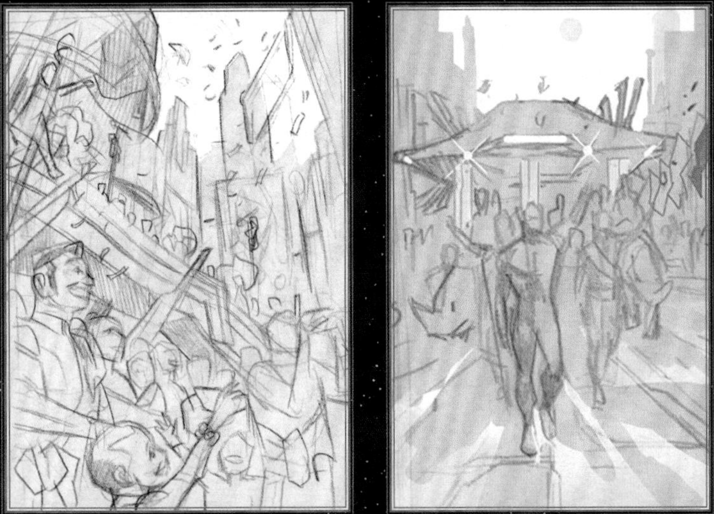

Daniel Acuña
15 COVER SKETCHES

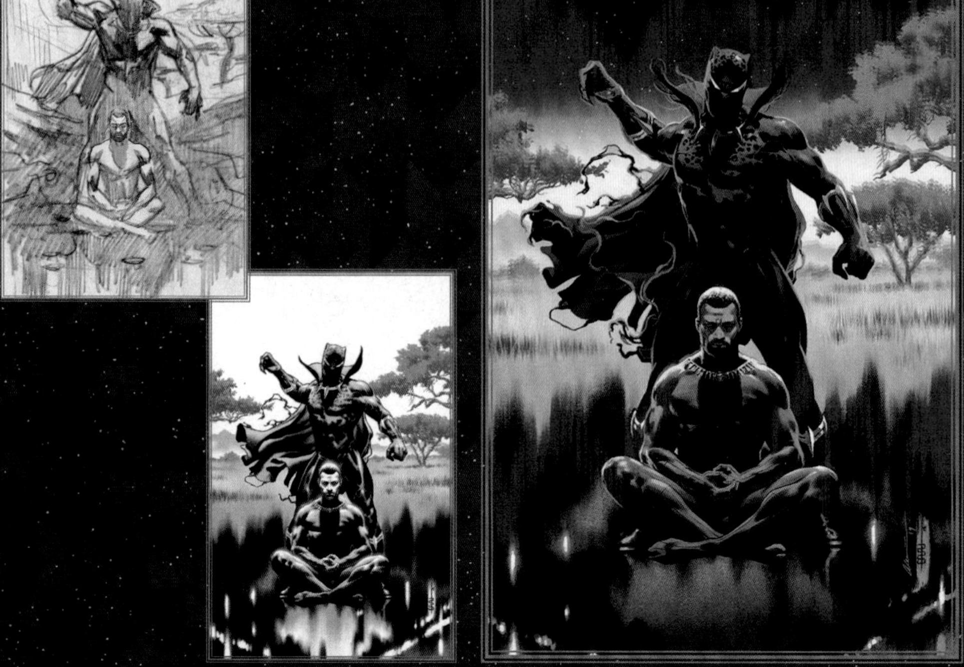

PENCILS & COLORS **Daniel Acuña** INKS **CAFU**
16 COVER PROCESS

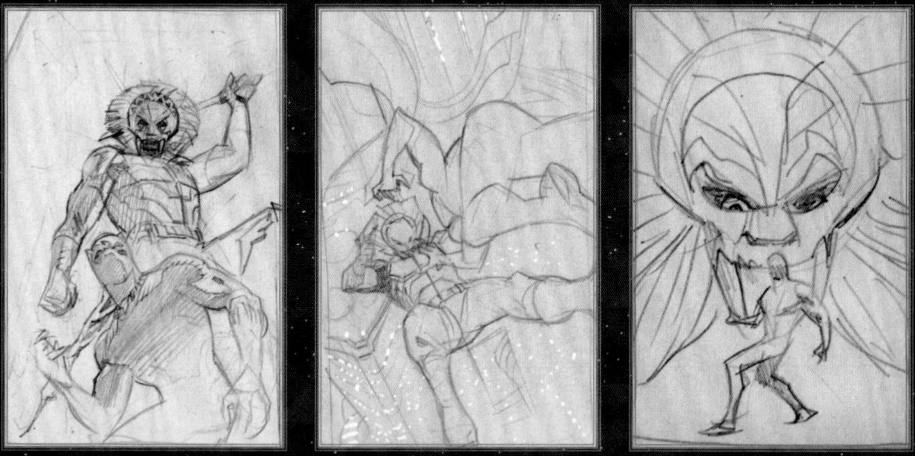

Daniel Acuña
17 COVER SKETCHES

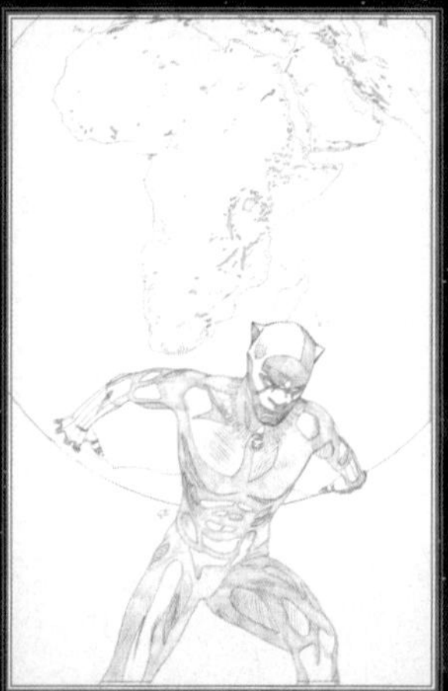

Daniel Acuña
18 COVER PENCILS